CALIFORNIA BUNGALOWS

The 1911 Ye Planry Catalog

Copyright © 2013 by Schiffer Publishing Ltd.
Originally Copyright 1910 by Ye Planry Building Co., (Inc.)

Library of Congress Control Number: 2013940210

All rights reserved. No part of this work may be reproduced or used in any form or by any means—graphic, electronic, or mechanical, including photocopying or information storage and retrieval systems—without written permission from the publisher.

The scanning, uploading, and distribution of this book or any part thereof via the Internet or via any other means without the permission of the publisher is illegal and punishable by law. Please purchase only authorized editions and do not participate in or encourage the electronic piracy of copyrighted materials. "Schiffer," "Schiffer Publishing, Ltd. & Design," and the "Design of pen and inkwell" are registered trademarks of Schiffer Publishing, Ltd.

ISBN: 978-0-7643-4454-1
Printed in China

Published by Schiffer Publishing, Ltd.
4880 Lower Valley Road
Atglen, PA 19310
Phone: (610) 593-1777; Fax: (610) 593-2002
E-mail: Info@schifferbooks.com

For our complete selection of fine books on this and related subjects, please visit our website at www.schifferbooks.com. You may also write for a free catalog.

This book may be purchased from the publisher. Please try your bookstore first.

We are always looking for people to write books on new and related subjects. If you have an idea for a book, please contact us at proposals@schifferbooks.com

Schiffer Publishing's titles are available at special discounts for bulk purchases for sales promotions or premiums. Special editions, including personalized covers, corporate imprints, and excerpts can be created in large quantities for special needs. For more information, contact the publisher.

In Europe, Schiffer books are distributed by
Bushwood Books
6 Marksbury Ave.
Kew Gardens
Surrey TW9 4JF England
Phone: 44 (0) 20 8392 8585; Fax: 44 (0) 20 8392 9876
E-mail: info@bushwoodbooks.co.uk
Website: www.bushwoodbooks.co.uk

"YE PLANRY" BUNGALOWS

FOURTH EDITION
1911

A BOOK CONTAINING MANY NEW AND ATTRACTIVE TYPES OF CALIFORNIA HOMES WITH MUCH INFORMATION CONCERNING THEM

PUBLISHED BY
YE PLANRY BUILDING COMPANY (Inc.)
212 MERCANTILE PLACE, LOS ANGELES

A. S. BARNES, President
E. B. RUST, Secretary

PREFACE TO THE FACSIMILE EDITION

Ye Planry was one of several companies to offer plans for bungalow-style homes in the early 20th century. It was a time of rising expectations, when emerging middle class families were seeking homes of their own that were affordable, well designed, and of good quality. The bungalow was just the answer.

The principals of the company were Arthur S. Barnes (1882–1975), President, and Edward Butler Rust (1883–1958), Secretary, young architects who started Ye Planry in their mid-twenties. The influence that the Arts & Crafts Movement and the philosophy of Gustav Stickley and others had on them is evident in the 102 designs in this catalog. The concern with both economy and design is underlined in the introductory essay by Rust. The materials to be used were well selected and a great deal of attention was given to the ergonomics of the house; i.e. proper ventilation, windows, lighting, closets, appliances, and storage space. In addition, design details, such as lighting fixtures and hardware, were considered integral to the whole of the house.

Ye Planry's principal business was in home design, though they did some building. They sold detailed architectural plans for the homes shown on these pages, including specifications for the quality of materials, wiring and fixtures, plumbing, heating, cement for walkways, paint, and even screens for the windows. Complete lumber lists were included with the plans, carefully and precisely compiled to avoid over-expenditure. A set of plans cost $10 for the first copy and $2.50 for each duplicate copy. For another $2.50, legal contracts for the contractor, customized with the appropriate names, could be obtained. The company was also happy to customize a plan, or create an entirely new design, to meet the customer's needs, for a "reasonable fee."

Ye Planry was based in Los Angeles, and California comprised the majority of its sales. But as Rust makes clear, the company sold thousands of its more than 900 plans throughout the "entire country." The prices quoted in this catalog reflect the fact that building costs varied widely by region, but the reader is assured that they are "fair average estimates that should in all cases cover a well built and finished home."

Because of the careful thought that went into their design and the choice of quality materials, many of these bungalows are still standing and occupied. They have become treasured examples of Arts & Crafts architecture that continue to serve their families well into the 21st century.

FOREWORD

E. B. RUST

THE modern Bungalow fills a world-wide demand for a home combining the elements of convenience, attractive appearance and low cost; different from the old-fashioned cottage with its steep roof, elaborate mill-work and box-like rooms, yet not startling in that difference; up-to-date in every particular, yet not "faddish"; a home that preserves its simplicity and charm, though the choice of materials necessarily differs with the locality.

While the word "Bungalow" conveys the idea of a low, rambling, one-story dwelling, the bungalow lines and details of construction have entered so largely into all classes of houses that there has evolved what might be well termed a two-story bungalow, though it is popularly referred to as the "Swiss Chalet." The peculiar advantage of this style lies in its comparatively low cost relative to the number of rooms. This is due to its compactness, as it covers little ground, has few breaks in outline and is therefore much easier to frame and roof over, and all the rooms are insured cross-ventilation.

Another transition has brought about the "Story-and-a-half." This is the result of building originally one or two small rooms under the slope of the roof, and adding other rooms until in many cases the second floor covers the entire area of the first, yet the main roof, being built down to the line of the first story ceiling, preserves the low, broad lines of the one-story. This type has given rise to much discussion where lots are sold under a restriction demanding that only two-story houses be built. While these restrictions have been variously interpreted, the concensus of opinion is that where the second story is practically as large as the first, with the up-stairs rooms full height throughout, the house is legally a two-story.

The "Mission Style" is a much abused term generally applied to anything with exterior plastering. As a matter of fact the Mission style is extremely plain, with no ornate staff work or elaborate colonnades, but with simple arches and roof lines. The exterior walls are of rough-cast plaster and the roof of terra cotta or galvanized iron tiles. The latter have the advantage of being considerably lighter than the clay tiles, and somewhat lower in initial cost, but this is offset in a few years by the necessity of renewing the paint.

The "California Style" is a term applied to a house built of 1"x12" vertical boards with battens over the joints outside, and frequently on both sides. The boards may be covered on the interior with burlap or heavy painted canvas, as there is no plaster, and generally no studding unless the climatic conditions require a more rigid frame. The advantage of this type lies in its comparatively low cost and facility of construction. It makes an ideal summer home but is too lightly built for severe winter weather, unless the exterior walls be sheathed horizontally and shingled, in which case the cost will nearly equal that of a plastered house.

For exterior finish, dressed lumber is used less and less for two reasons: first, it is not in keeping with the bungalow style, and second, it is more expensive, requiring two or three coats of paint where one of stain will answer for an unfinished surface. Shingles, shakes, unsurfaced siding or rough plaster for the walls; tile, patent roofing or shingles for the roofs; concrete, brick or native stone for the foundation; wood, hollow tile, concrete, brick and stone for the frame—all have their use. In response to many inquiries concerning the comparative merits and expense of different materials, it may be here stated that in general, frame construction is at least ten per cent cheaper than masonry, although in a locality where lumber is brought a great distance and stone, brick, etc., are near at hand, it is obvious that the reverse will be the case.

One of the favorite materials for exterior finish of the walls is shakes, a distinctly Western product, originally made by sawing the giant redwoods into three foot sections and splitting them off by hand. Sawed shakes are now generally used, being cheaper. They resemble shingles somewhat, but are of a uniform width of six inches, do not taper, and are thirty-six inches long, while the shingles are sixteen inches in length and vary in width. They may be used full length and laid as much as twenty-four inches to the weather by doubling the courses, or sawed in two and laid six to eight inches to the weather.

Heavy, rough timbers are used to support the wide overhanging roof and in the construction of porches and pergolas. Dark red brick, preferably laid in black mortar, cobblestones in gray mortar, cement stone, cut stone and rough plaster are all used for porch columns, exterior chimneys, etc., and cement, brick, or the large square Spanish tiles make appropriate outdoor floors.

Exterior color schemes are subject to infinite variety according to individual tastes. The favorite colors are soft brown, green or olive stains for the walls, with trimmings a shade darker or lighter for contrast. The roof may have the same tone as the walls, or perhaps better in many cases, it may be white or frosted.

In designing roofs, climate is the first consideration. The low, wide projecting roof is picturesque and satisfactory where the weather is not extreme, but is not practical and must be not only steeper, but more heavily constructed where snow or heavy rain storms are encountered. And the the slope of the roof will determine its projection. A steep roof would be illogical and appear heavy if it also had a wide overhang, while a very flat roof should extend not less than four feet beyond the walls.

In arrangement the bungalow is as varied as the requirements of many thousands of home-builders have made it, but the general idea is consistently the same; the rooms must be of good size, the windows should be on as many sides of each room as possible, and the communication between rooms as perfect as study can make it, avoiding unnecessary passage through intermediate rooms to gain one's objective. This can be done only by careful consideration of the requirements and mode of living of the individual: bearing in mind that a multiplicity of doors in a bed room or living room results in a loss of needed wall space, but that two or three doors in a long hall means that the hall is not sufficiently "busy" and should be discarded. When possible the bed rooms and bath should be secluded and the bath accessible independently of the bed rooms; the kitchen, screen porch with its laundry tubs, and servant's quarters in another part; and the dining room, den and living room constituting the third group. In case there is a basement, it should be near the center to insure the furnace pipes having approximately equal runs to the various rooms. The hall, like the stairway, is one of the utilitarian features, and should be in proportion to the house. A long passage in a five room bungalow would be out of place, but is an absolute necessity where there are many rooms.

Interior finish is plain almost to severity, with simplicity the keynote and straight lines predominating, doing away with all dust-catching mouldings. The materials used will of course vary in different localities. In the east oak costs but little more than good pine finish, while in the west it costs four times as much. The slash-grain Oregon Pine makes an exceptionally handsome interior wood as it readily takes the satin finish generally used. Oak may be successfully treated with ammonia fumes and waxed, preserving a uniform shade throughout, and omitting the paste filler, which has a tendency to darken the open parts of the grain. This method is somewhat more expensive than the usual method of stain, shellac and wax, and should only be adopted where the wood can be especially selected for uniform grain and texture. The more costly woods, such as walnut and mahogany, are seldom used as their effect is not brought out except with a glossy finish. White Cedar makes an excellent material where the finish is to be enameled, as the grain is not pronounced and is easily covered by four or five coats of white paint and enamel. Redwood is particularly beautiful in grain and the finish it takes, but is objectionable if there are small children as it is rather easily marred.

For interior decoration there is an infinite variety of schemes, depending in each case on individual preference and the character of the finish detail. An important factor in interior color schemes, which makes most general suggestions valueless, is the exposure of the rooms. However, rich colors seem right for the den, living room and dining room, with lighter colors in the bed rooms. The plaster is generally left with a sand finish, laid perfectly true and even, but without the very smooth surface unless wall paper or tapestry is to be used.

Hardware is massive and finished to match the interior decoration; in the living room and dining room hammered copper, bronze or oxidized silver, in the bed rooms dull brass, in the bath and kitchen nickeled finish. The electric fixtures should have the same finish as the hardware. At a slight additional cost, the fixtures may be specially designed and executed in hammered copper or brass. Shown herewith are a few of our original designs in hammered copper; a candle-stick, a card-receiver, and a reading lamp.

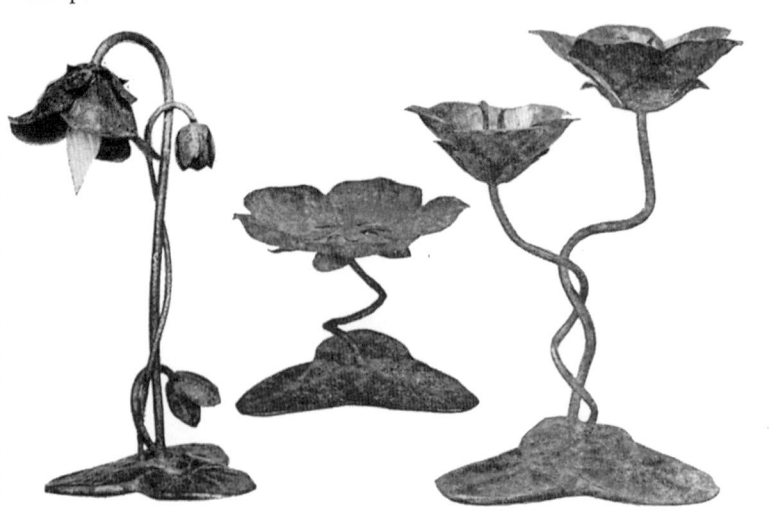

The floors should be of oak as largely as possible. They may be either quarter sawed or straight oak, seven-eighths inch thick, or where cost must be considered, the three-eighths inch floor is satisfactory, provided a good quality of tar paper is laid beneath to keep dampness from warping the floor. Maple floors are good in bed rooms or where there is no heavy furniture to mar them. In the kitchen a pine floor covered with linoleum seems to give the most satisfaction as it may be frequently washed without damage. The bath room may have a similar floor where tile is too expensive.

The porch is an excellent index of the owner's temperament, many desiring a board, hospitable front porch with hammocks and inviting chairs, while others prefer a small entrance porch, and for the family outdoor life a more secluded side porch or patio, with perhaps a pergola leading to a summerhouse.

The pergola may be described as two parallel beams resting on wood or masonry posts, with smaller cross-beams above. Vines should be trained over the pergola, making a delightful arbor, porte cochere, or covering for a porch.

The patio is reminiscent of early days when the house was built around a court, affording an outdoor spot for the women and children, who could not safely venture on the street. It is now usually left open on one side, with access through long French windows from the living room or dining room, though sometimes still enclosed on all sides and often with a glass sky-light overhead; or it may be screened and converted into an outdoor sleeping apartment.

The reception hall is a modification of the eastern reception hall, without the double-entrance door made necessary by a rigorous winter climate. The vestibule can be easily added when required, or sliding doors substituted for the cased openings frequently used. The stairway usually starts from the reception hall, if there be one, or otherwise either from the living room or a rear hallway. It should be in proportion to the size and general character of the house. A large open stair is a handsome addition to the home, but would be out of place, and too expensive for the modest story-and-a-half.

The living room is the family gathering place and should have as the distinctive feature a cheerful open fireplace, which may be of stone, brick, tile or plaster. The plastered mantel is only used where there is no paneling, as it should be tinted to match the walls. Where so treated the effect is exceptionally pleasing, and has the added advantage of being the least expensive of mantels. There may be either a picture mould near the ceiling or a picture rail of convenient height with the walls below either paneled in wood or with plaster panels divided by battens, or vertical strips of wood. The living room ceiling may be beamed, or it may have a large cove, making a dome, and indirect lighting used. This is accomplished by using an electric fixture in the form of a bowl hung on chains, with a highly polished reflector. The bulbs are arranged inside this bowl and the light is reflected against the ceiling and "spills" over the room in a soft glow toned by the tint of the ceiling, giving perfect illumination without the glare usually attendant upon electric lighting. This system is equally appropriate for the music room.

The den is usually a small room with built-in bookcases and perhaps a desk, mantel or window seat. The walls may be appropriately paneled in leather, basket matting or canvas, the last making a durable wall-covering capable of a great variety of decoration. The ceiling may be beamed, or what is better, if the room is not large, a wood cornice or coved ceiling.

The dining room has a built-in buffet, wood or leather paneled walls and beamed ceiling. The buffet may be of infinite variety, from a simple ledge to the elaborate one built entirely across an outside wall, with windows over the counter shelf and art glass back of the china cupboards. Mirrors, leaded glass, leather panels, plate-glass shelves, all have their appropriate places. A bay with its cosy window seat adds attractiveness to the dining room.

The kitchen is usually finished in ivory or gray enamel or varnished in the natural color, and is complete in every particular, having range, sink, drawers, cupboards, bins, moulding board, and cold air cabinet, arranged with a view to saving steps. The drainboard may be of sugar pine or one of the patent preparations resembling cement but with more resilience. The walls should be of hard plaster ruled to imitate tile, and enameled, giving a surface easy to keep clean and more durable than tile, as in a frame building where there is sure to be some settlement, the tiles are liable to work loose. A hood over the range is a particularly desirable and inexpensive feature. It is framed down to a height of seven feet above the floor, plastered, and slopes on the inside to a ventilator which draws the fumes from cooking out through the roof.

A breakfast room opening from the kitchen is a novel feature gaining favor. It is finished in light tones and should have, where possible, an east exposure to get the morning sun.

Bed rooms should be large, well ventilated, and arranged always with a space for bed and other furniture, a matter often overlooked until too late. Popular adjuncts of the bed room are the separate dressing room, or boudoir, and the screened sleeping room, the latter of distinct hygienic benefit as well as a delightful sitting room.

Closets should be as large and numerous as possible and should have either an outside window or a screen ventilator in the ceiling. Built-in hat- and shoe-boxes are desirable and the plaster should be painted or enameled to prevent the plaster from rubbing off on the clothing. The linen closet is usually built in the hall or bath room and is complete with cupboards, drawers and cabinet. Cedar makes an excellent material for linen cabinets and closets as its odor excludes moths.

The bath room is finished in white enameled woodwork, with tinted walls above the wainscot, which should be of enameled hard plaster as in the kitchen. Where space affords there may be a built-in cabinet for towels, medicine, etc., with hinged seat and a large mirror.

The height of a ceiling should always be in proportion to the size of the room. The average sized room has a ceiling from nine to nine and a half feet high. In small rooms, such as a bath room, or in a long narrow hall, the ceiling should be not over seven and a half feet, to avoid the appearance of a well. In larger rooms, the ceiling is best if sloping at the sides, as otherwise it will, through optical illusion, give the impression of sagging in the center.

by having windows on two or more sides of the room can proper ventilation be secured. Opalescent glass is good where light is required but no outlook, as in a bathroom.

The photographs in this book are all of our own work, and have been taken with a view of giving, not a number of homes of any one style, but as great a variety as possible in order to show more adequately the scope of our work. We have not found it ne-

Perhaps no one subject requires more study of individual conditions than windows. They are primarily intended to admit light and air, but are subject to varied treatment. They are so constructed as to exclude dust and rain, and should be made to be opened, except where the view demands a large stationary plate glass. Also they should be grouped rather than scattered, and so placed that the wall-space lends itself to a pleasing arrangement of furniture. Moreover, it should be remembered that only

Building prices will vary twenty-five per cent and more throughout the United States, and in some cases different contractors in the same locality have been known to vary by fifteen to twenty per cent in their bids on the same building. We have, however, given fair average estimates which should in all cases cover a well built and finished house, with the exception of unusually expensive or elaborate features, unless conditions out of the ordinary are to be met.

The drawings include floor plans with all dimensions, door and window sizes, location of electric lights and switches, four eleva- cessary or fitting to photograph others' houses and publish them as our own, as we have over nine hundred plans to select from and have been embarrassed in making a choice rather than at a loss for material. We have, however, been obliged to use several pen sketches of houses, having excellent floor plans, but which have not been built where we could secure photographs, or were not completed in time.

The estimates given are of necessity approximate.

tions, foundation plan carefully figured and the bearings worked out to prevent settlement of any part of the house. A roof plan is included where necessary, and large scale details of all interior features always furnished. One of our first considerations in preparing plans for out-of-town clients is meeting local conditions. **The bungalow is as practical as any type of home, in any locality,** provided it is properly designed and built. Letters on file in our office from thousands of thoroughly satisfied home builders and investors throughout the entire country, have convinced us that our plans do meet local conditions in a manner that leaves no opening for criticism.

The specifications with reference index are most complete, taking up every part of the construction, size of timbers and quality of workmanship and material throughout. The notes given with the plans on the following pages are of necessity brief, but the specifications in each case provide for electric wiring and fixtures, screens for all windows, finish hardware, cement walks, painting, tinting, plumbing, etc.—in short, a complete home ready for occupancy.

Our lumber lists are as accurate as it is possible to make them. Every piece of timber is carefully billed as to size and quality, and every part of the finish lumber specified in proper lengths to avoid any splicing. Special care is taken to avoid ordering too much or too little material and incurring extra charge for cartage.

With one or two exceptions, the price of complete plans, specifications and details of any one of the houses shown in this book, or of our eight hundred other stock plans is Ten Dollars. Duplicate sets where more than one set is required on the same building, will be furnished at Two Dollars and Fifty cents each. The lumber bills are Five Dollars each. The plans will be sent by express C. O. D. with privilege of examination. If they are not satisfactory, they may of course be returned. Orders for stock plans will be filled immediately. Order plans by number given under the sketch of the floor plan, not by page number.

For Two Dollars and a Half we will put a building contract into legal form. In this case the owner should send us his full name, the name of the contractor in full, and the legal description, according to the terms of the deed, of the ground on which the house is to be erected. We also furnish individual contracts; that is to say, those covering particular parts of the work, such as the masonry, woodwork or painting.

When special plans are required our fee is most reasonable, being based on the number of rooms rather than on the cost of the house, unless exceptionally elaborate work is contemplated. In the case of special plans, it is our rule to require a deposit of twenty-five per cent of the total fee with the order. On receipt of this, we prepare pencil sketches of the floor plans and elevations, to be submitted for correction and approval before completing the working plans. No other payment is due until the plans are completed and inspected by the client. In ordering special plans, all the data possible should be given, such as direction of storms, points of the compass, slope of the building site, local materials to be used, etc., as well as a rough outline of the size, general arrangement and number of rooms required.

Where alterations to a plan not otherwise satisfactory are required, or sketches and specifications of additional features in a house already built, our charge is in proportion to the work involved. When additions to, or deviations from the stock specifications only are required, or suggestions concerning color schemes, decorating or finish, there is no extra charge. Before ordering special plans, it should be remembered that we have over nine hundred plans in stock, only a few of which are shown herewith, and among these nine hundred are many plans quite similar to the ones given, but differing in one or more respects, a breakfast room or screen sleeping room added, a stairway, providing for rooms under the roof, or other variations, and it is more than possible that a stock plan can be found to answer the requirements. When it seems advisable we will send several plans for examination.

Having been in this line of business for over six years—since the origin of the modern bungalow, in fact—we are on the ground floor, both figuratively and literally. Our experience has been largely in the line of meeting the requirements of the average homebuilder, though many of the buildings here shown will give an example of the larger plans we are often called upon to prepare. The plans are all entirely practical, homes having been built after each from one to fifty times and more. We have furnished plans for over five thousand thoroughly satisfied homebuilders and investors throughout the United States, Canada and Mexico, and even further, and are in a position to meet the demands of a prospective builder in any locality. Our plans being originally designed in each case for a home, are always "homelike" and as such, make the best houses for investment.

Respecting our standing we refer our clients to:

National Hardwood Co.

Los Angeles Trust & Savings Bank.

Cost $2700.00 to $3000.00.

Foundation concrete, porch and terrace floors cement, plastered mantel, porch and chimneys plastered with brick corbels. Shakes on walls and shingles on roof. Pine finish throughout. Oak floors in living and dining rooms, den and breakfast room. Paneled wainscot and beamed ceiling in dining room, indirect lights in living room and den. Finish in living and dining rooms and den stained and waxed, other finish and bath room and kitchen wainscot enameled.

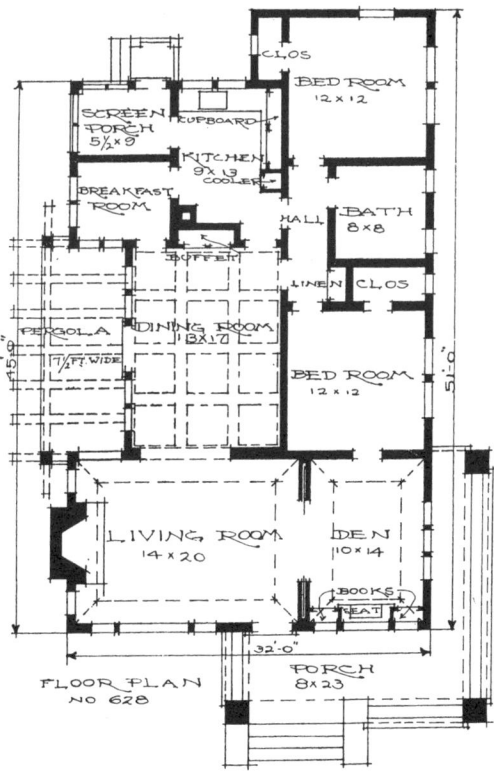

Plans as shown or reversed, $10.00.

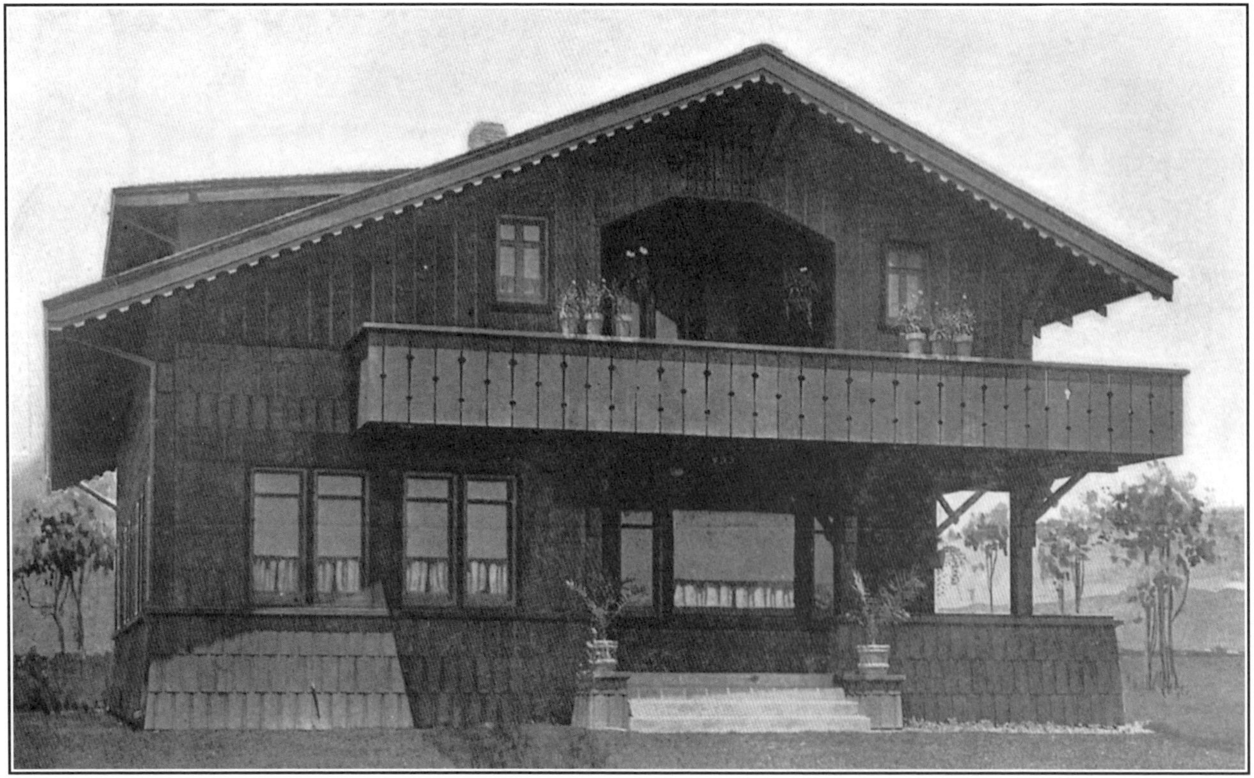

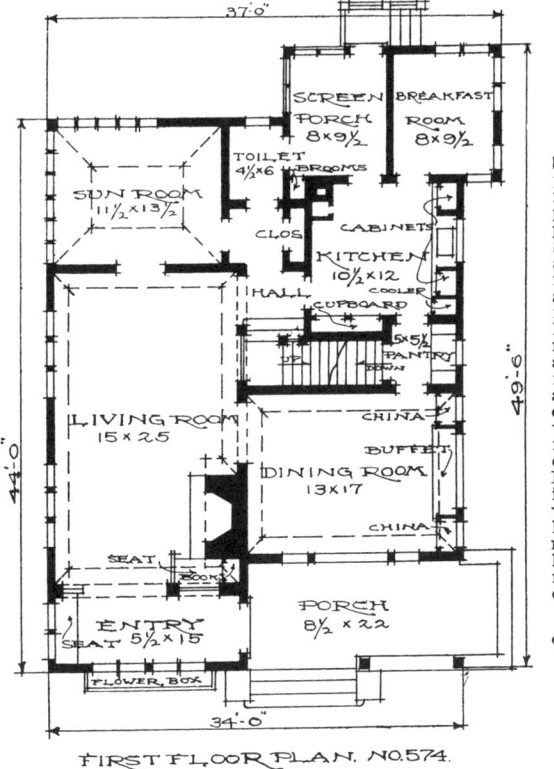

Cost $3700.00 to $4000.00.

Foundation and basement concrete, porch floor cement, chimneys plastered, mantel pressed brick. Shakes on walls and shingles on roof. Oak floors, stained and waxed finish in entry, living and dining rooms, sun-room and halls; other floors pine. Balance of finish enameled, also wainscot in bath room, toilet, kitchen and pantry. Plaster paneling in dining room, wood cornice in living and dining rooms, indirect lighting in sun-room. Furnace included.

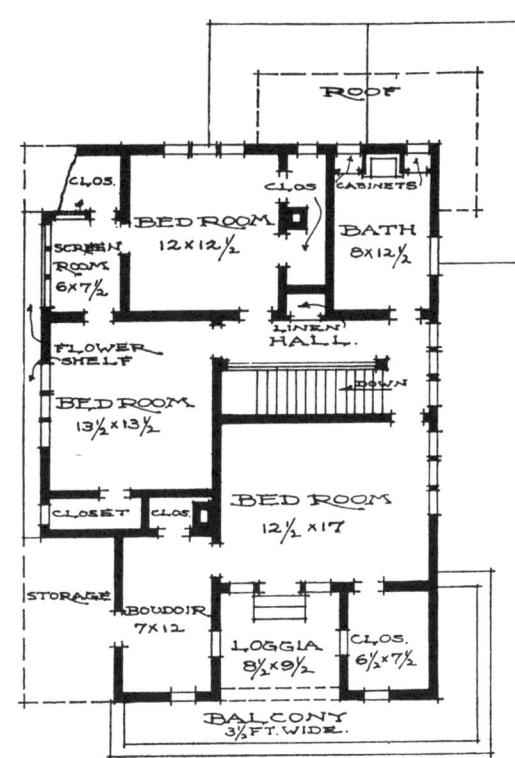

Plans as shown or reversed, $10.

FIRST FLOOR PLAN. NO. 574.

SECOND FLOOR PLAN. NO. 574.

Cost $1800.00 to $2000.00.

Foundation concrete, porch and chimney cobblestones, shingled walls and roof, mantel tile. Pine finish throughout. Stained and waxed finish and oak floors in living room and dining room. Ceiling beams and paneled wainscot in dining room. Indirect lighting and plaster paneling in living room. Kitchen finish varnished, other finish, and bath room and kitchen wainscot enameled.

Plans as shown or reversed, $10.00.

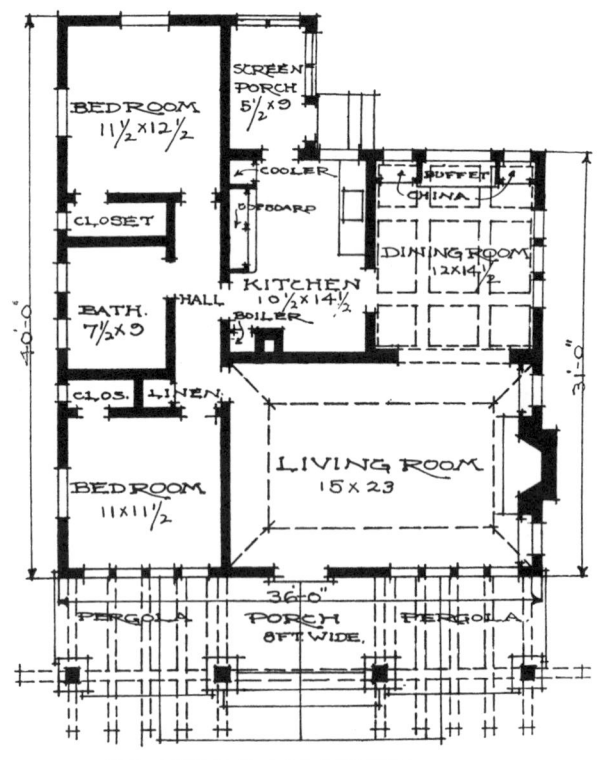

FLOOR PLAN NO. 754.

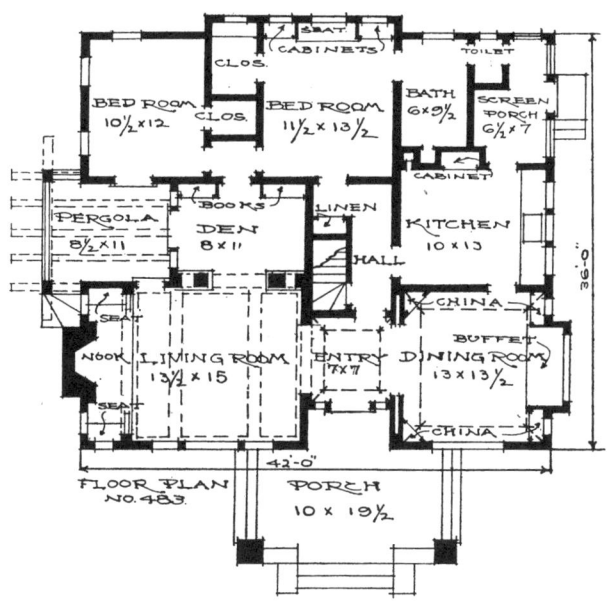

Cost $2200.00 to $2450.00.

Foundation and basement concrete, porch, pergola and basement floors cement. Porch and chimneys cobblestones, mantel tile. Redwood siding to window sill, shingles above and on roof. Oak floors, and stained and waxed finish in living and dining rooms, reception hall, and den. Other floors pine, other finish and kitchen and bath room wainscot enameled. Paneled wainscot in dining room, plaster panels in den, beamed ceiling in living room, wood frieze in reception hall, den and dining room.

Plans as shown or reversed, $10.00.

NO. 747.
DONE AT
"Ye Planry"

FIRST FLOOR PLAN NO. 747.

SECOND FLOOR PLAN NO. 747.

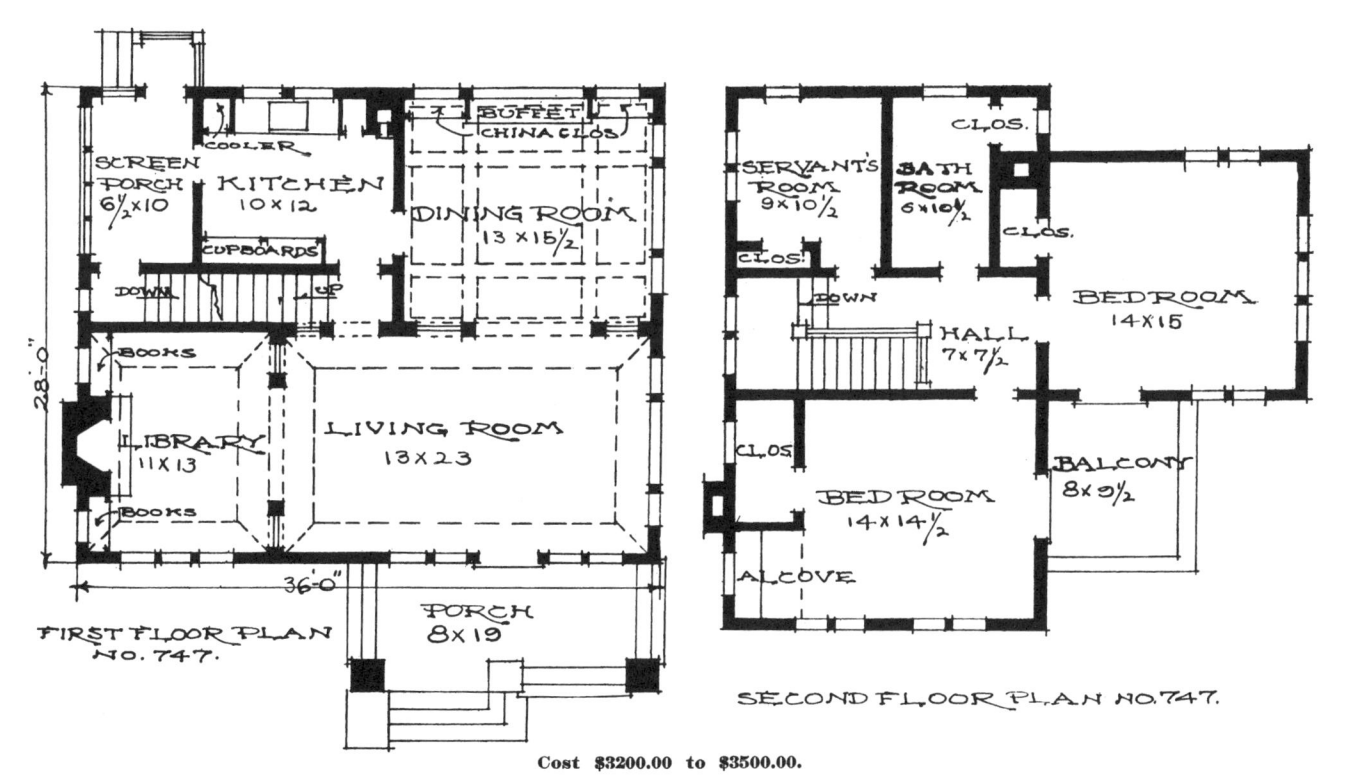

Cost $3200.00 to $3500.00.

Foundation and basement concrete, porch and chimneys brick, porch and basement floors cement, mantel tile. Shakes on walls, composition roof. Oak floors, stained and waxed finish in living and dining rooms and library, other floors pine. Other finish, and kitchen and bath room wainscot enameled. Beamed ceiling and paneled wainscot in dining room, indirect lighting and plaster paneling in living room and library. Furnace included.

Plans as shown or reversed, $10.00.

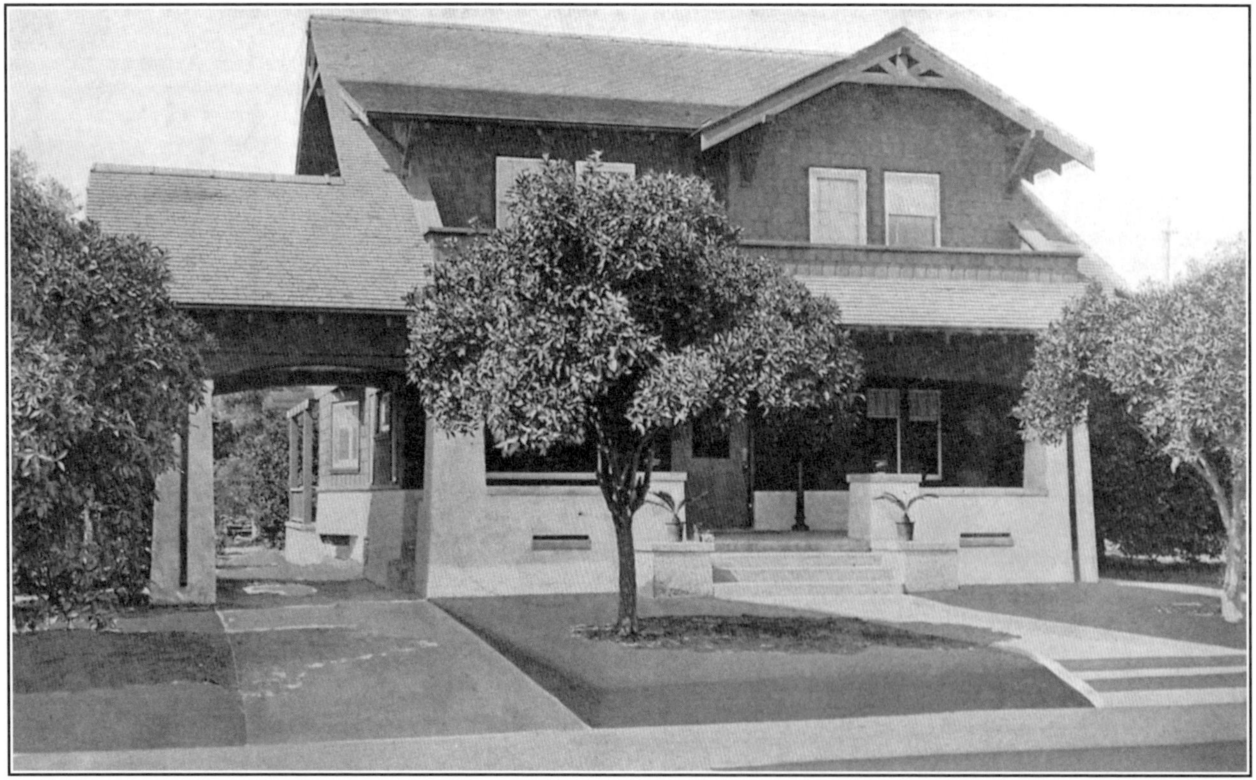

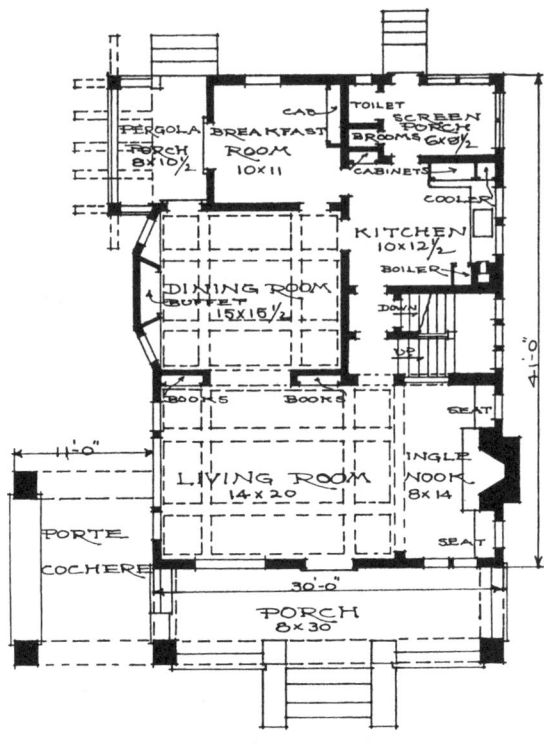

Cost $3800.00 to $4100.00.

Foundation and basement concrete; porch and basement floors cement; chimneys, walls to window sills and front porch rough plaster; shakes above plaster and shingles on roof. Tile mantel. Pine finish throughout. Oak floors except kitchen and bath, beamed ceilings and paneled wainscot in living and dining rooms. Plaster paneling in breakfast room. Finish stained and waxed except kitchen; bath room and bed rooms finish, and kitchen and bath room wainscot enameled. Screen room finish varnished. Furnace pipes included.

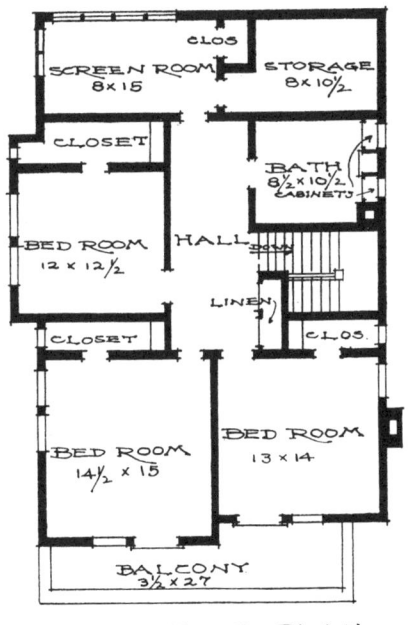

Plans as shown or reversed, $10.00.

Cost $2700.00 to $3000.00.

Foundation and basement concrete, porch and basement floors cement, porch and chimney brick, mantel pressed brick. Shakes on walls and shingles on roof. Beamed ceilings, stained and waxed finish, and oak floors in living and dining rooms and den. Paneling in dining room, plaster wainscot in kitchen and bath room enameled. Finish in bed rooms, bath and kitchen varnished. Furnace included.

Plans as shown or reversed, $10.00.

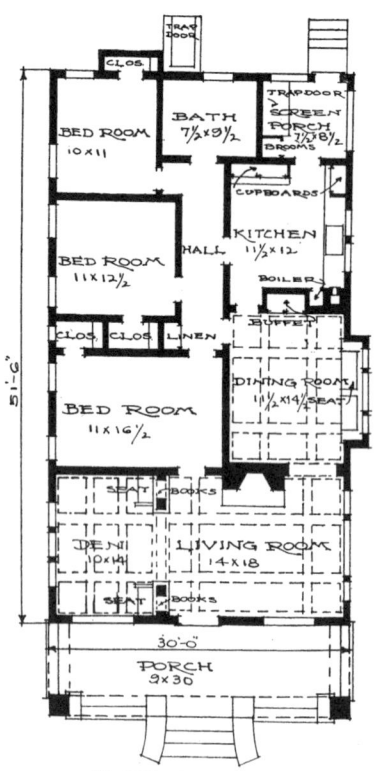

FLOOR PLAN NO. 377

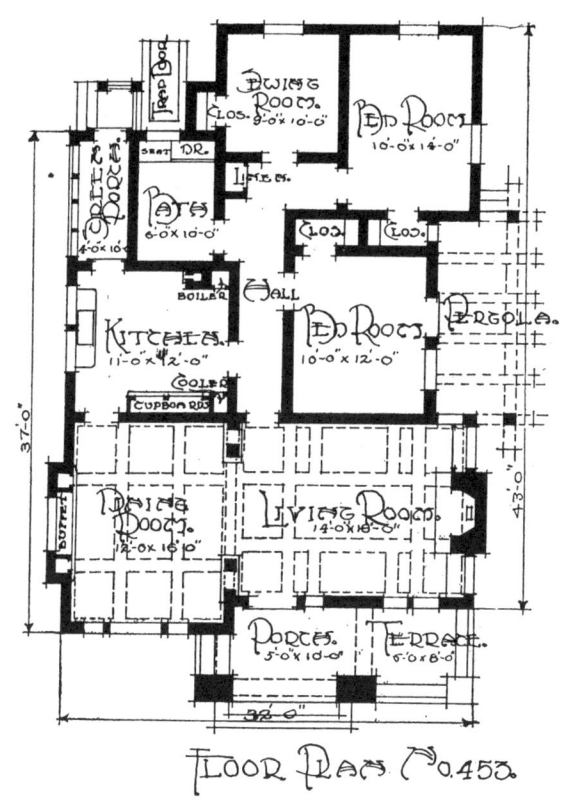

Cost $2000.00 to $2200.00.

Foundation and basement concrete, porch and chimneys rough plaster, porch, pergola and basement floors cement, shakes on walls and shingles on roof. Oak floors, stained and waxed finish, beamed ceilings, and paneled wainscot in living and dining rooms; other finish enameled, other floors pine. Furnace pipes included.

Plans as shown or reversed, $10.00.

Floor Plan No. 453.

31

Cost $1500.00 to $1650.00.

Foundation and chimney brick, plastered mantel, porch floor pine, redwood siding on walls and shingles on roof. Pine finish throughout. Stained and waxed finish and oak floors in living and dining rooms, other floors pine. Plaster panels and ceiling beams in dining room. Indirect lighting in living room. Kitchen finish varnished; other finish, and bath room and kitchen wainscot enameled.

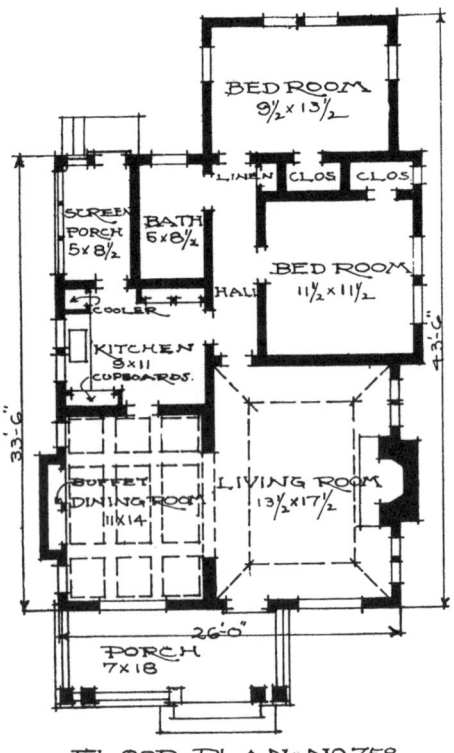

Plans as shown or reversed $10.00.

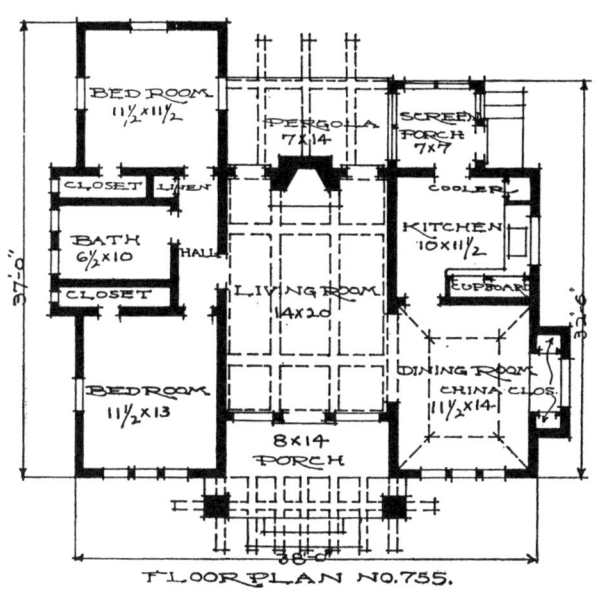

Cost $2000.00 to $2200.00.

Foundation and chimney brick, mantel pressed brick, porch floor pine, vertical 1"x12" boards and battens to window sills, shakes above and on roof. Pine finish throughout. Plaster panels, stained and waxed finish and oak floors in living and dining rooms; other floors pine. Indirect lighting in dining room, beam ceiling in living room. Kitchen finish varnished; other finish, bath room and kitchen wainscot enameled.

Plans as shown or reversed, $10.00.

FLOOR PLAN NO. 755.

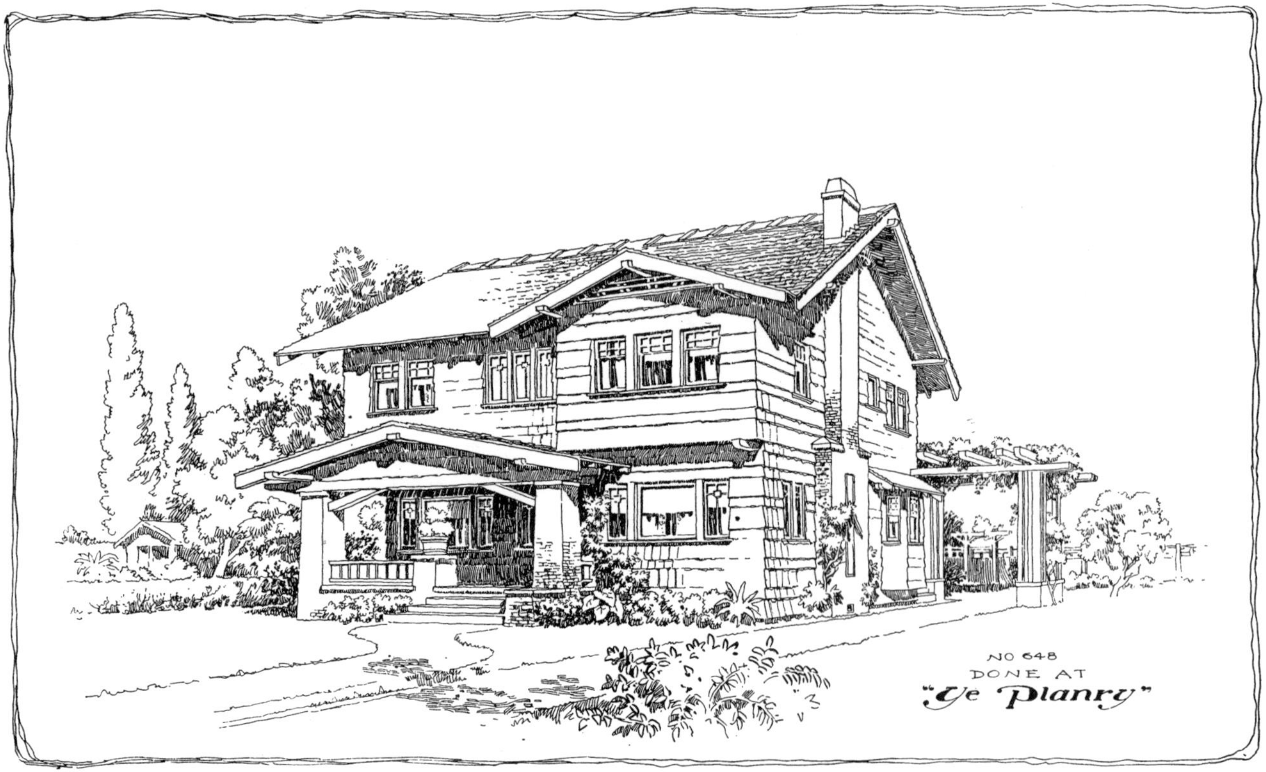
NO 648
DONE AT
"Ye Planry"

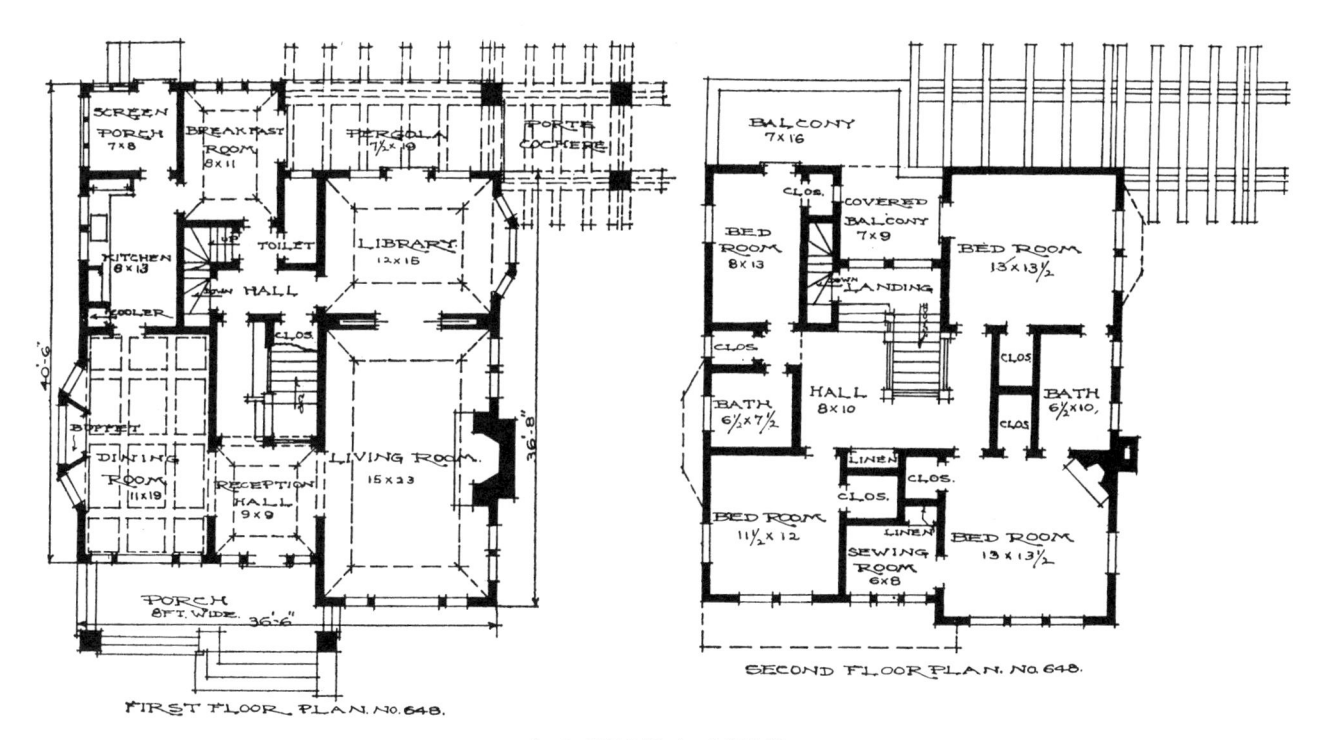

Cost $3900.00 to $4300.00.

Foundation and basement concrete; porch, pergola and basement floors cement; porch, pergola and chimney brick. Tile mantel. Shakes in alternating courses on walls and shingles on roof. Pine finish throughout. Oak floors throughout except pine in kitchen and bath rooms. Paneled wainscot and ceiling beams in dining room, indirect lighting in reception hall, living room, library and breakfast room. Downstairs finish, except in kitchen and breakfast room, stained and waxed. Other finish, and kitchen and bath room wainscots enameled. Furnace included.

Plans as shown or reversed, $10.00.

35

36

Cost $15,000.00 to $16,500.00.

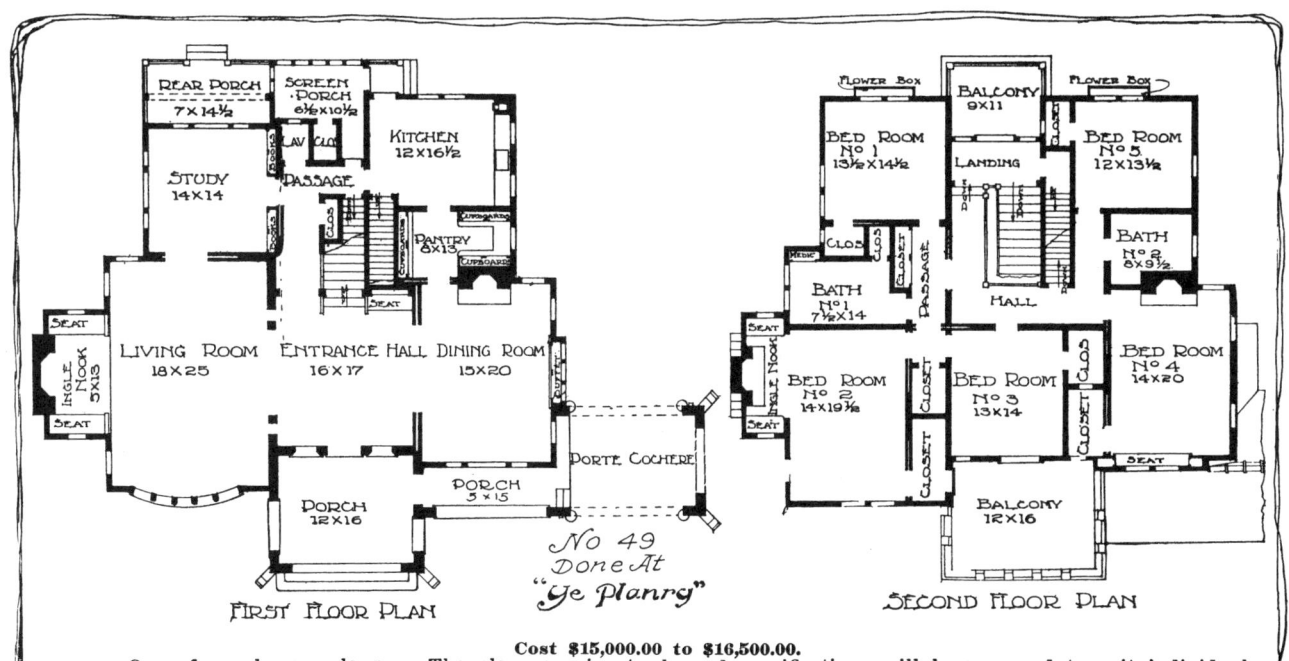

One of our larger plans. The plans are in stock, and specifications will be prepared to suit individual preference. The porch, chimneys, and living room mantel are of sandstone, and the walls half timber and plaster, with slate roof. Interior finish down-stairs may be pine, oak, etc. Up-stairs finish enameled white cedar, with mahogany doors. Oak floors throughout. A furnace is included and there are servants' quarters in the attic.

Plans as shown or reversed with specially prepared specifications, $25.00.

NO 645
DONE AT
"Ye Planry"

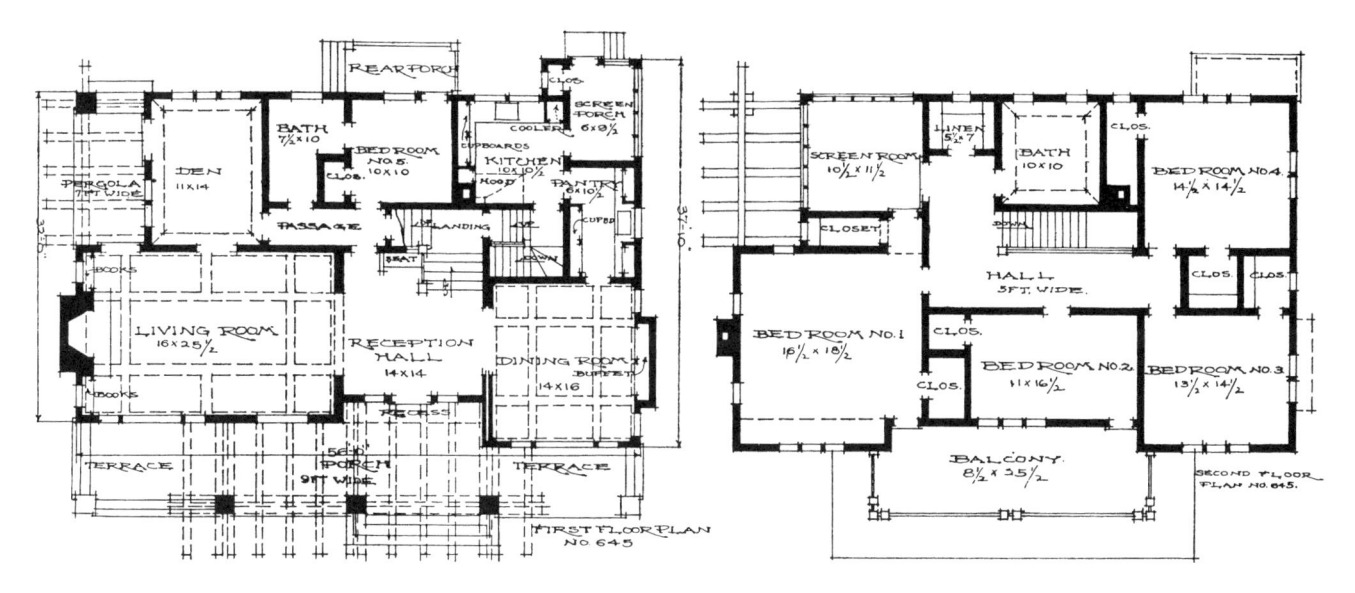

Cost $7500.00 to $8250.00.

Foundation and basement concrete; basement, pergola and porch floors cement; mantel tile; porch, chimneys and first story walls rough plastered, shakes above; composite roof. Oak floors throughout first story except pine in kitchen, bath and pantry; maple floors throughout second story except pine in screen room, and tile floor in bath. The first story finish stained and waxed, pine except dining room, bath and pantry. Dining room oak. Screen room finish stained redwood. All other finish enameled white cedar. Veneered oak panels in dining room, imitation leather panels in reception hall and living room. Furnace included.

Plans as shown or reversed, $10.00.

40

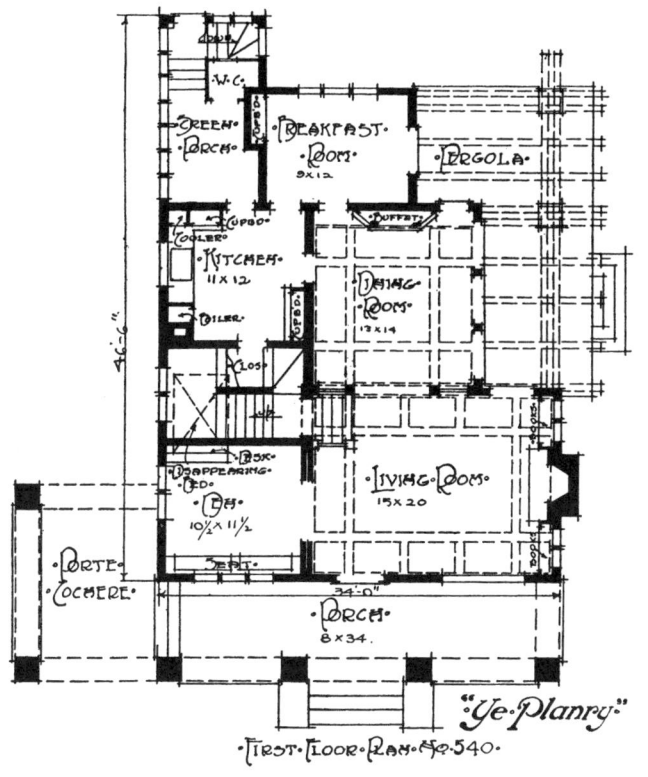

Cost $3800.00 to $4200.00.

Foundation and basement concrete, basement, porch and pergola cement. Porch, chimneys and pergola rough plaster. Pressed brick mantel, shakes on walls and shingles on roof. Kitchen, breakfast room, and up-stairs floors pine, others oak. Pine finish throughout, stained and waxed in living, dining rooms and den. Other finish, and bath room and kitchen wainscot enameled. Beamed ceiling in living and dining rooms. Paneled wainscot in dining room and den, plaster panels in breakfast room. Disappearing bed in den. Furnace included.

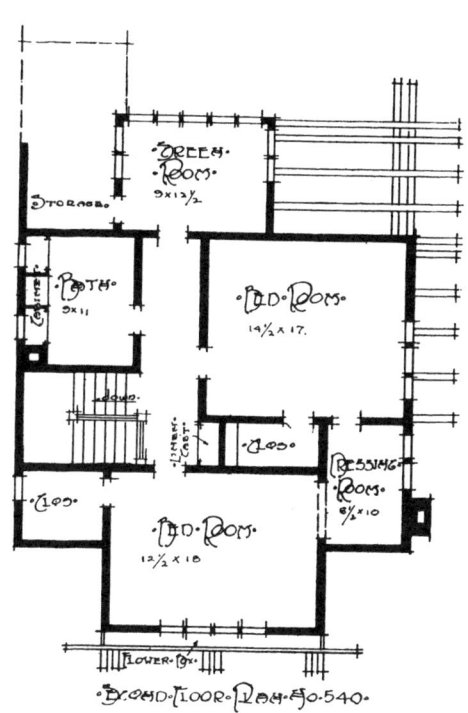

Plans as shown or reversed, $10.00.

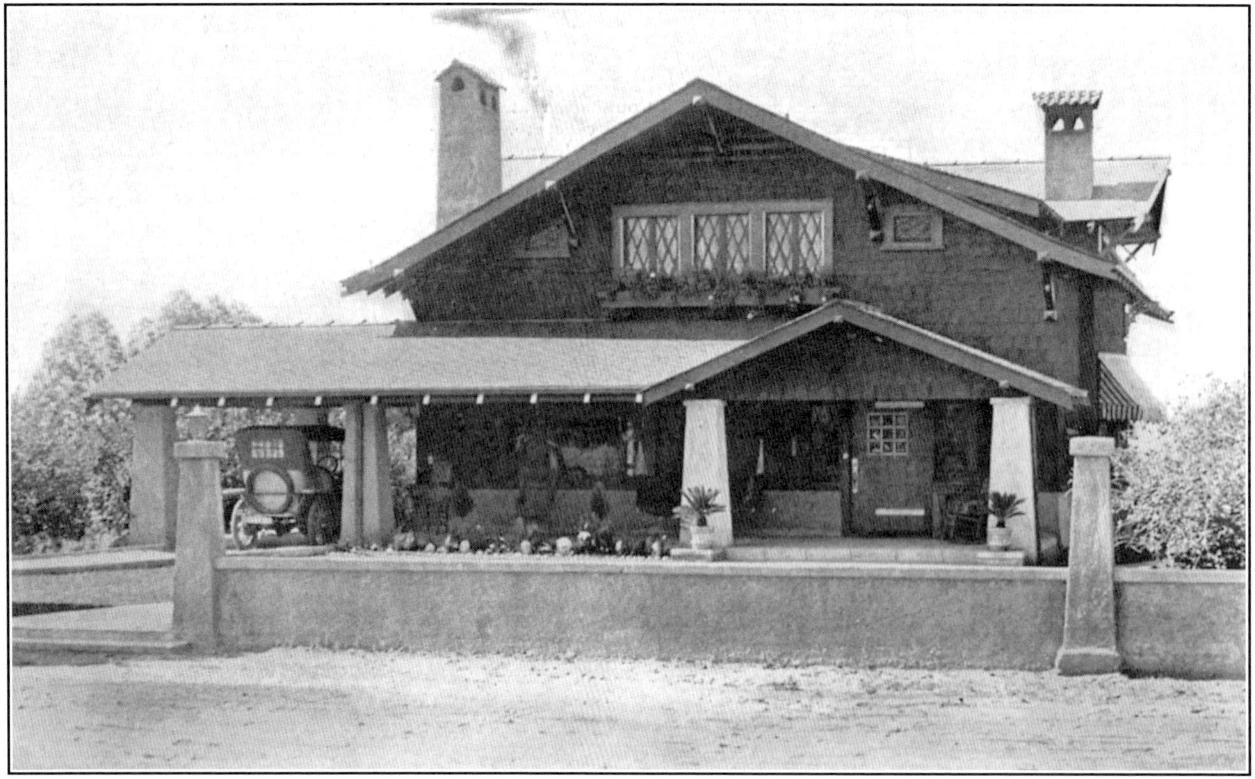

Cost $4800 to $5300.

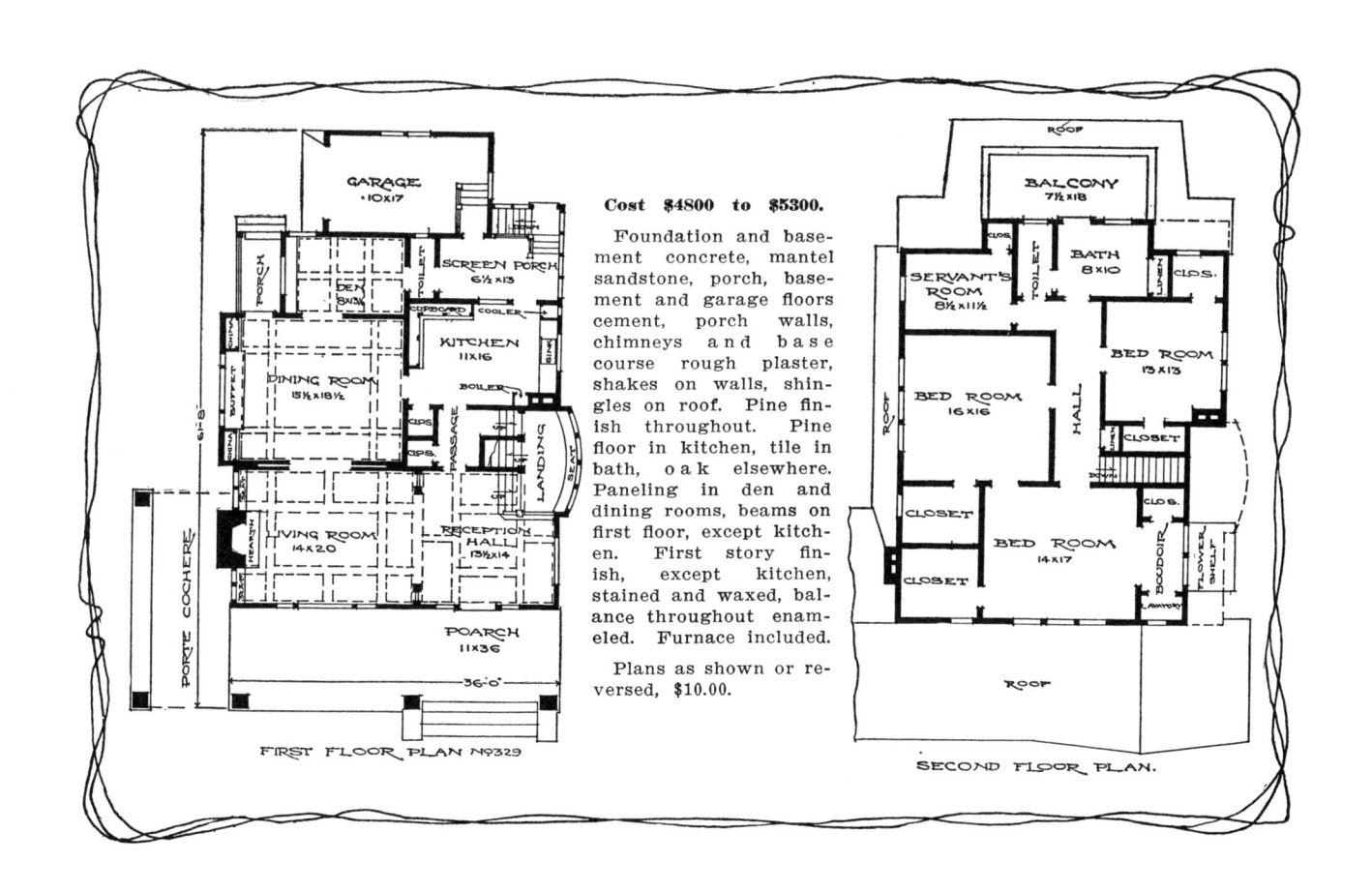

Foundation and basement concrete, mantel sandstone, porch, basement and garage floors cement, porch walls, chimneys and base course rough plaster, shakes on walls, shingles on roof. Pine finish throughout. Pine floor in kitchen, tile in bath, oak elsewhere. Paneling in den and dining rooms, beams on first floor, except kitchen. First story finish, except kitchen, stained and waxed, balance throughout enameled. Furnace included.

Plans as shown or reversed, $10.00.

Cost $1650.00 to $1800.00.

Foundation concrete, porch floor cement, porch and chimneys plaster, mantel pressed brick. Shingled walls and roof. Pine finish throughout. Stained and waxed finish and oak floors living and dining rooms, other floors pine. Plaster panels and ceiling beams in dining room. Indirect lighting in living room. Kitchen finish varnished, other finish and bath room and kitchen wainscot enameled.

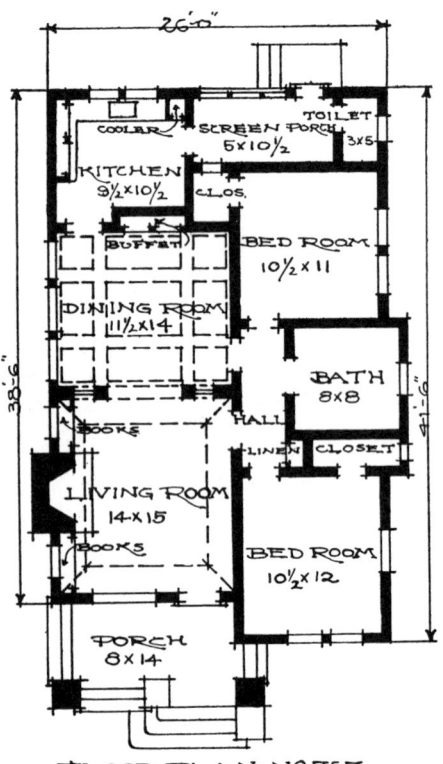

Plans as shown or reversed, $10.00.

Cost $1800.00 to $2000.00.

Foundation and chimney brick, mantel pressed brick, porch floor pine, redwood siding on walls and shingles on roof. Pine finish throughout. Stained and waxed finish, and oak floors in living and dining rooms. Ceiling beams and paneled wainscot in dining room, indirect lighting and plaster paneling in living room. Kitchen finish varnished, other finish, and bath room and kitchen wainscot enameled.

Plans as shown or reversed, $10.00.

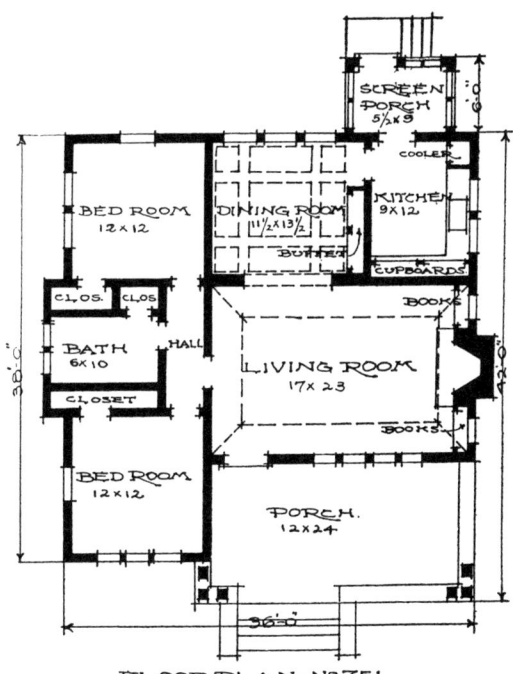

FLOOR PLAN.—NO. 751.

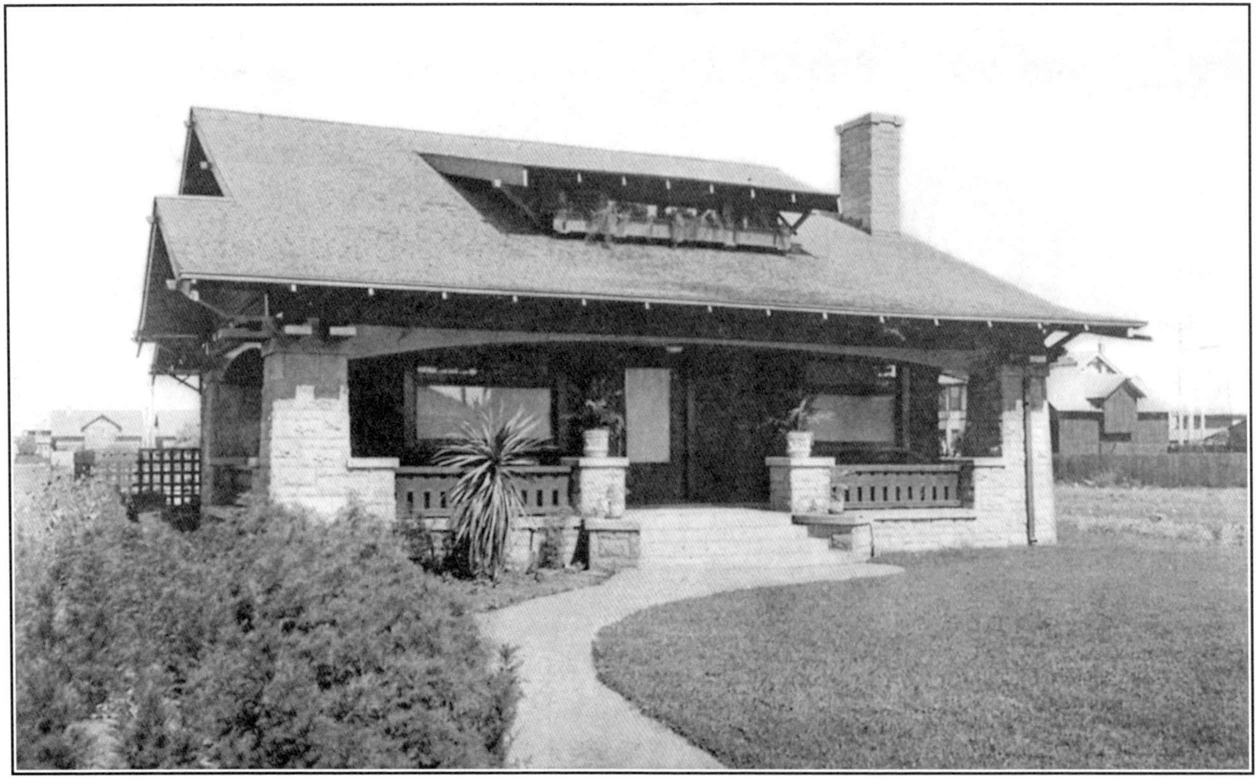

No. 308
Done At "Ye Planry"

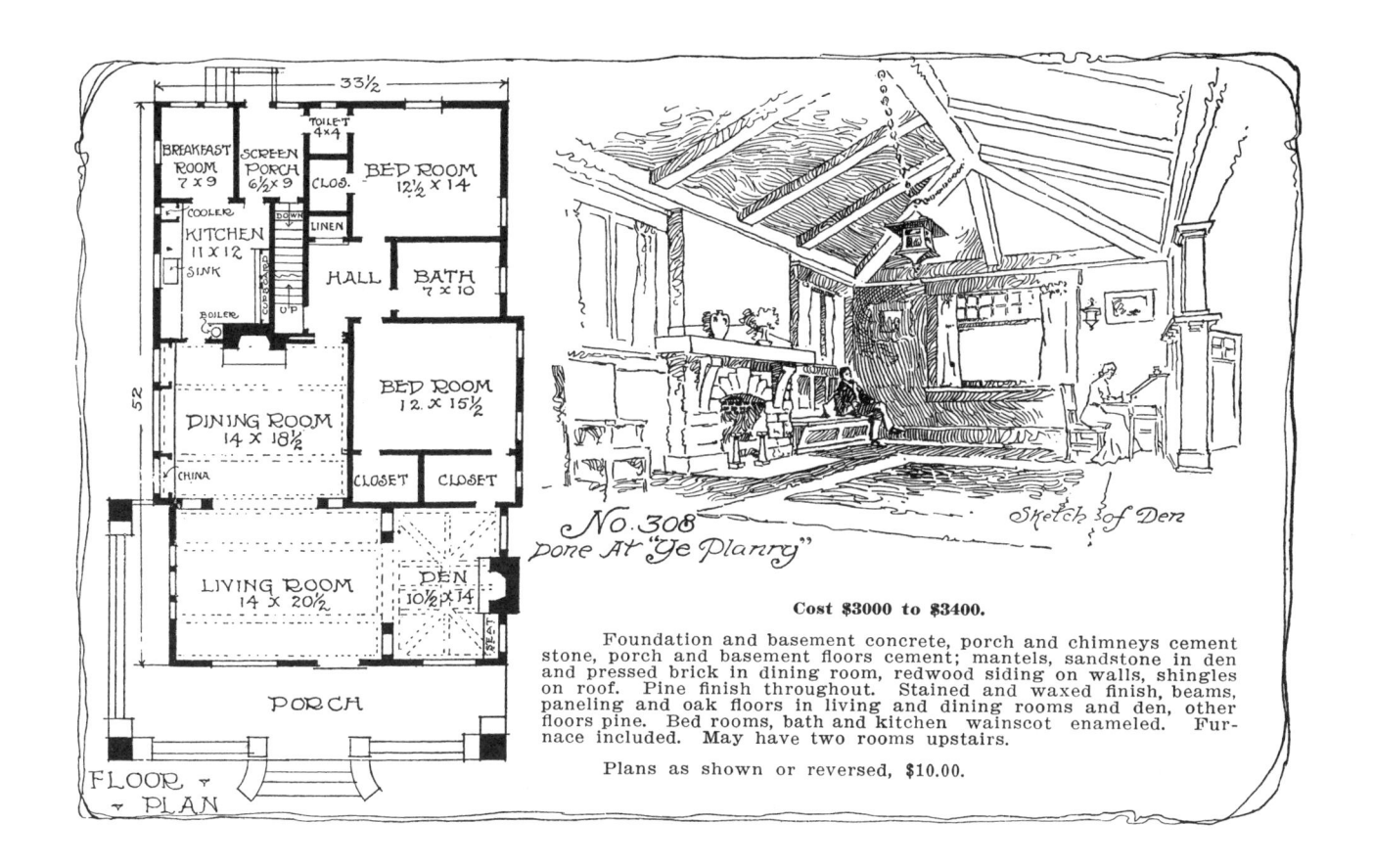

Sketch of Den

Cost $3000 to $3400.

Foundation and basement concrete, porch and chimneys cement stone, porch and basement floors cement; mantels, sandstone in den and pressed brick in dining room, redwood siding on walls, shingles on roof. Pine finish throughout. Stained and waxed finish, beams, paneling and oak floors in living and dining rooms and den, other floors pine. Bed rooms, bath and kitchen wainscot enameled. Furnace included. May have two rooms upstairs.

Plans as shown or reversed, $10.00.

Cost $3500.00 to $3800.00.

Basement and foundation concrete, porch and basement floors cement, porch and chimneys rough plaster. Mantel tile. Shakes on walls and composition roof. Oak floors except pine in kitchen, bath room and screen rooms. Waxed redwood finish and indirect lighting in living and dining rooms. Basket-matting panels and waxed redwood finish in screen rooms. Enameled white cedar finish elsewhere. Enameled wainscot in kitchen and bath. Imitation leather panels in dining room, plaster panels in living room. Furnace included.

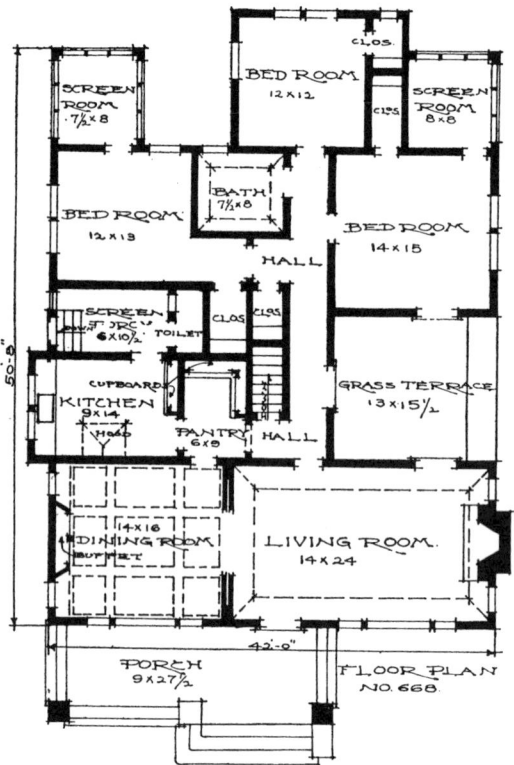

Plans as shown or reversed $10.00.

Cost $2300.00 to $2550.00.

Foundation concrete, porch floor cement, rough plaster on chimney, porch and walls to window sills. Shakes above and shingles on roof. Pressed brick mantel. Oak floors, paneled wainscot and stained and waxed finish in nook, living and dining rooms and library; other floors pine. Other finish, and kitchen and bath room wainscot enameled. Paneled ceiling in nook. Wall bed in library, indirect lighting in living and dining rooms.

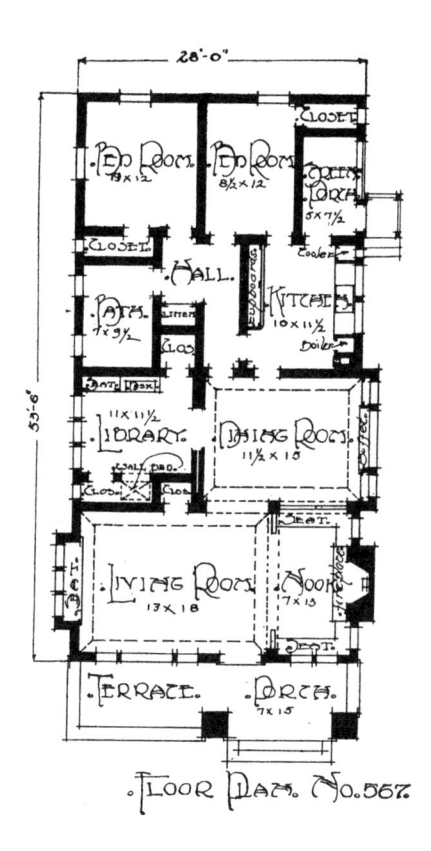

Plans as shown or reversed, $10.00.

Plan No. 542
"Ye Planry"

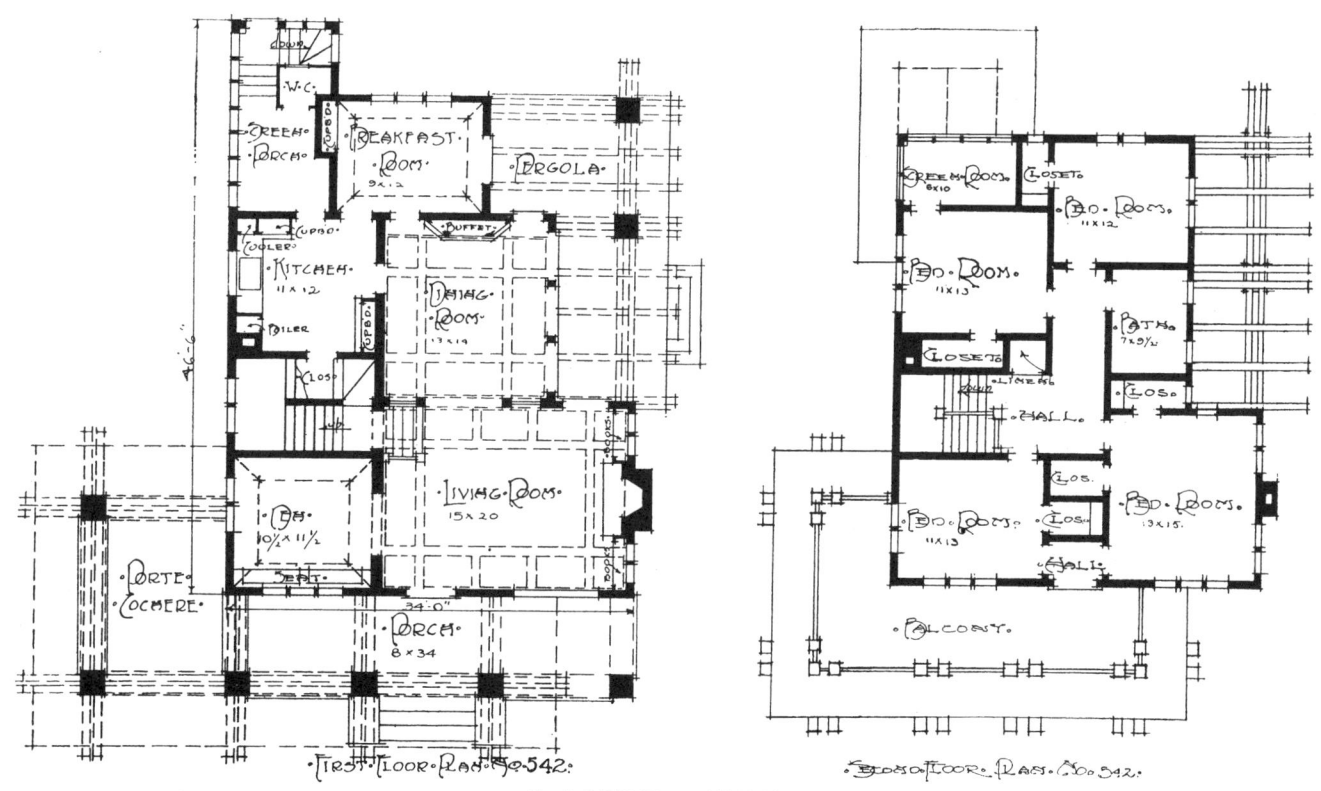

Cost $4200.00 to $4600.00.

Foundation and basement concrete, porch and chimney plastered with brick caps, porch, pergola and basement floors cement. Shakes alternating 8" and 16" to weather on walls, and composition roof. Tile mantel. Oak floors throughout except kitchen. Pine finish stained and waxed in living and dining room, library and hall, balance of finish enameled white cedar. Plaster paneling in living room and library. Veneered pine paneling in dining room. Beamed ceilings in living and dining rooms, indirect lighting in den and breakfast room. Enameled plaster wainscot in bath and kitchen. Furnace included.

Plans as shown or reversed, $10.00.

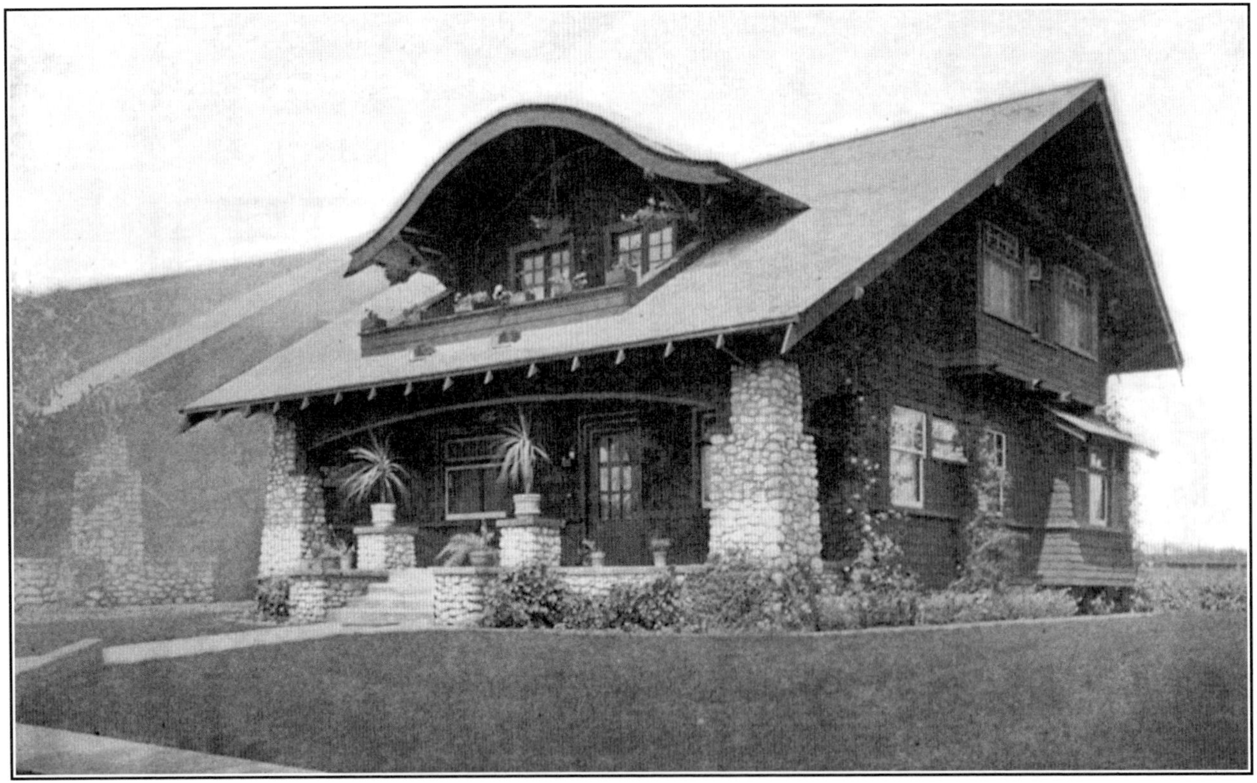

Cost $3000.00 to $3300.00.

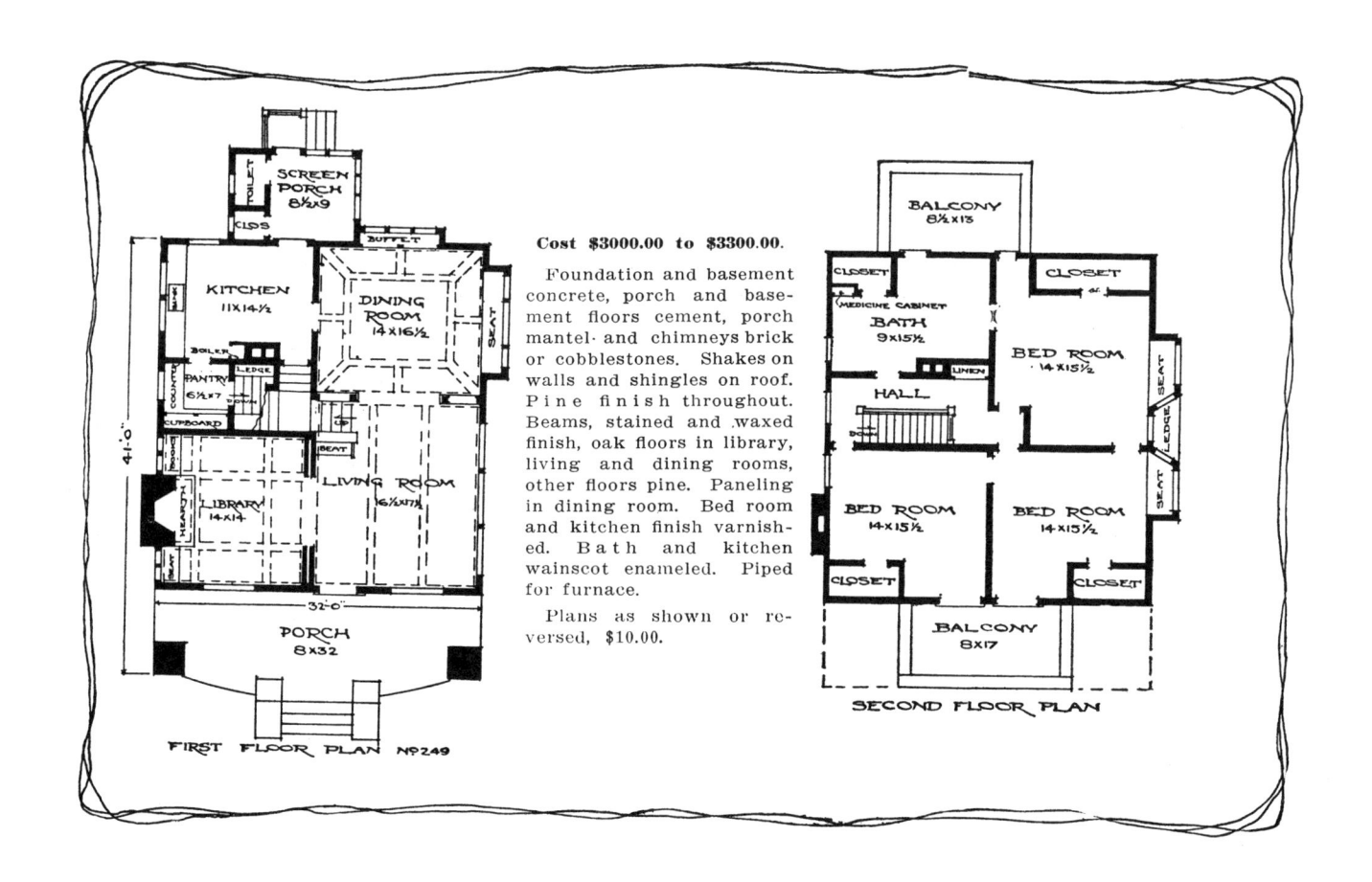

Foundation and basement concrete, porch and basement floors cement, porch mantel and chimneys brick or cobblestones. Shakes on walls and shingles on roof. Pine finish throughout. Beams, stained and waxed finish, oak floors in library, living and dining rooms, other floors pine. Paneling in dining room. Bed room and kitchen finish varnished. Bath and kitchen wainscot enameled. Piped for furnace.

Plans as shown or reversed, $10.00.

NO. 759.
DONE AT
"Ye Planry"

Cost $1500.00 to $1650.00.

Foundation and chimney brick, brick mantel, porch floor pine, redwood siding on walls and shingles on roof. Pine finish throughout. Oak floors, stained and waxed finish, plaster panels and indirect lighting in living and dining rooms. Other floors pine. Kitchen finish varnished; other finish, and bath room and kitchen wainscot enameled.

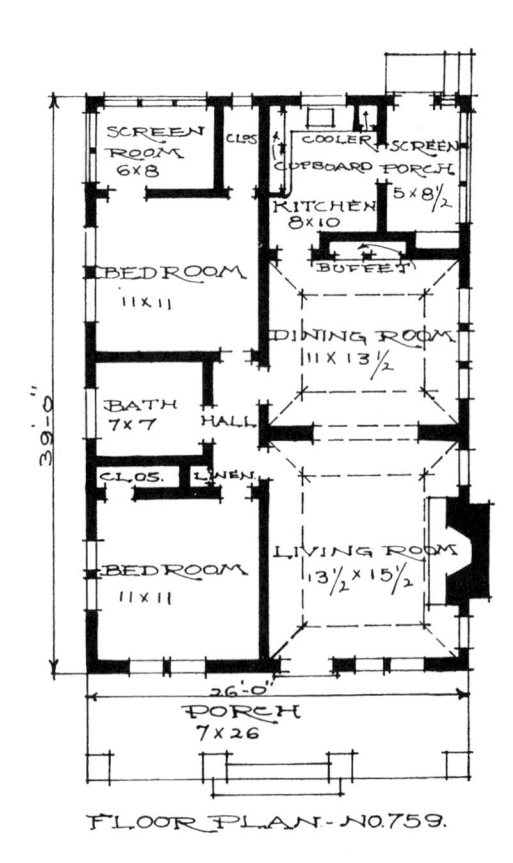

Plans as shown or reversed, $10.00.

FLOOR PLAN - NO. 759.

Cost $2400.00 to $2600.00.

Foundation concrete, porch and chimneys cement stone, porch floor cement, mantel sandstone and brick. Redwood siding on walls and shingles on roof. Pine finish throughout. Oak floors in living and dining rooms and den. Wood panels in dining room, imitation leather in den. Ceiling beams in living and dining rooms. Breakfast alcove, living and dining rooms and den finish stained and waxed, balance of finish, and kitchen and bath room wainscot enameled. Wall-bed included.

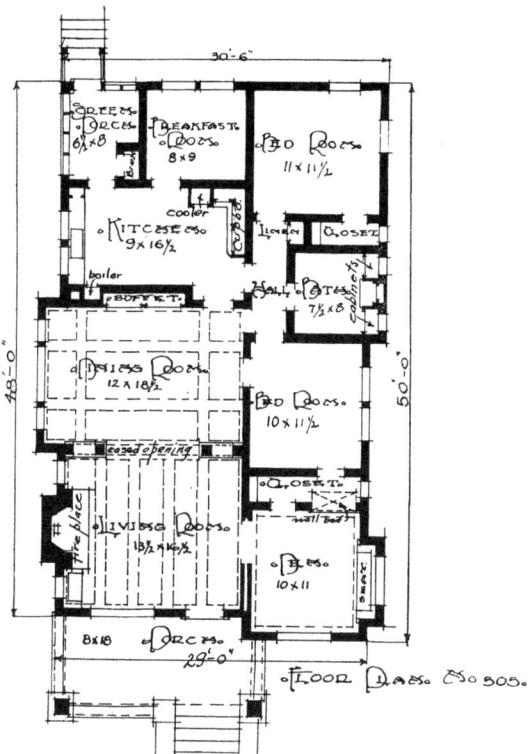

Plans as shown or reversed, $10.00.

NO 513
DONE AT
"Ye Planry"

Cost $4500.00 to $5000.00.

Foundation and basement concrete, basement floor cement, porch and terrace floors Spanish tiles, shakes on walls and composition roof. Mantels tile. Pine finish throughout, except white birch in living and dining rooms. Oak floors throughout. Veneered paneling and beam ceiling in living room, plaster paneling in dining and breakfast rooms. Finish in living and dining rooms stained mahogany color and waxed. Other finish, and kitchen and bath room wainscot enameled. Furnace included.

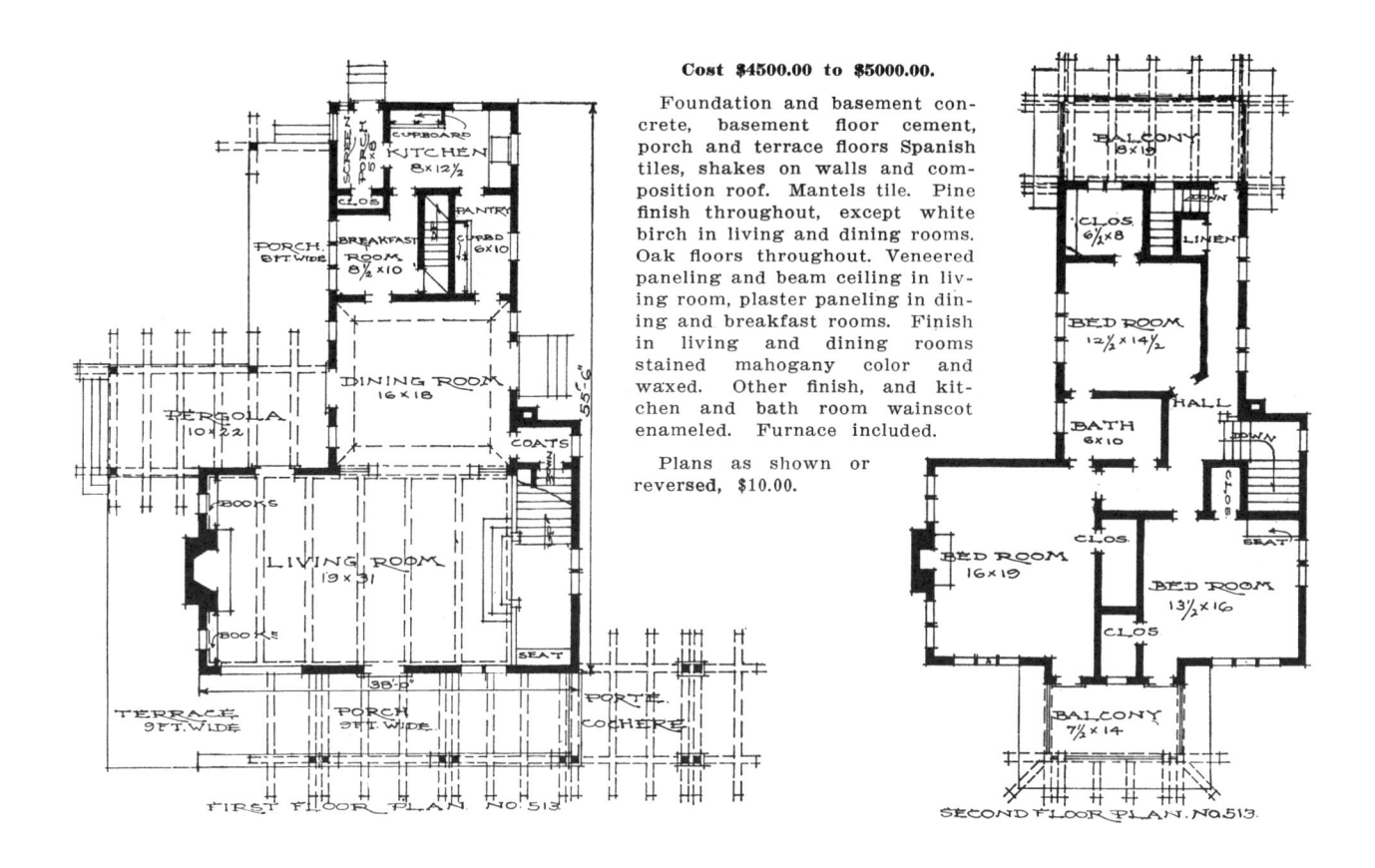

Plans as shown or reversed, $10.00.

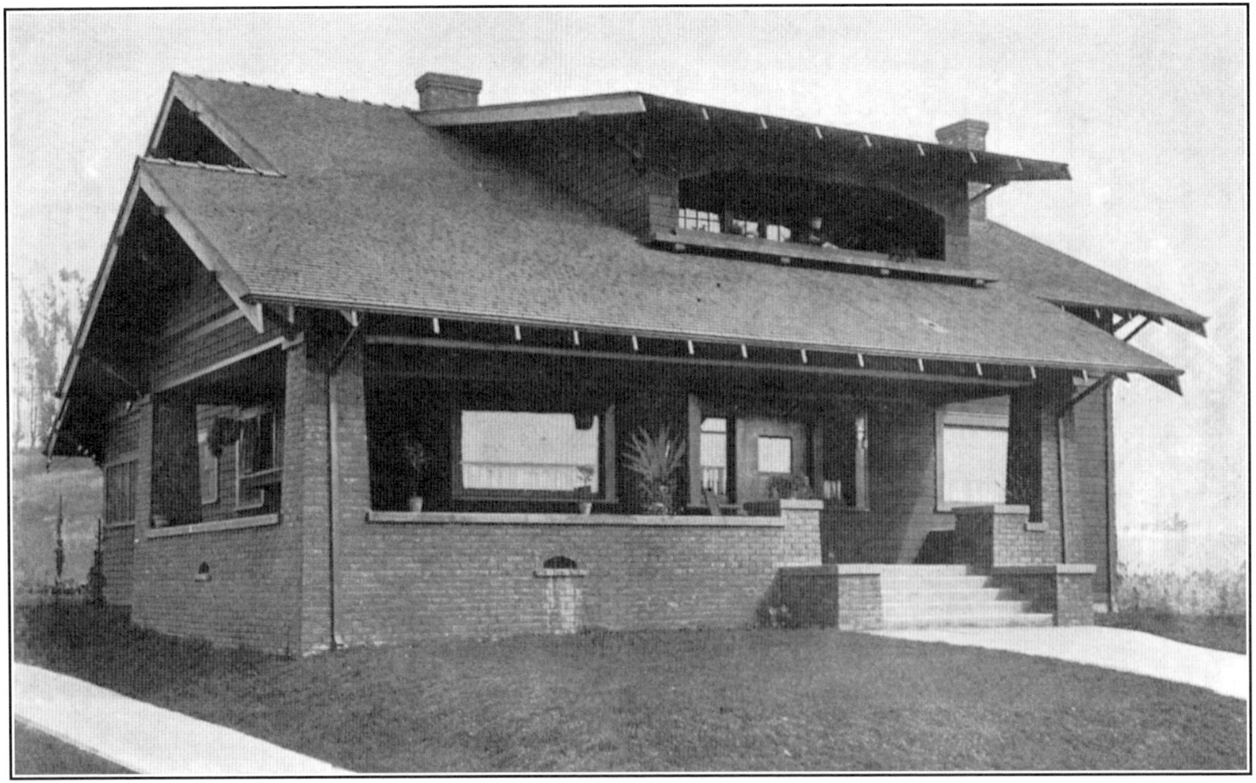

Cost $3700.00 to $4000.00.

Foundation and basement concrete, porch and basement floors cement, porch and chimneys brick, mantel pressed brick. Redwood siding to top of windows, shingles above and on roof. Pine finish throughout. Oak floors on first story except kitchen, other floors pine. Paneling in dining room, beamed ceiling in living and dining rooms and library. Downstairs finish stained and waxed, except kitchen finish **varnished.** Balance of finish and bath and kitchen wainscot enameled. Furnace included.

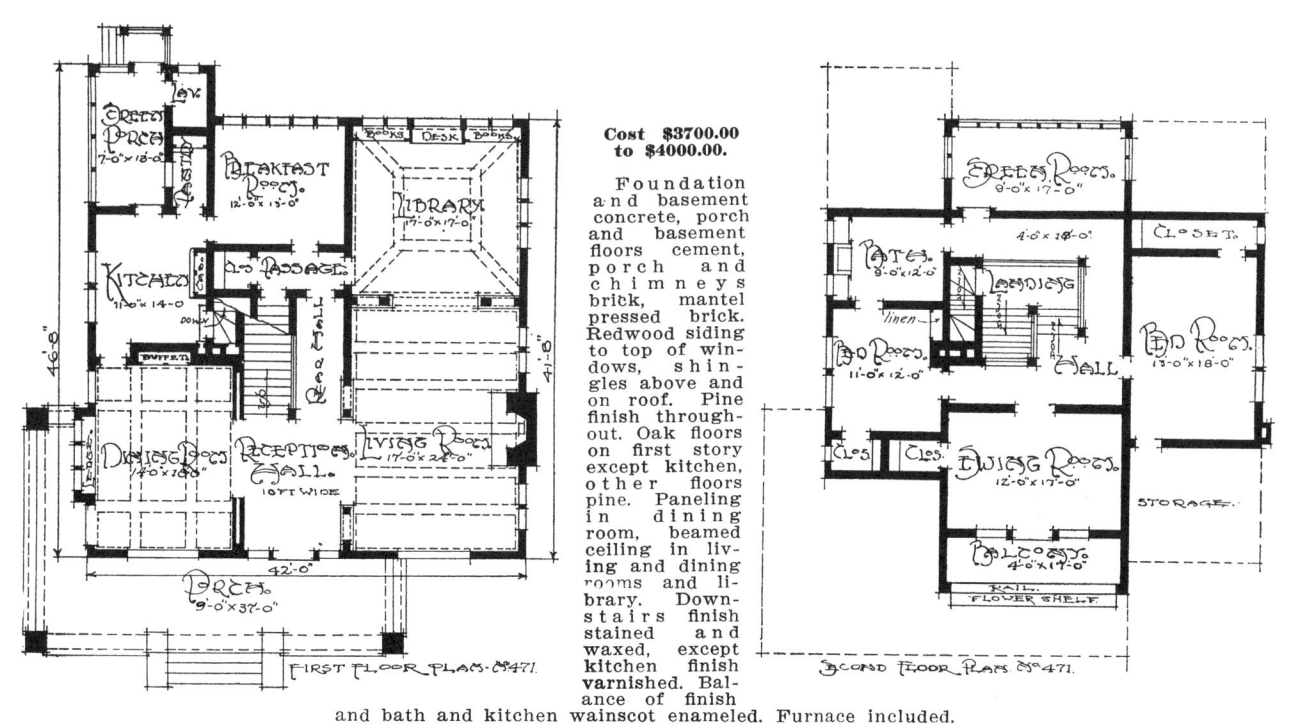

Plans as shown or reversed, $10.00.

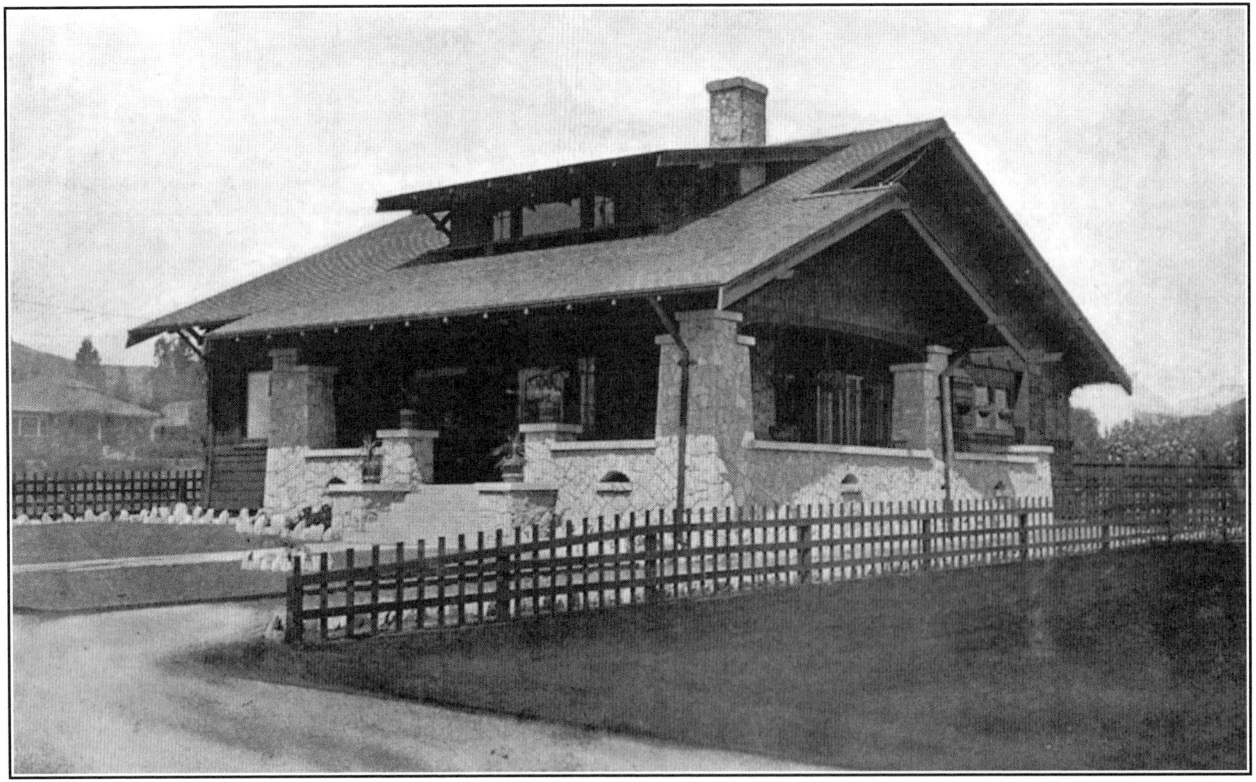

Cost $3500.00 to $3850.00.

Foundation and basement concrete, basement, patio, and porch floors cement. Porch and chimneys split granite boulders. Mantel tile. Redwood siding to top of windows, shakes above and shingles on roof. Pine finish throughout, stained and waxed in den, living, dining and breakfast rooms and rear bed room. Finish in other rooms, and kitchen and bath room wainscot, enameled. Oak floors throughout, except pine in kitchen and tile in bath room. Paneled wainscot in living, dining and breakfast rooms. Beamed ceiling in living and dining rooms; composition drain board in kitchen. May have two rooms on second floor. Furnace included.

Plans as shown or reversed, $10.00.

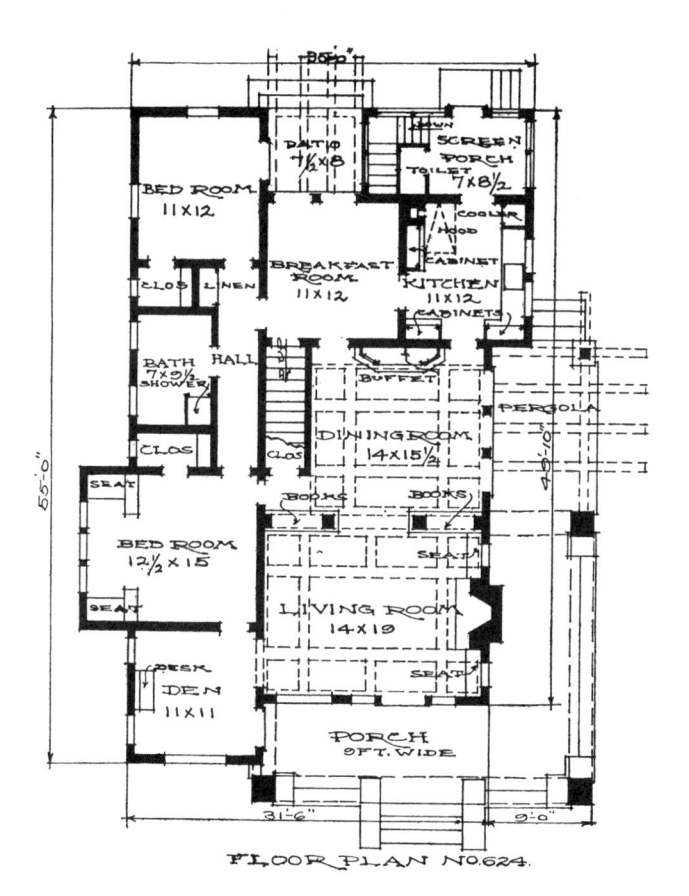

FLOOR PLAN NO. 624.

61

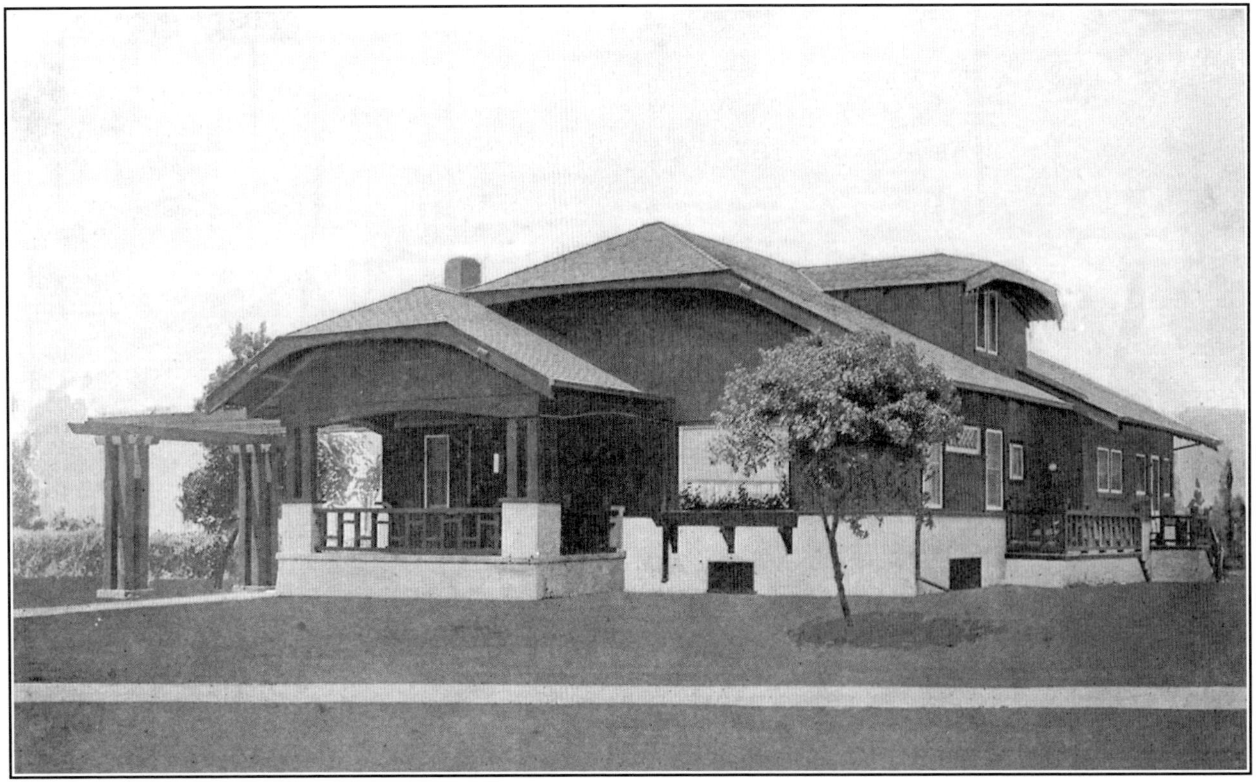

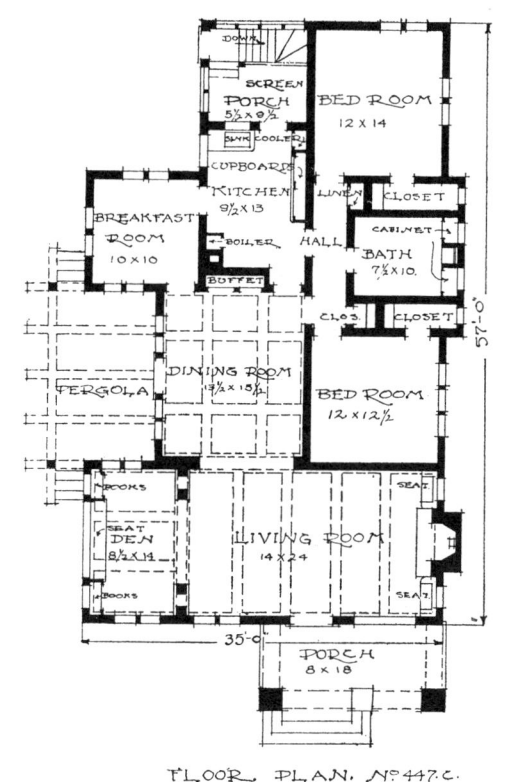

Cost $3600.00 to $3900.00.

Foundation and basement concrete, porch and basement floors cement, side porch floor pine, mantel tile. Porch, chimney and walls to window sills rough plastered, shakes above and shingles on roof. Pine finish throughout. Oak floors on first story except pine in kitchen and bath room. Stained and waxed finish and paneling in living and dining rooms, balance of finish, and kitchen and bath room wainscot, enameled. Trunk room, servant's room and screened sleeping balcony on second floor. Furnace included.

Plan No. 447-C shown herewith may be adapted to either this exterior or to No. 447 on page 76.

Plans as shown or reversed, $10.00.

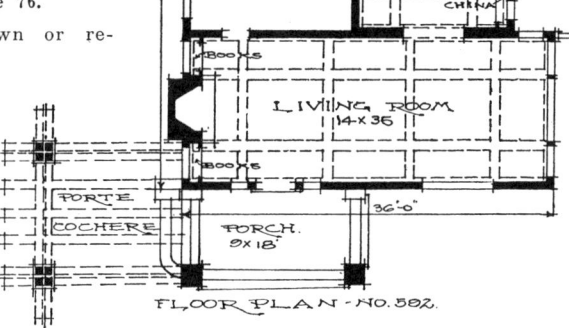

63

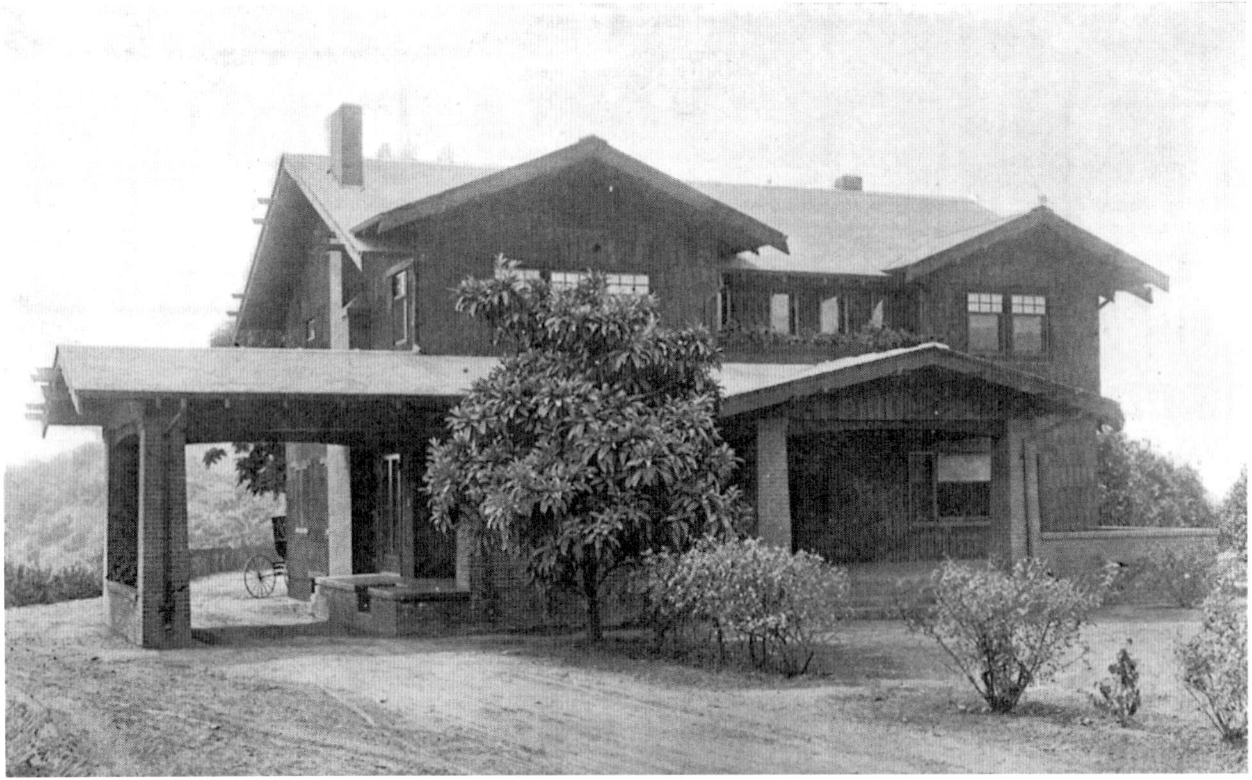

Cost $7500.00 to $8250.00.

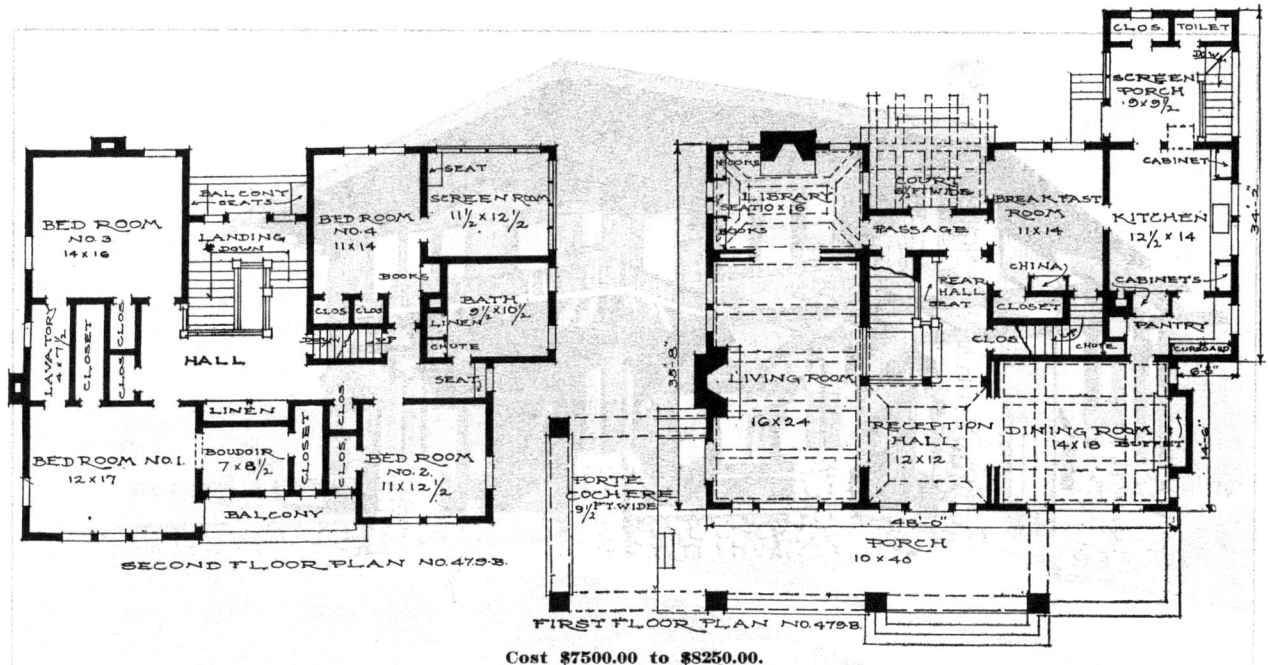

Foundation and basement concrete, porch and chimneys brick; porch, court, and basement floors cement. Mantels, stone in living room, pressed brick n library. Shakes on walls and shingles on roof. Pine finish throughout first story except oak in dining room; yellow pine in kitchen, breakfast room and pantry, also entire second story. Tile floor in bath room, oak floor entire first story, kitchen and up-stairs floors pine. Beam ceilings in dining and living rooms and library. Veneered panels, oak in dining room with tapestry above, pine in library and living room. Basket paneling walls and ceiling in screen room, illustrated on page 17. Down-stairs finish except pantry, kitchen and breakfast room stained and waxed, balance of finish and bath room and kitchen wainscot enameled. Solar heater and furnace included.

Plans as shown or reversed, $10.00.

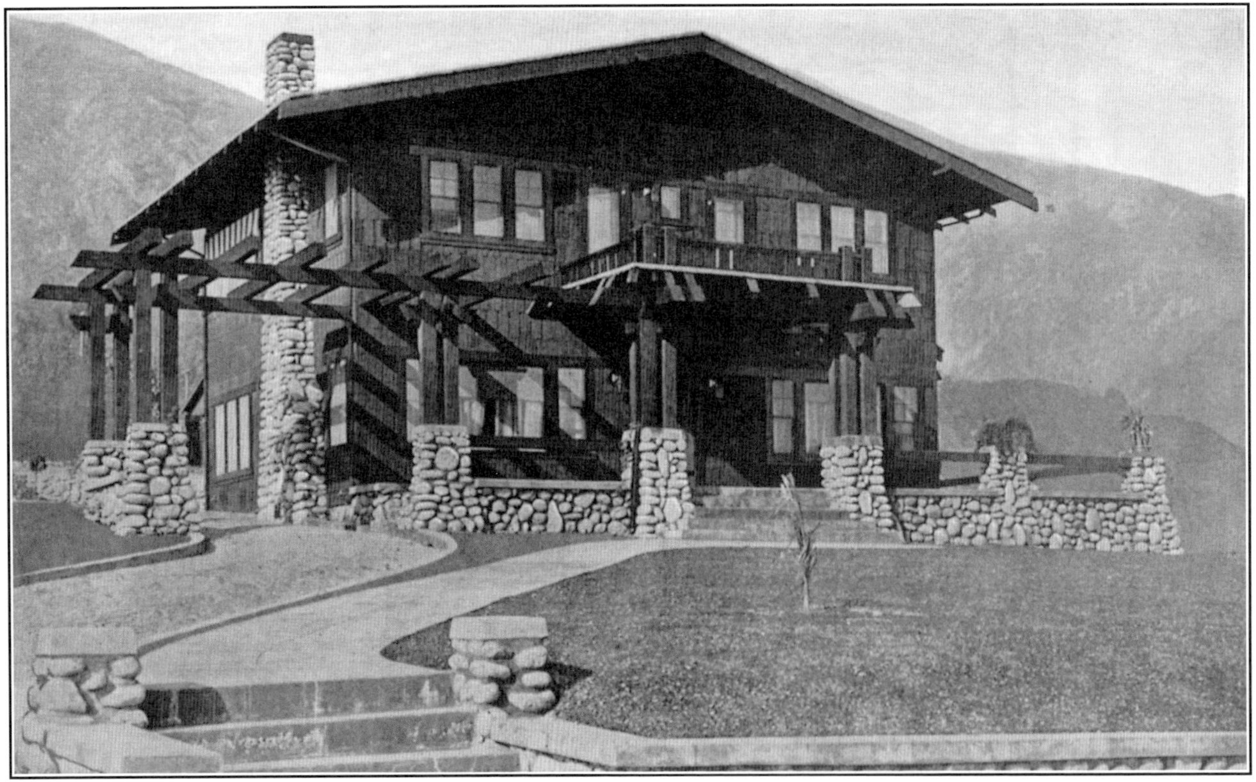

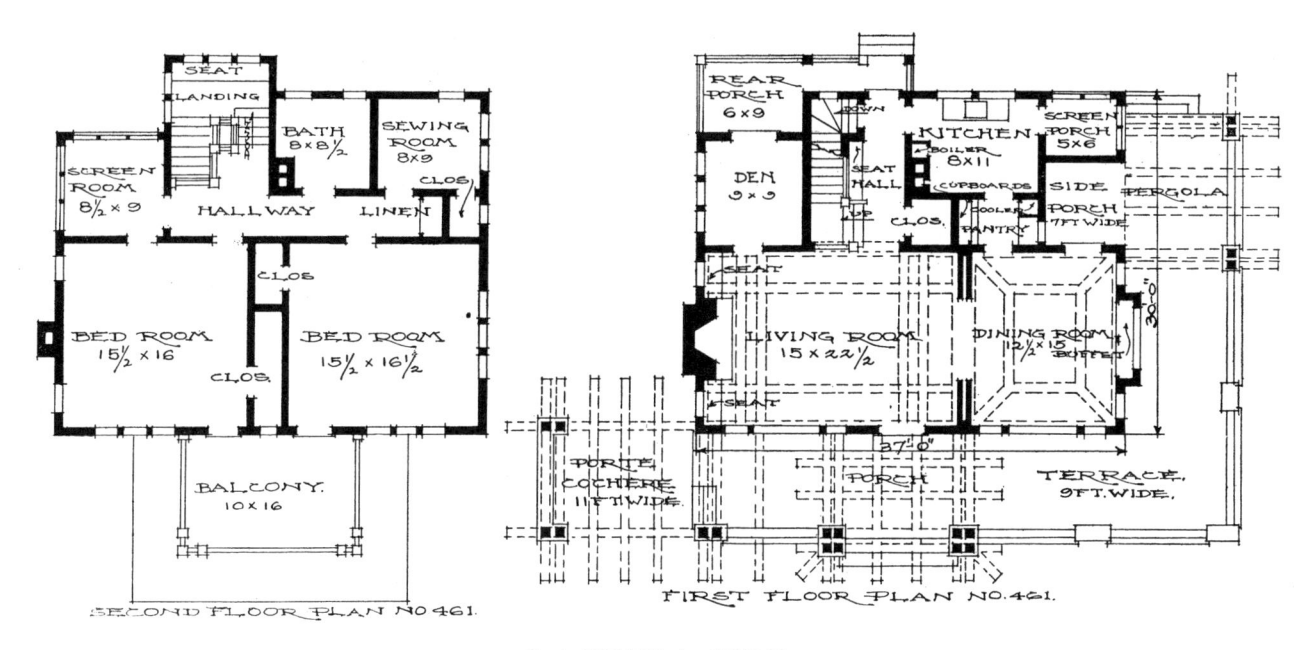

Cost $3800.00 to $4200.00.

Foundation and basement concrete, basement, porch and terrace floors cement, rear porch floor pine, porch and chimneys cobblestones, mantel pressed brick. Shakes on walls and composition roof. Kitchen and second story floors pine, balance oak. Paneling in dining room, beamed ceilings in living and dining rooms. Pine finish throughout, stained and waxed, except enameled finish in bath, varnished finish in kitchen, pantry and servant's room. Enameled wainscot in bath, kitchen and pantry. Furnace included.

Plans as shown or reversed, $10.00.

Cost $2200.00 to $2400.00.

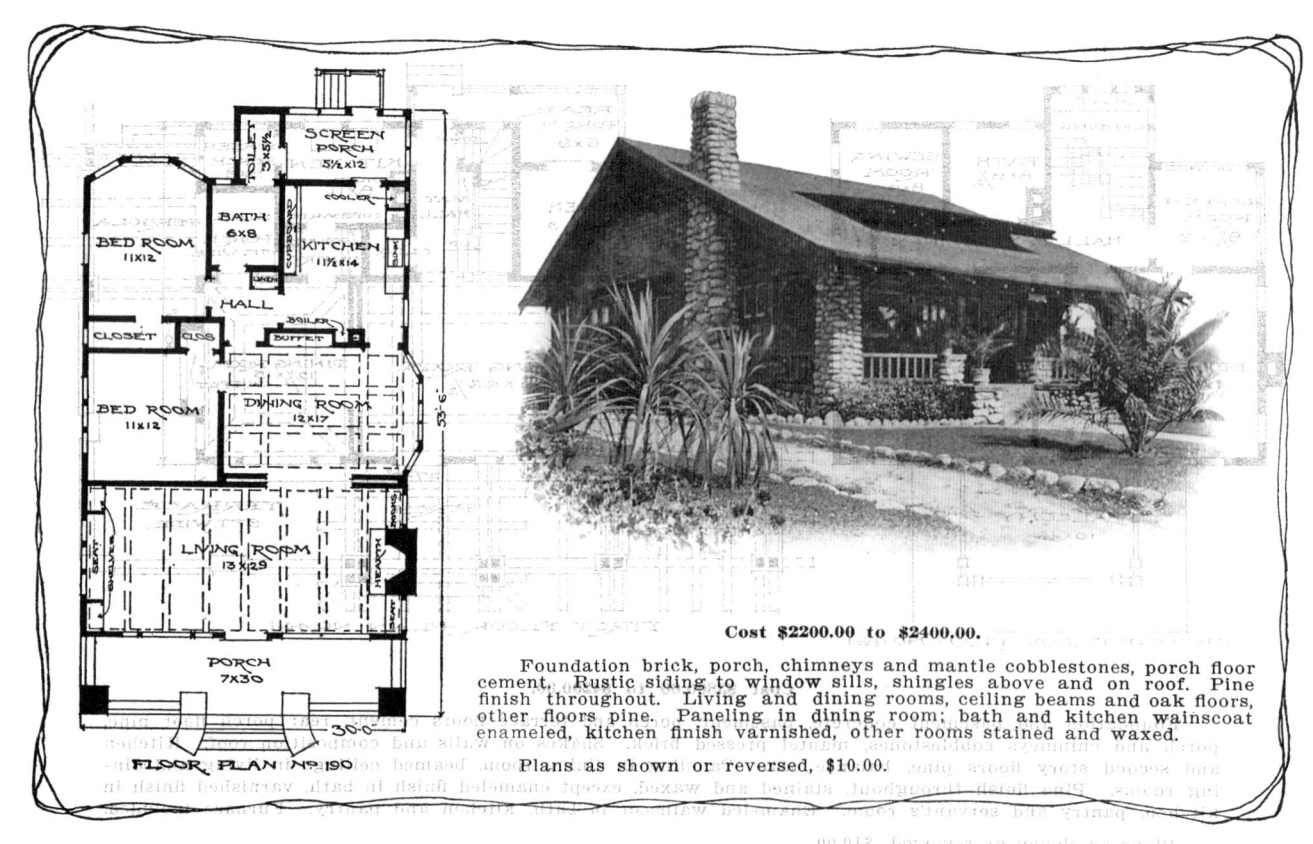

Foundation brick, porch, chimneys and mantle cobblestones, porch floor cement. Rustic siding to window sills, shingles above and on roof. Pine finish throughout. Living and dining rooms, ceiling beams and oak floors, other floors pine. Paneling in dining room; bath and kitchen wainscoat enameled, kitchen finish varnished, other rooms stained and waxed.

Plans as shown or reversed, $10.00.

Cost $1600.00 to $1750.00.

Foundation, chimney and porch brick, porch floor cement, shingled walls and roof. Pine finish throughout. Stained and waxed finish and oak floors in living and dining rooms. Ceiling beams and paneled wainscot in dining room. Indirect lighting and plaster paneling in living room. Kitchen finish varnished; other finish, and bath room and kitchen wainscot enameled.

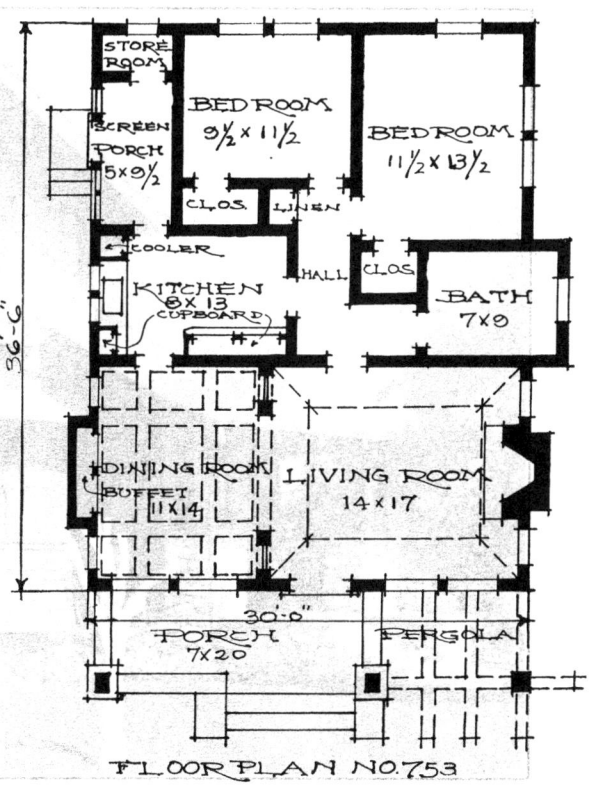

Plans as shown or reversed, $10.00.

FLOOR PLAN NO. 753

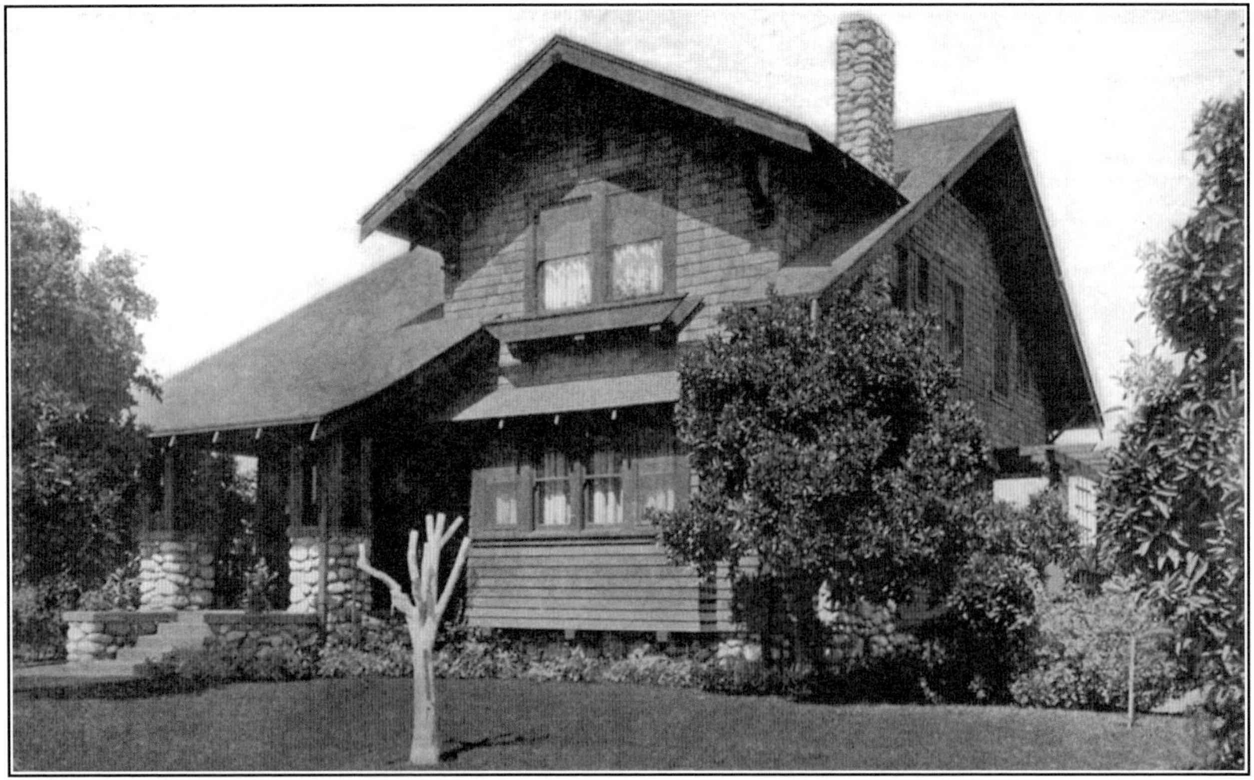

Cost $3000 to $3300.

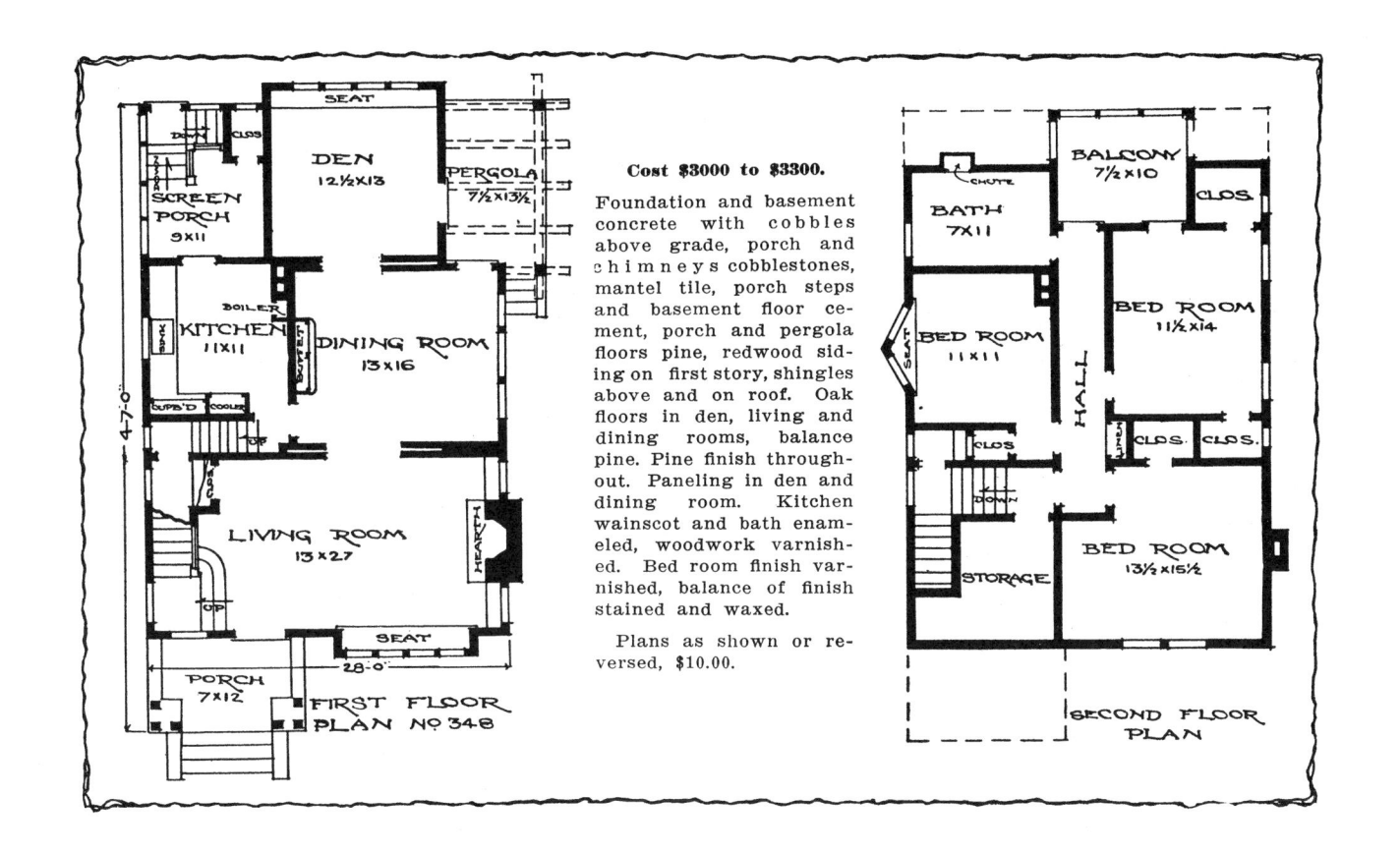

Foundation and basement concrete with cobbles above grade, porch and chimneys cobblestones, mantel tile, porch steps and basement floor cement, porch and pergola floors pine, redwood siding on first story, shingles above and on roof. Oak floors in den, living and dining rooms, balance pine. Pine finish throughout. Paneling in den and dining room. Kitchen wainscot and bath enameled, woodwork varnished. Bed room finish varnished, balance of finish stained and waxed.

Plans as shown or reversed, $10.00.

72

Cost $7500.00 to $8000.00

Foundation and basement concrete, cement floors in court, basement and porch. Tile mantel, walls rough plaster on metal lath, Spanish tile roof. Pine finish throughout. Canvas floor in tower, pine floor in servants' room, storage and kitchen, tile in bath room, oak elsewhere. Beamed ceilings in living room and court. Finish in bath room, bed rooms and dressing room enameled, in kitchen, pantry and servant's room varnished. Other finish stained and waxed. Enameled wainscot in kitchen, pantry and bath rooms. **Furnace included.** Plans as shown or reversed, $10.00.

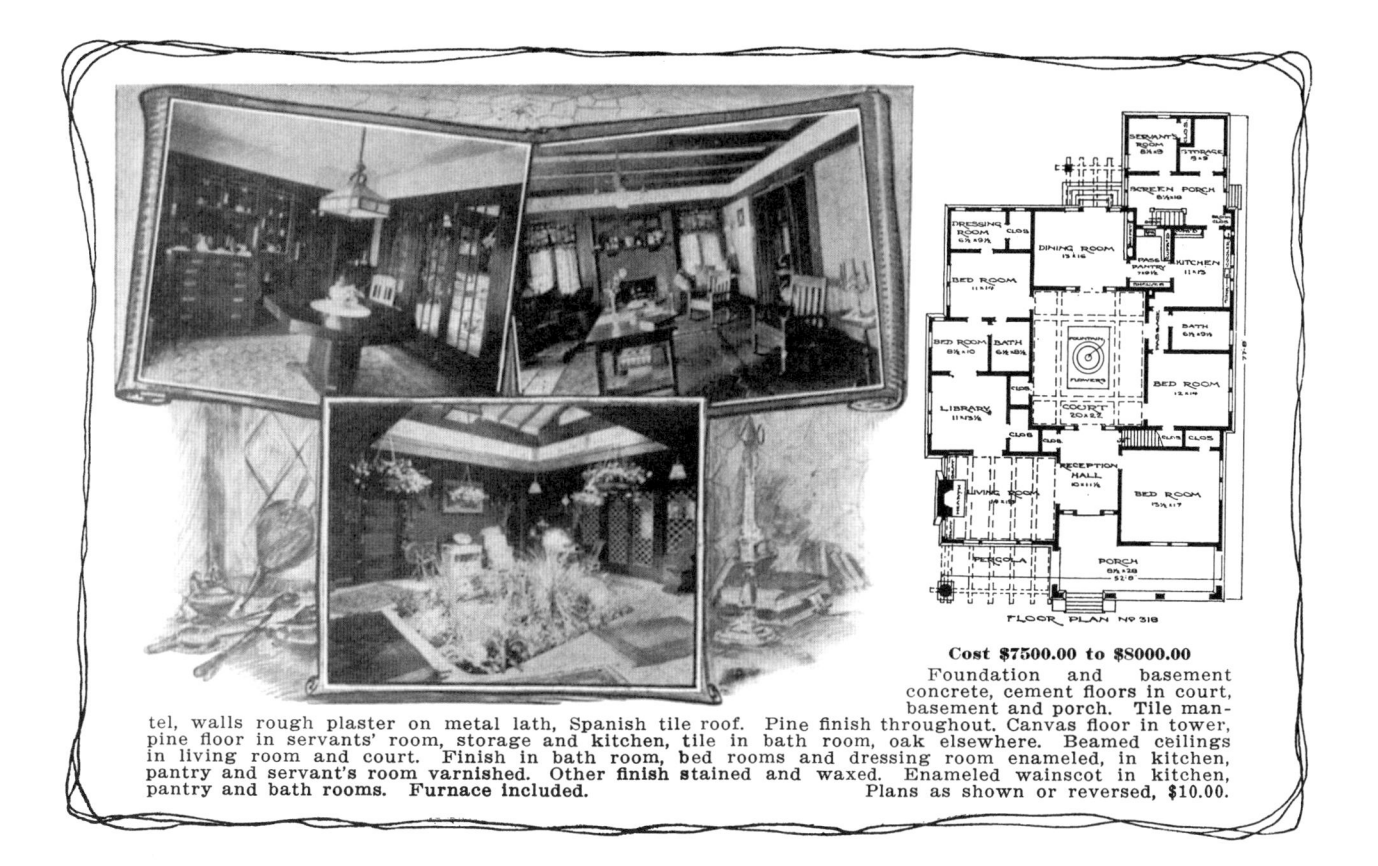

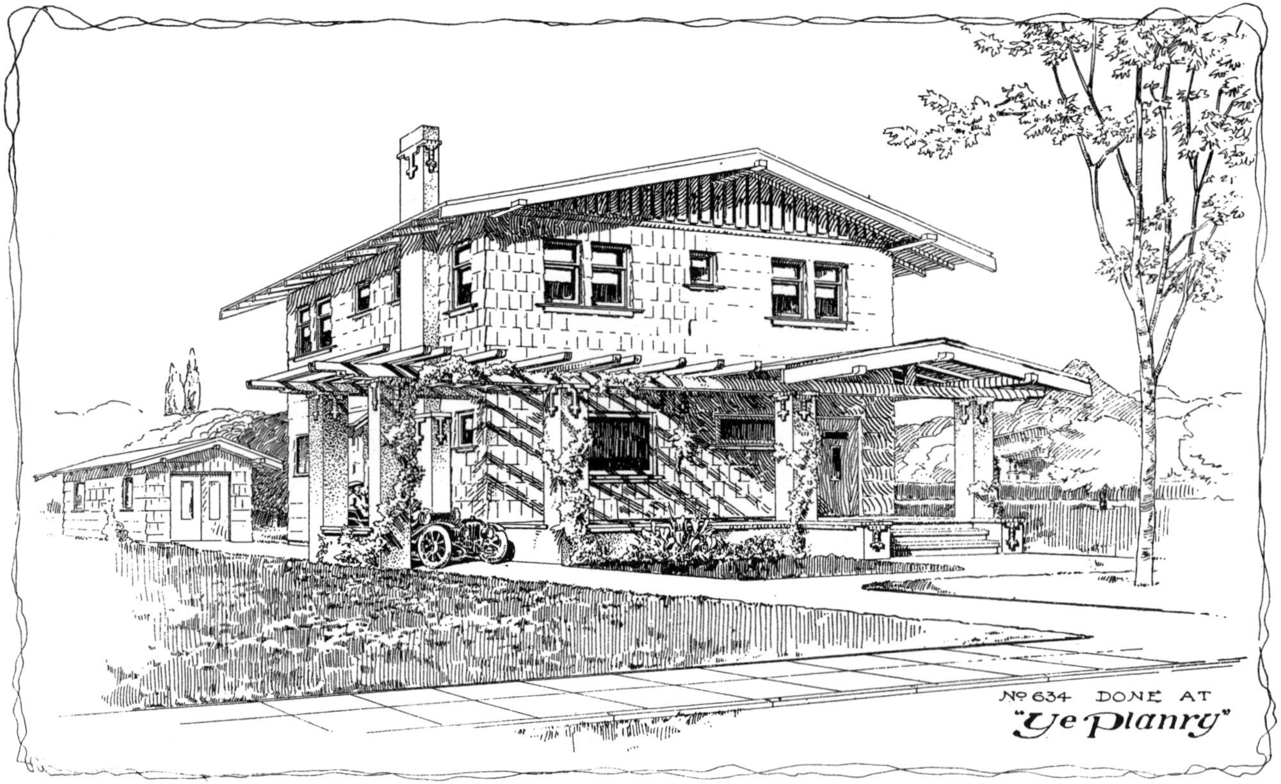
No 634 DONE AT
"Ye Planry"

Cost $3500.00 to $3850.00.

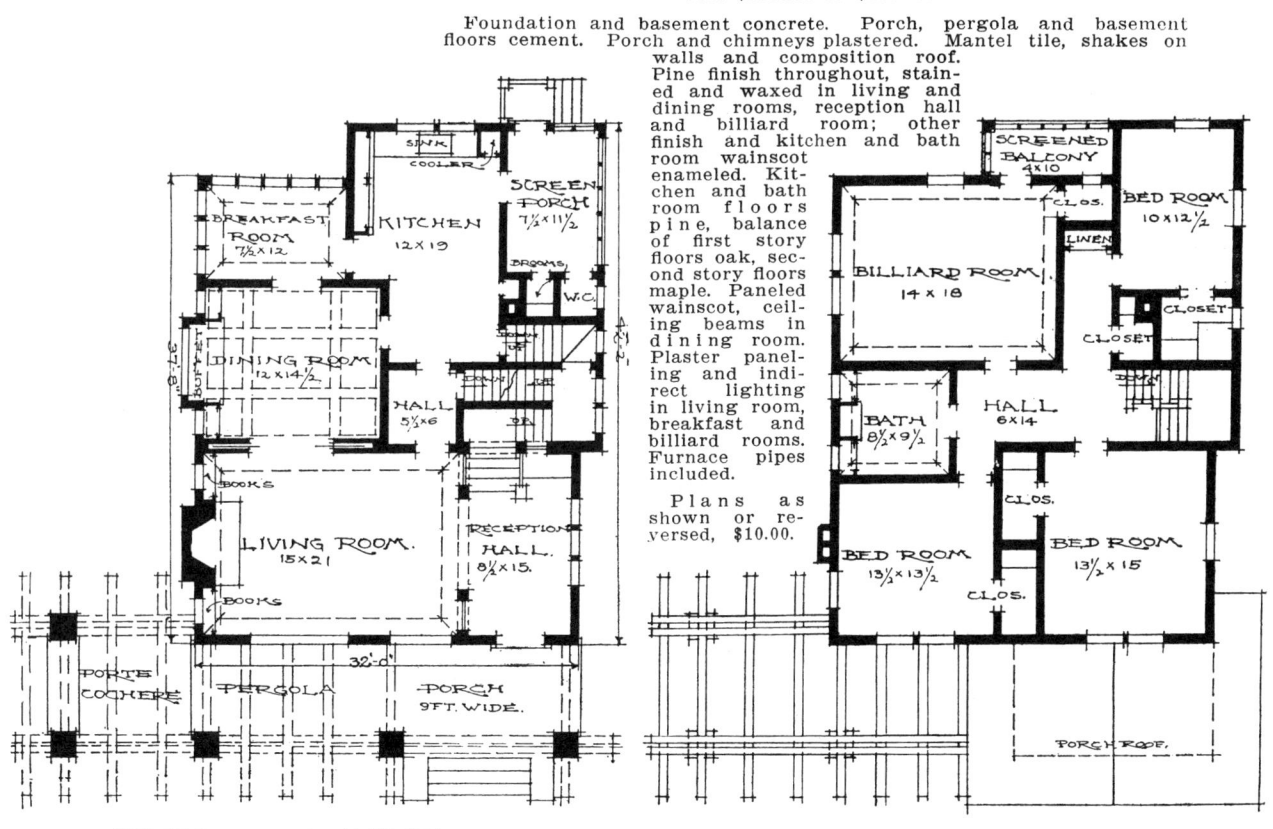

Foundation and basement concrete. Porch, pergola and basement floors cement. Porch and chimneys plastered. Mantel tile, shakes on walls and composition roof.

Pine finish throughout, stained and waxed in living and dining rooms, reception hall and billiard room; other finish and kitchen and bath room wainscot enameled. Kitchen and bath room floors pine, balance of first story floors oak, second story floors maple. Paneled wainscot, ceiling beams in dining room. Plaster paneling and indirect lighting in living room, breakfast and billiard rooms. Furnace pipes included.

Plans as shown or reversed, $10.00.

FIRST FLOOR PLAN NO. 634.

SECOND FLOOR PLAN NO. 634.

75

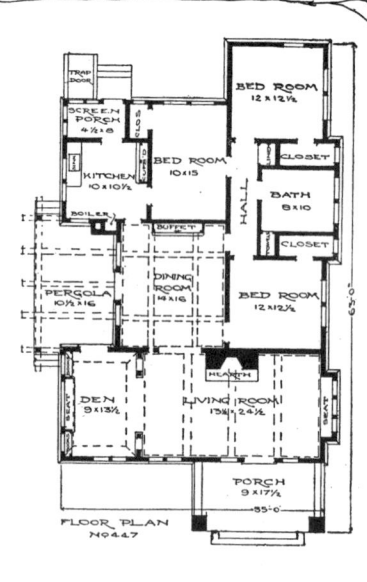

Cost $2500.00 to $2800.00.

Foundation and basement concrete, porch and chimneys cement stone, porch, basement and pergola floors cement, shakes on walls, shingles on roof. Mantel brick or tile. Pine finish throughout. Paneling, stained and waxed finish and oak floors in living and dining rooms and den, pine floors elsewhere. Beams in living and dining rooms, cove ceiling in den. Kitchen finish varnished, bed room, kitchen wainscot and bath enameled. Furnace extra.

Plans as shown or reversed, $10.00.

NO. 657.
DONE AT "Ye Planry"

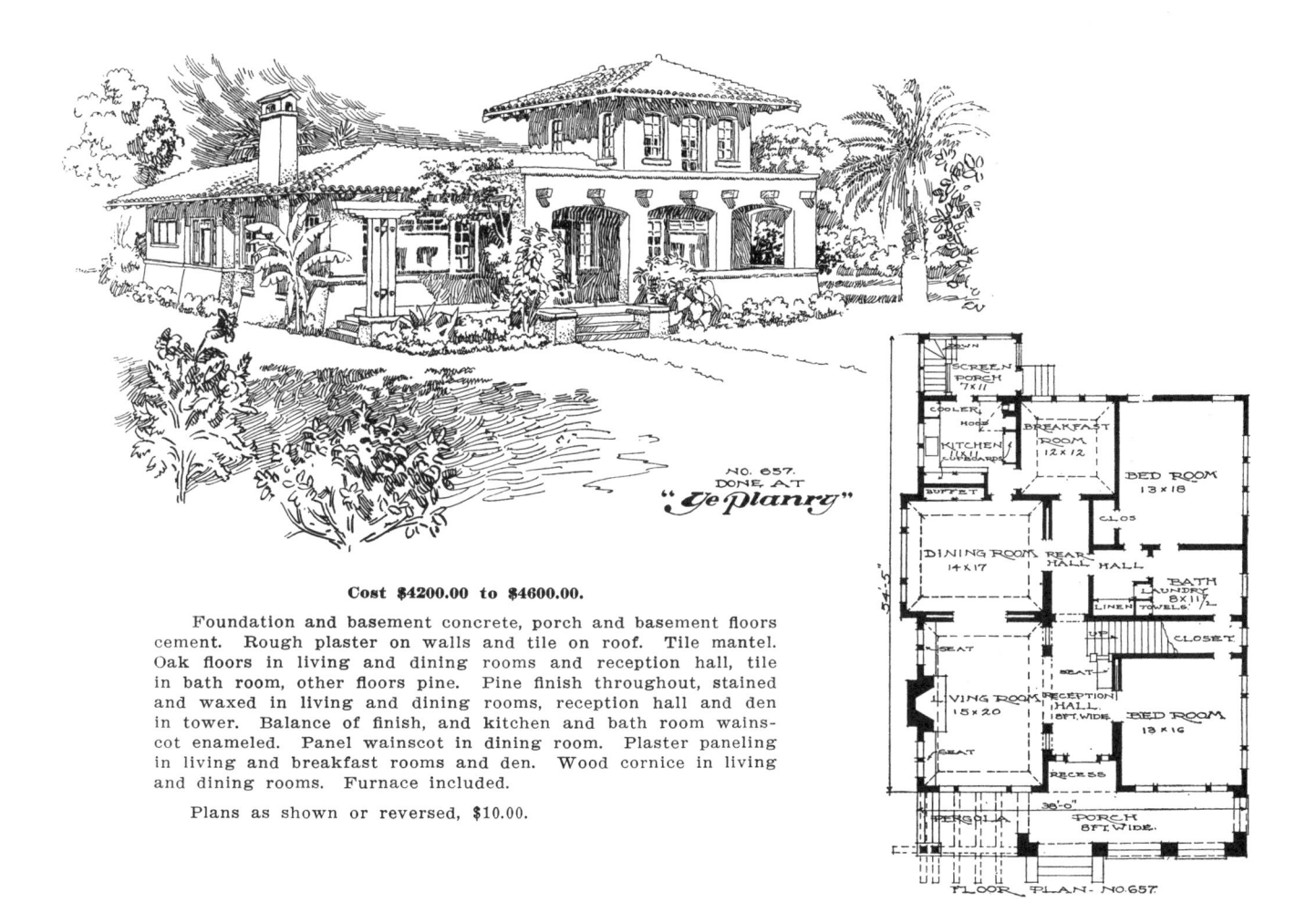

Cost $4200.00 to $4600.00.

Foundation and basement concrete, porch and basement floors cement. Rough plaster on walls and tile on roof. Tile mantel. Oak floors in living and dining rooms and reception hall, tile in bath room, other floors pine. Pine finish throughout, stained and waxed in living and dining rooms, reception hall and den in tower. Balance of finish, and kitchen and bath room wainscot enameled. Panel wainscot in dining room. Plaster paneling in living and breakfast rooms and den. Wood cornice in living and dining rooms. Furnace included.

Plans as shown or reversed, $10.00.

77

Cost $1800.00 to $2000.00.

Foundation and chimney brick, mantel tile, porch floor pine, redwood siding on walls and shingles on roof. Pine finish throughout. Stained and waxed finish and oak floors in living and dining rooms. Ceiling beams and paneled wainscot in dining room. Indirect lighting and plaster paneling in living room. Kitchen finish varnished, other finish and bath room and kitchen wainscot enameled.

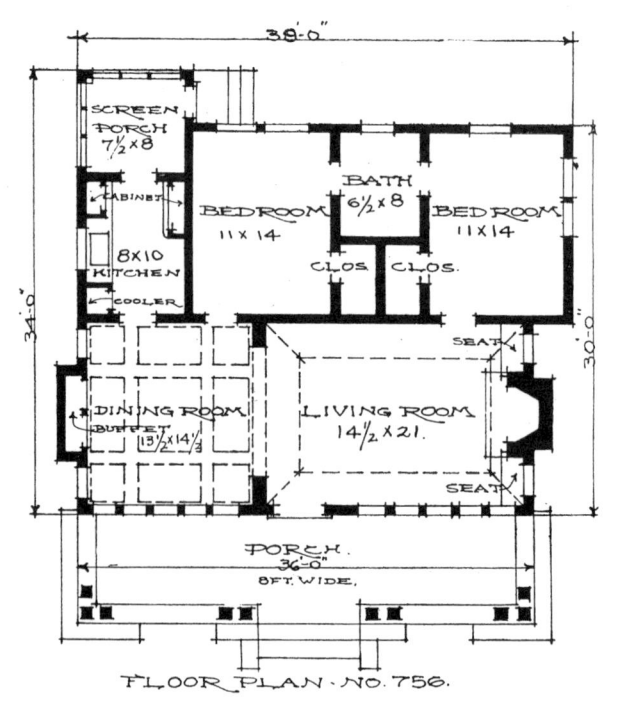

Plans as shown or reversed, $10.00.

Cost $1750.00 to $1900.00.

Foundation, porch and chimney brick, mantel tile. Porch floor cement. Redwood siding on walls and shingles on roof. Pine finish throughout. Stained and waxed finish, oak floors and indirect lighting in living and dining rooms. Paneled wainscot in dining room; kitchen finish varnished, other finish and bath room and kitchen wainscot enameled.

Plans as shown or reversed, $10.00.

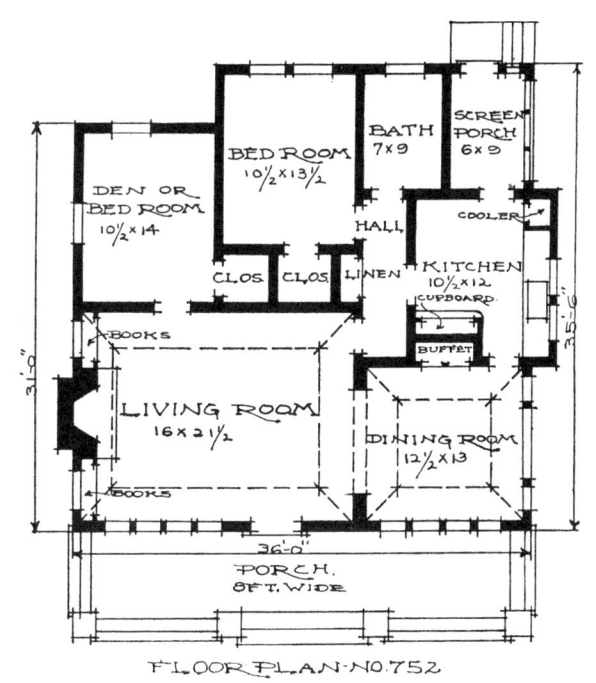

FLOOR PLAN NO. 752

SKETCH ~ No 314.
DONE AT
Ye Planry
SKETCH OF LIVING ROOM
SKETCH OF DINING ROOM

Cost $3700 to $4000

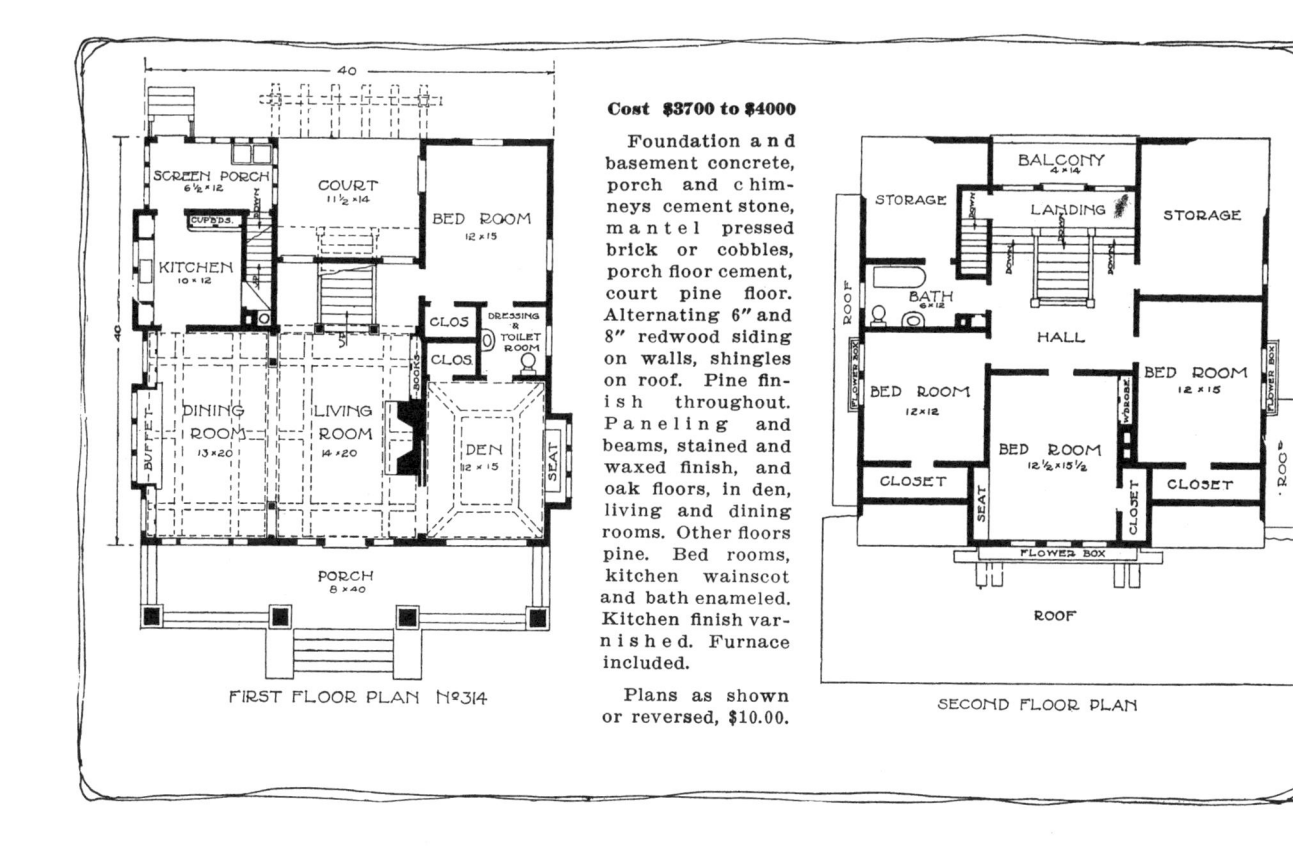

Foundation and basement concrete, porch and chimneys cement stone, mantel pressed brick or cobbles, porch floor cement, court pine floor. Alternating 6" and 8" redwood siding on walls, shingles on roof. Pine finish throughout. Paneling and beams, stained and waxed finish, and oak floors, in den, living and dining rooms. Other floors pine. Bed rooms, kitchen wainscot and bath enameled. Kitchen finish varnished. Furnace included.

Plans as shown or reversed, $10.00.

Stairway

No. 228
Doña A
"Ye Planry"

Cost $3500.00 to $3800.00.

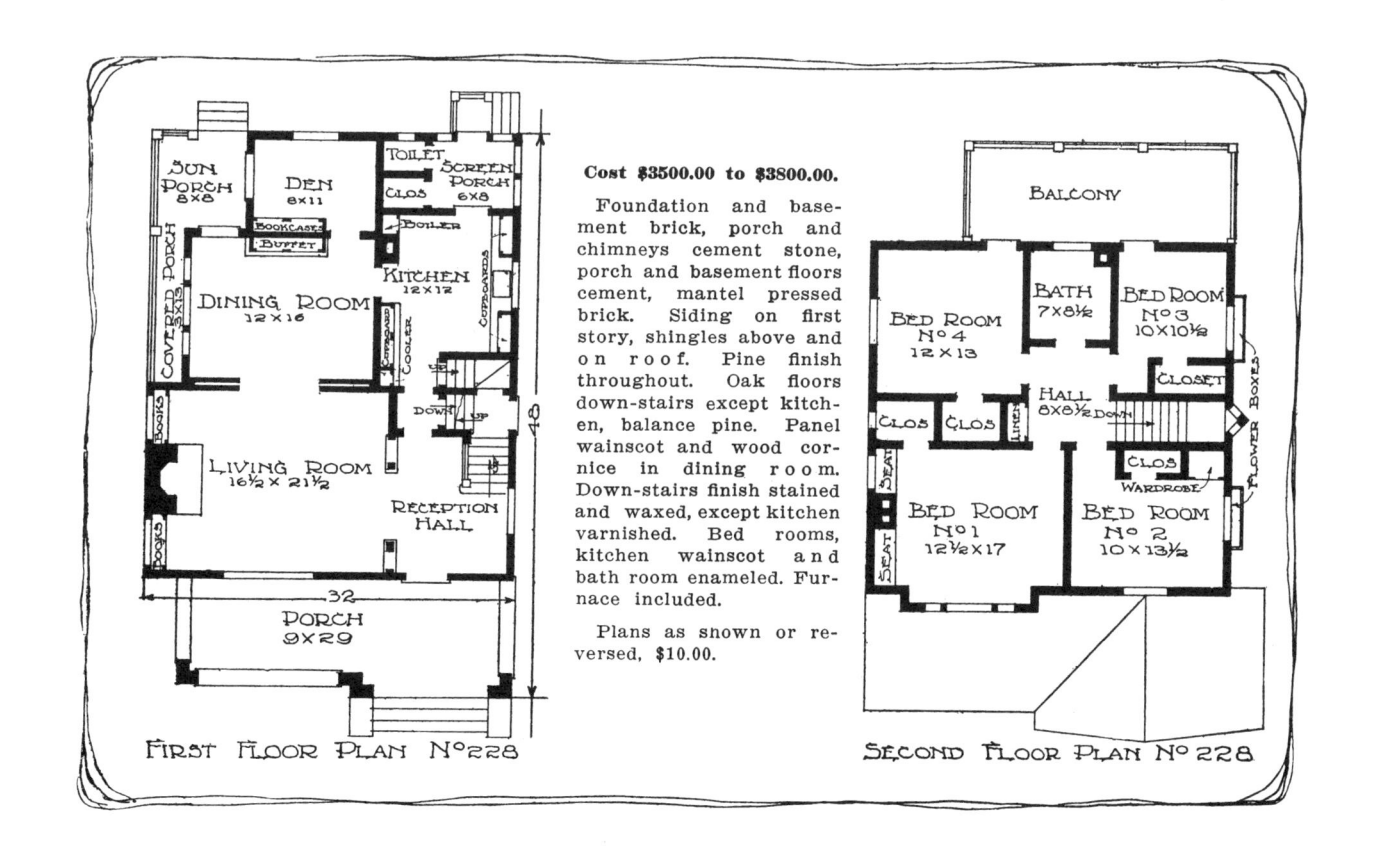

Foundation and basement brick, porch and chimneys cement stone, porch and basement floors cement, mantel pressed brick. Siding on first story, shingles above and on roof. Pine finish throughout. Oak floors down-stairs except kitchen, balance pine. Panel wainscot and wood cornice in dining room. Down-stairs finish stained and waxed, except kitchen varnished. Bed rooms, kitchen wainscot and bath room enameled. Furnace included.

Plans as shown or reversed, $10.00.

84

Cost $3200.00 to $3600.00.

Foundation and basement concrete, porch and basement floors cement, mantel pressed brick, shakes on walls and patent roofing. Pine finish throughout. Composition drain-board. Oak floors throughout except pine in kitchen and screen room. Wood paneling in dining room, imitation leather paneling in hall and living room. Downstairs finish stained and waxed except kitchen. Upstairs and kitchen finish and wainscot in bath room and kitchen enameled. Furnace pipes included.

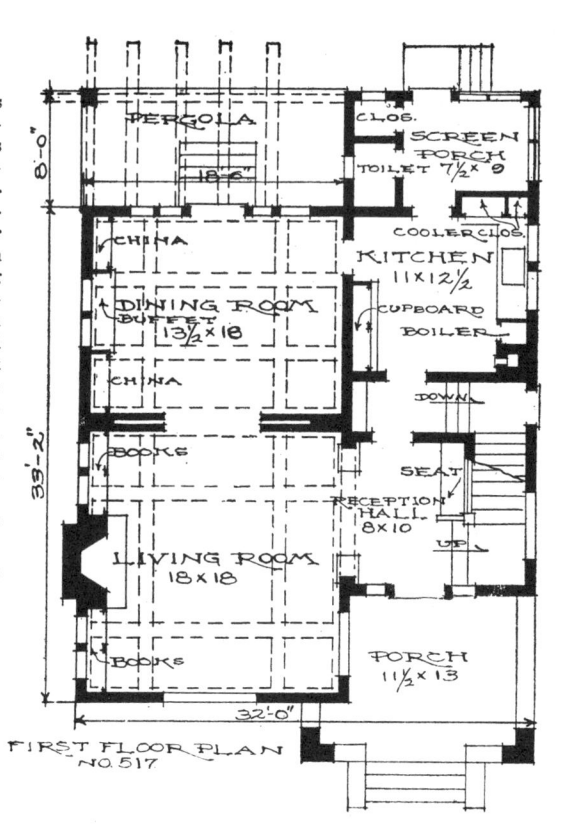

Plans as shown or reversed, $10.00.

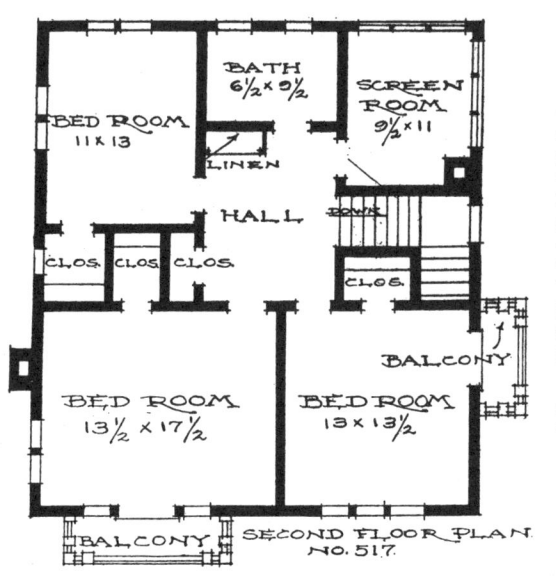

NO 700
DONE AT
Ye Planry

Cost $15,000.00 to $17,000.00.

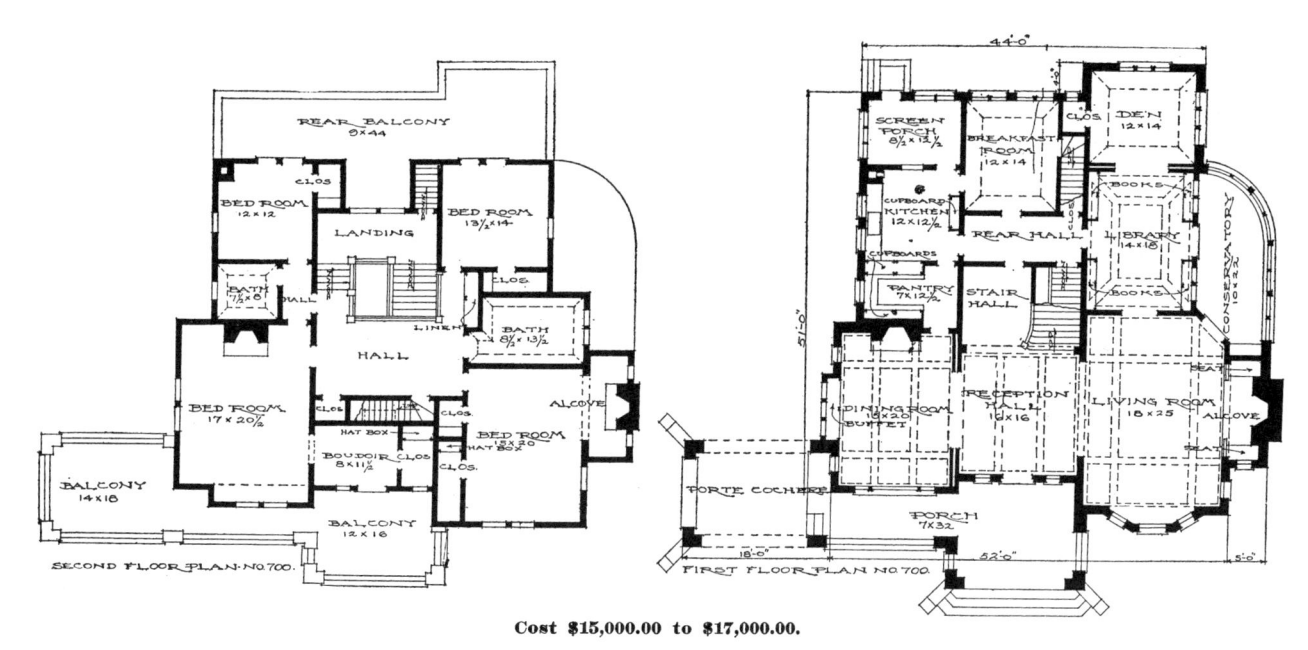

A "House with Seven Gables" similar in many respects to No. 49 on page 36-37; the plan is reversed and a conservatory, den and breakfast room added; the porch and chimneys are brick, and the first story walls half timber with brick panels, and the second story walls half timber and plaster. There are beamed ceilings and paneled wainscoting in the dining room, library, reception hall, and living room, and indirect lighting in the den and breakfast room. The first story floors are oak, except in the breakfast room, the bath room floors tile, and all other floors white maple. Kitchen, breakfast room and all up-stairs finish, and kitchen and bath room wainscot enameled. The living room mantel is stone, the other mantels tile. Furnace included.

Plans as shown or reversed, with special specifications calling for any desired finish material and treatment, $25.00.

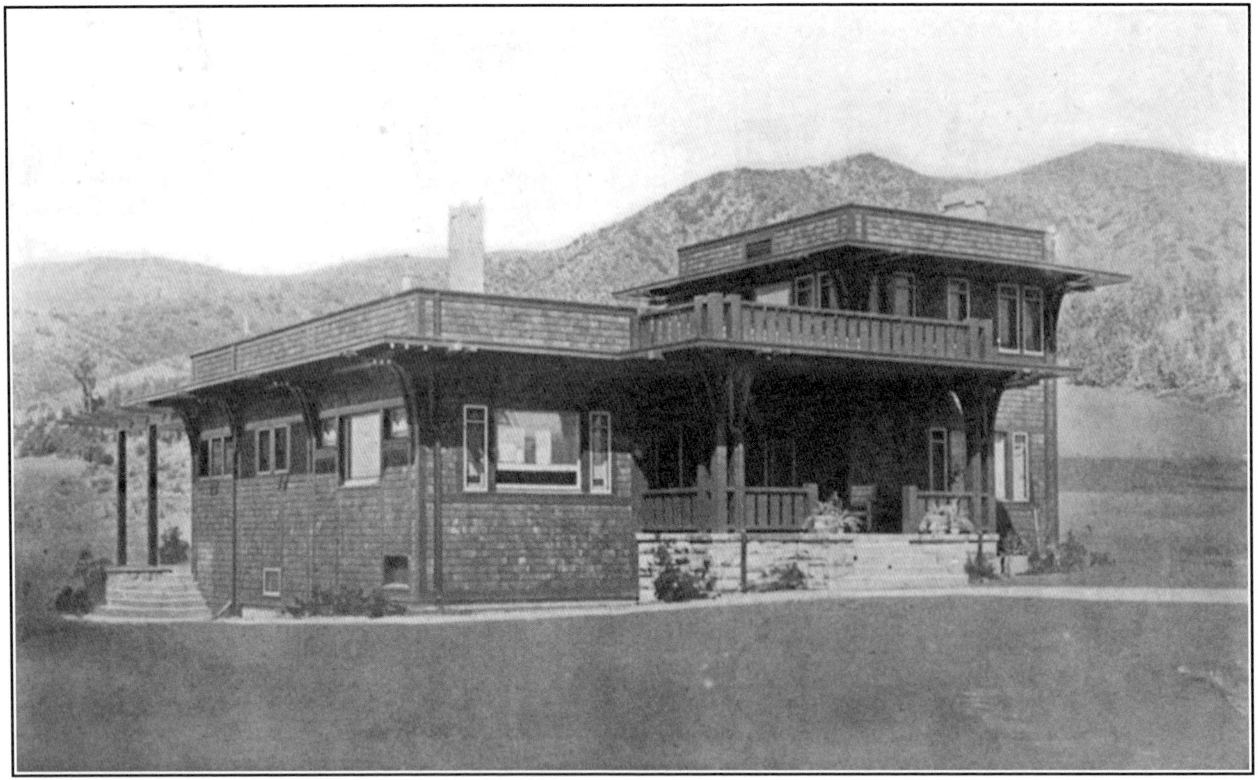

Cost $5500.00 to $6000.00.

Foundation and basement concrete, porch and basement floors cement. Porch and chimneys cement stone; mantels tile. Walls half timber and shingles, with patent roofing. Oak floors throughout except pine in kitchen, bath room and den in tower. Pine finish throughout. Paneling in living and dining rooms and reception hall. Indirect lighting in hall, living and dining rooms and parlor. Den and living room stained and waxed finish. All other interior finish enameled, gray in kitchen and ivory elsewhere. Enameled plaster wainscot in kitchen and bath room. Piped for furnace. Three-foot air chamber over entire house to exclude heat.

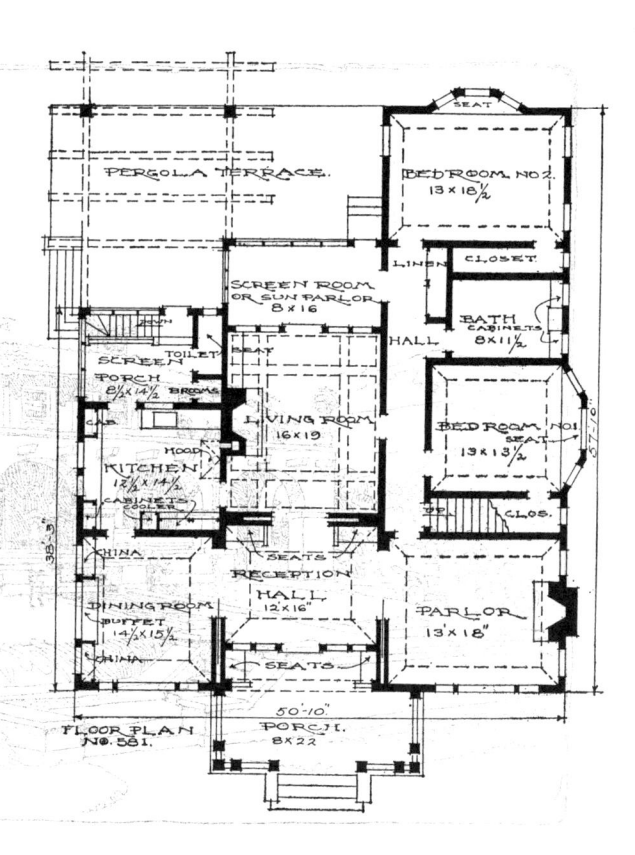

Plans as shown or reversed, $10.00.

No. 330.
Done At
"Ye Planry"

Cost $8500.00 to $9250.00.

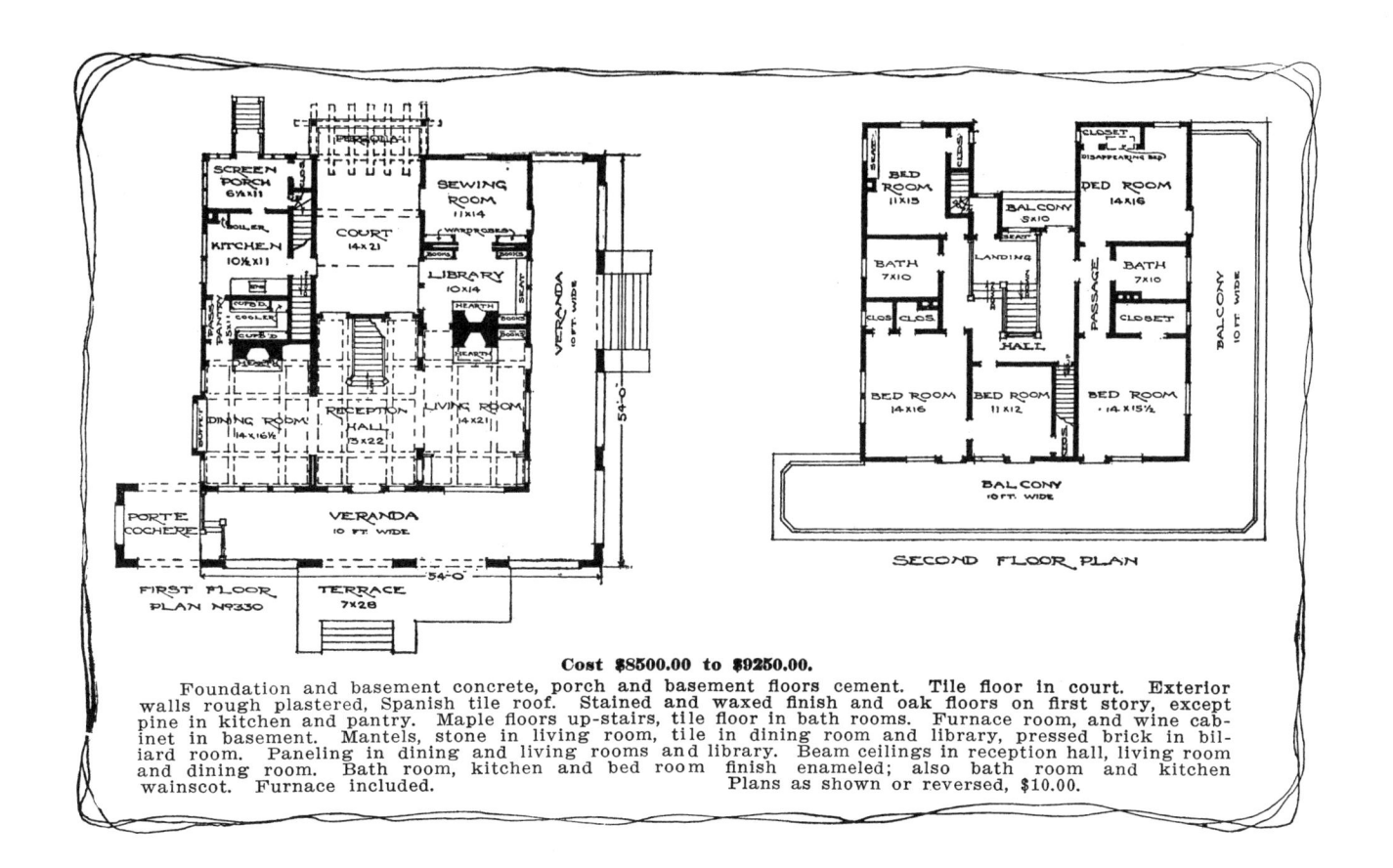

Foundation and basement concrete, porch and basement floors cement. Tile floor in court. Exterior walls rough plastered, Spanish tile roof. Stained and waxed finish and oak floors on first story, except pine in kitchen and pantry. Maple floors up-stairs, tile floor in bath rooms. Furnace room, and wine cabinet in basement. Mantels, stone in living room, tile in dining room and library, pressed brick in billiard room. Paneling in dining and living rooms and library. Beam ceilings in reception hall, living room and dining room. Bath room, kitchen and bed room finish enameled; also bath room and kitchen wainscot. Furnace included.

Plans as shown or reversed, $10.00.

92

Cost $7500.00 to $8000.00.

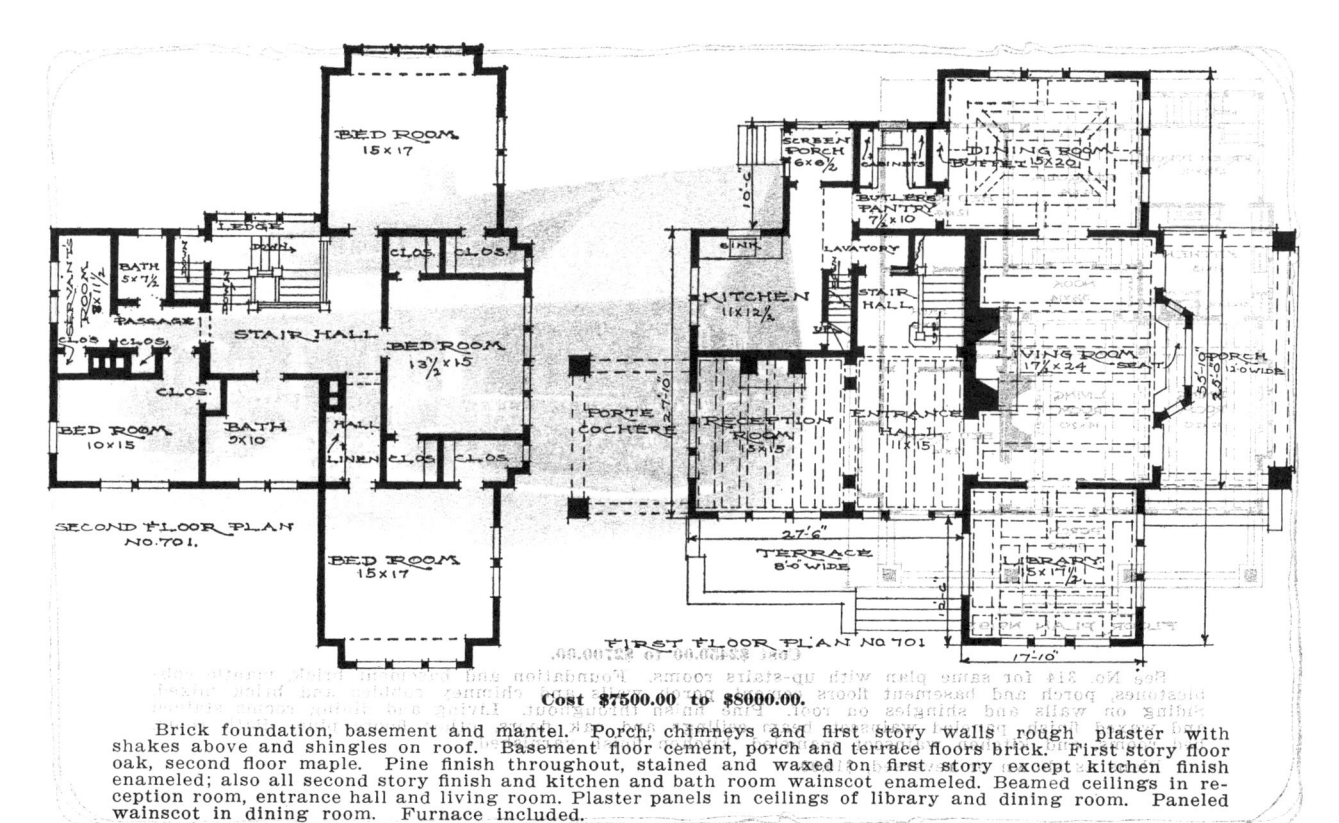

Brick foundation, basement and mantel. Porch, chimneys and first story walls rough plaster with shakes above and shingles on roof. Basement floor cement, porch and terrace floors brick. First story floor oak, second floor maple. Pine finish throughout, stained and waxed on first story except kitchen finish enameled; also all second story finish and kitchen and bath room wainscot enameled. Beamed ceilings in reception room, entrance hall and living room. Plaster panels in ceilings of library and dining room. Paneled wainscot in dining room. Furnace included.

Plans as shown or reversed, $10.00.

Cost $2450.00 to $2700.00.

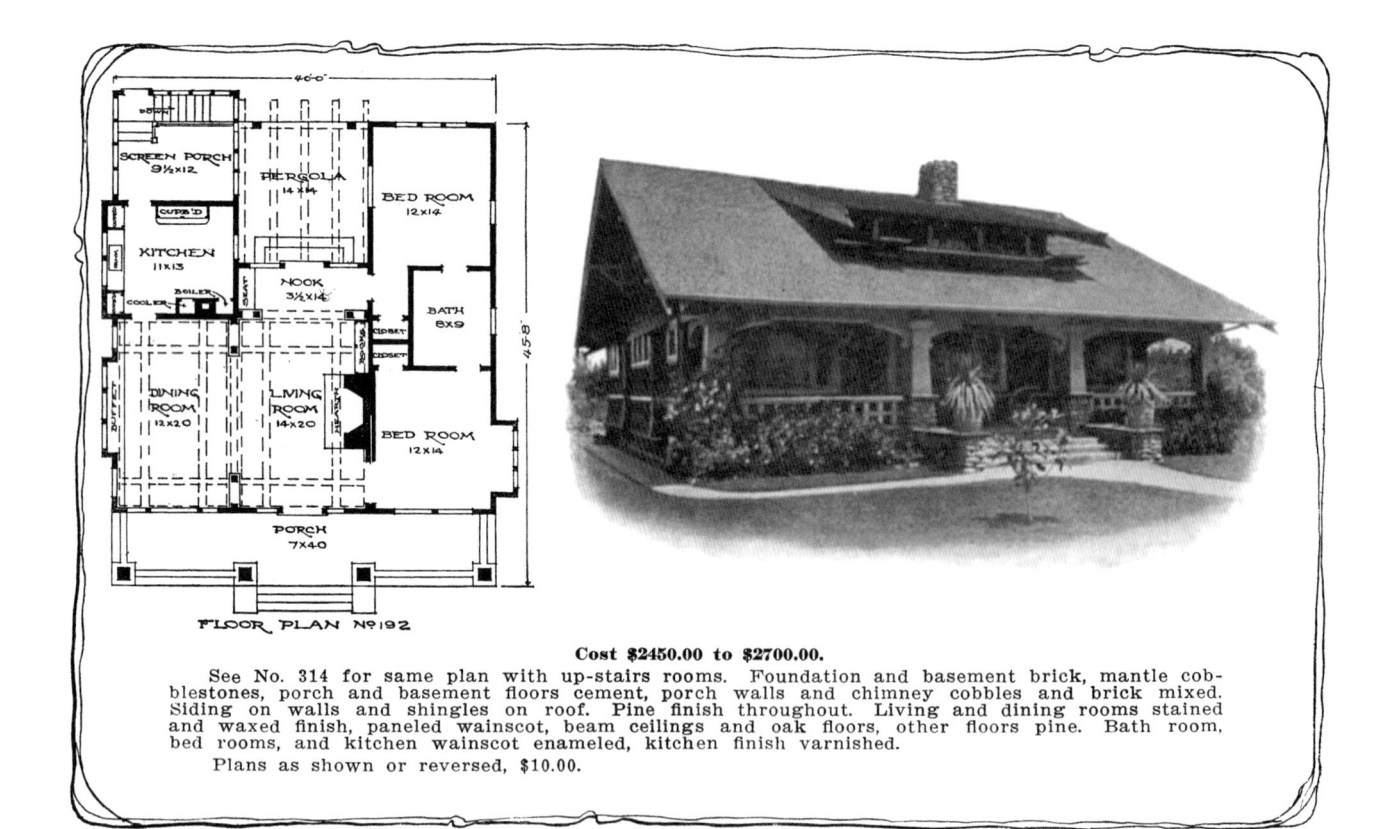

See No. 314 for same plan with up-stairs rooms. Foundation and basement brick, mantle cobblestones, porch and basement floors cement, porch walls and chimney cobbles and brick mixed. Siding on walls and shingles on roof. Pine finish throughout. Living and dining rooms stained and waxed finish, paneled wainscot, beam ceilings and oak floors, other floors pine. Bath room, bed rooms, and kitchen wainscot enameled, kitchen finish varnished.

Plans as shown or reversed, $10.00.

Cost $3200.00 to $3500.00.

Foundation and basement concrete, porch floor cement, chimneys and porch cement stone, mantel pressed brick, shakes on walls and shingles on roof. Oak floors throughout except pine in kitchen and bath. Paneled wainscot in den, imitation leather paneling in dining room, ceiling beams in dining room. Indirect lighting in den and living room. Stained and waxed finish in den, living and dining rooms; balance of finish, and kitchen and bath room wainscoting enameled. Furnace included.

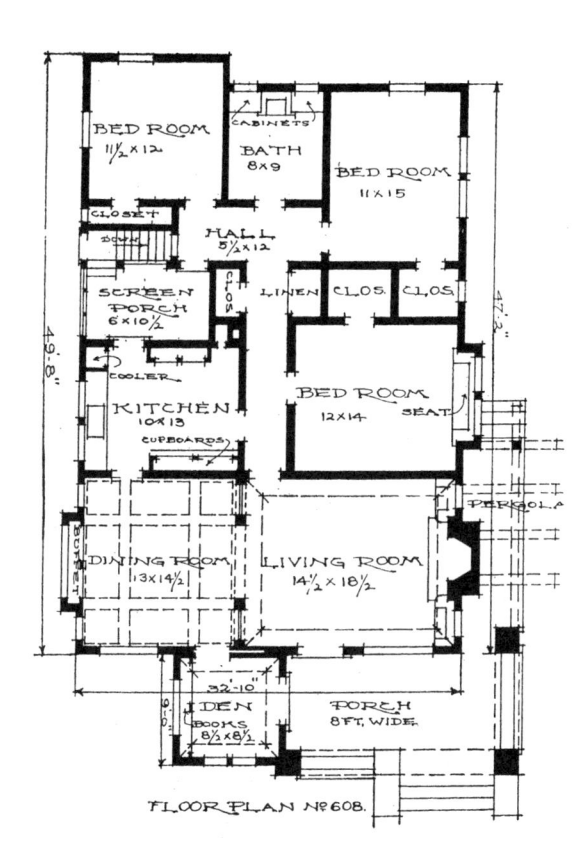

Plans as shown or reversed, $10.00.

95

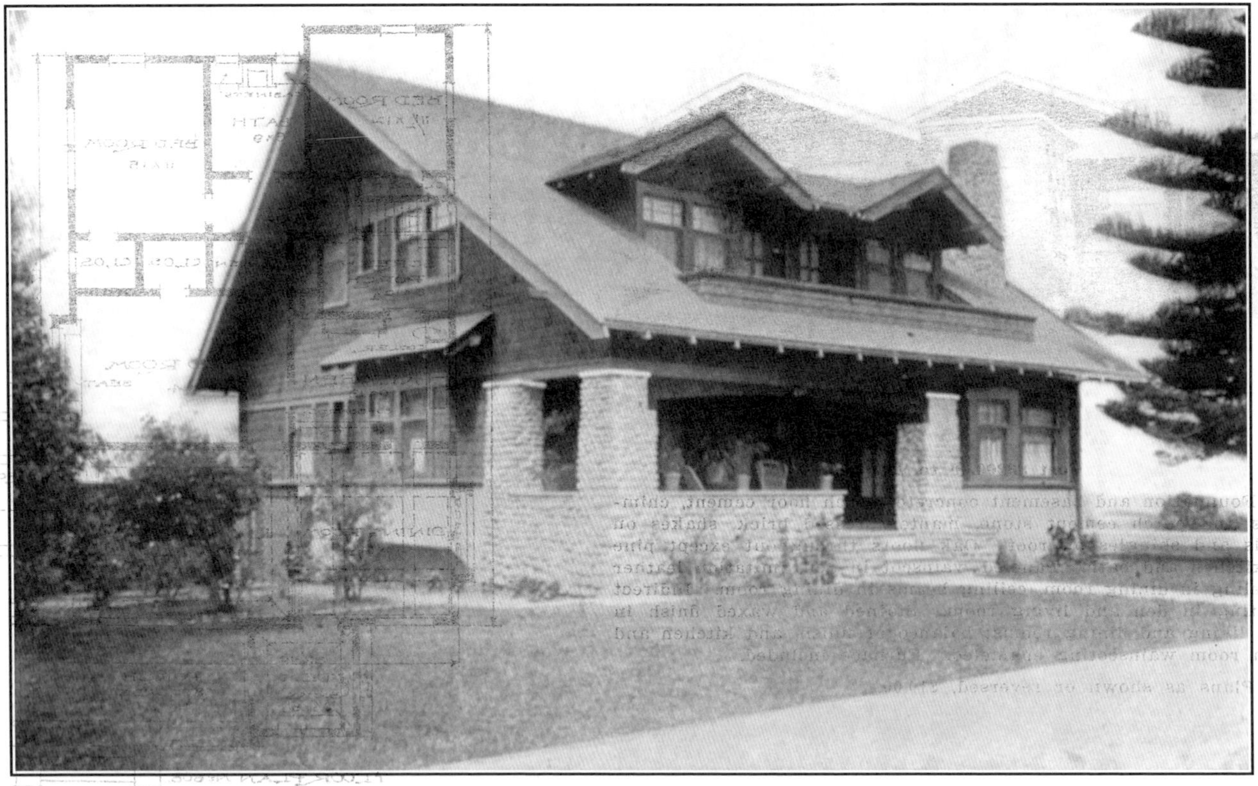

Cost $4000.00 to $4400.00.

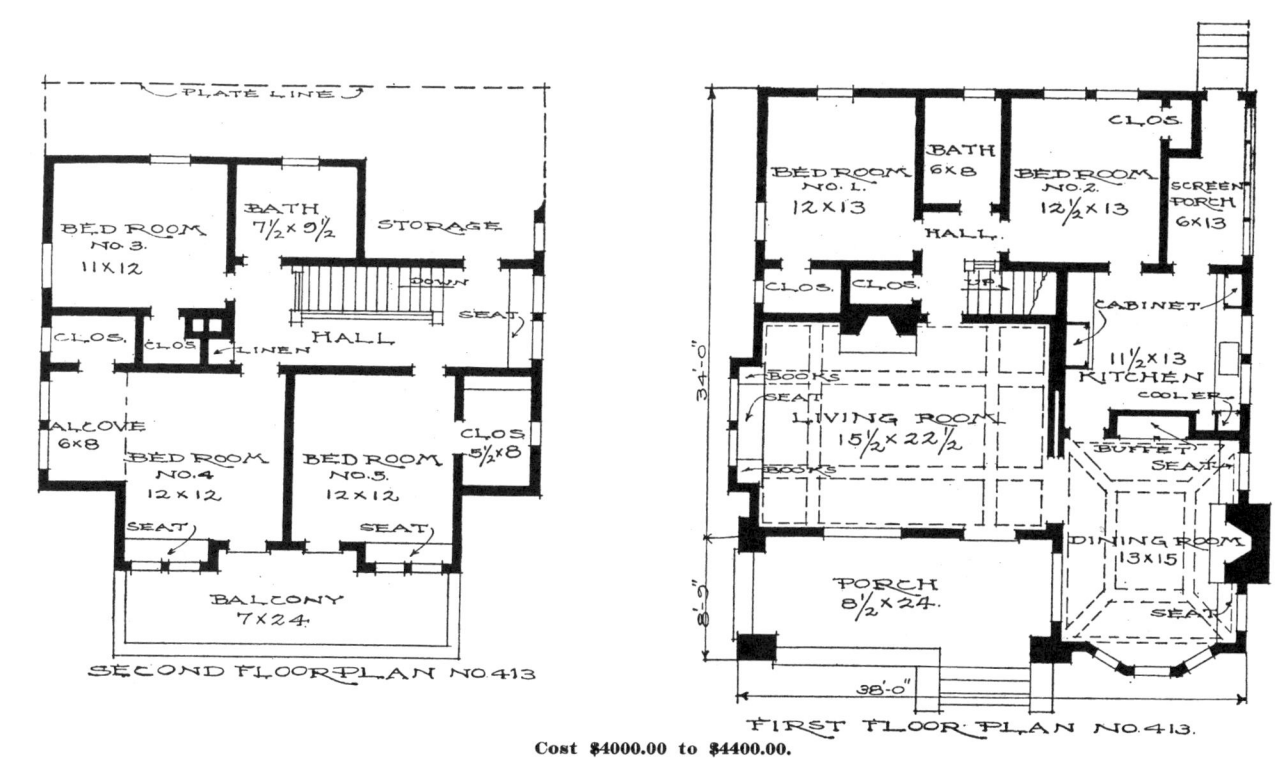

Foundation concrete, porch and chimneys cobble-stones, porch floor cement, mantels tile. Plastered walls to window sills, shakes to top of first story windows, shingles above and on roof. Oak floors, ceiling beams, and stained and waxed finish in living and dining rooms. Other floors pine. Finish in bed room No. 1 and first story bath room and kitchen and bath room wainscots enameled; other finish varnished. Basement and furnace $200.00 extra.

Plans as shown or reversed, $10.00.

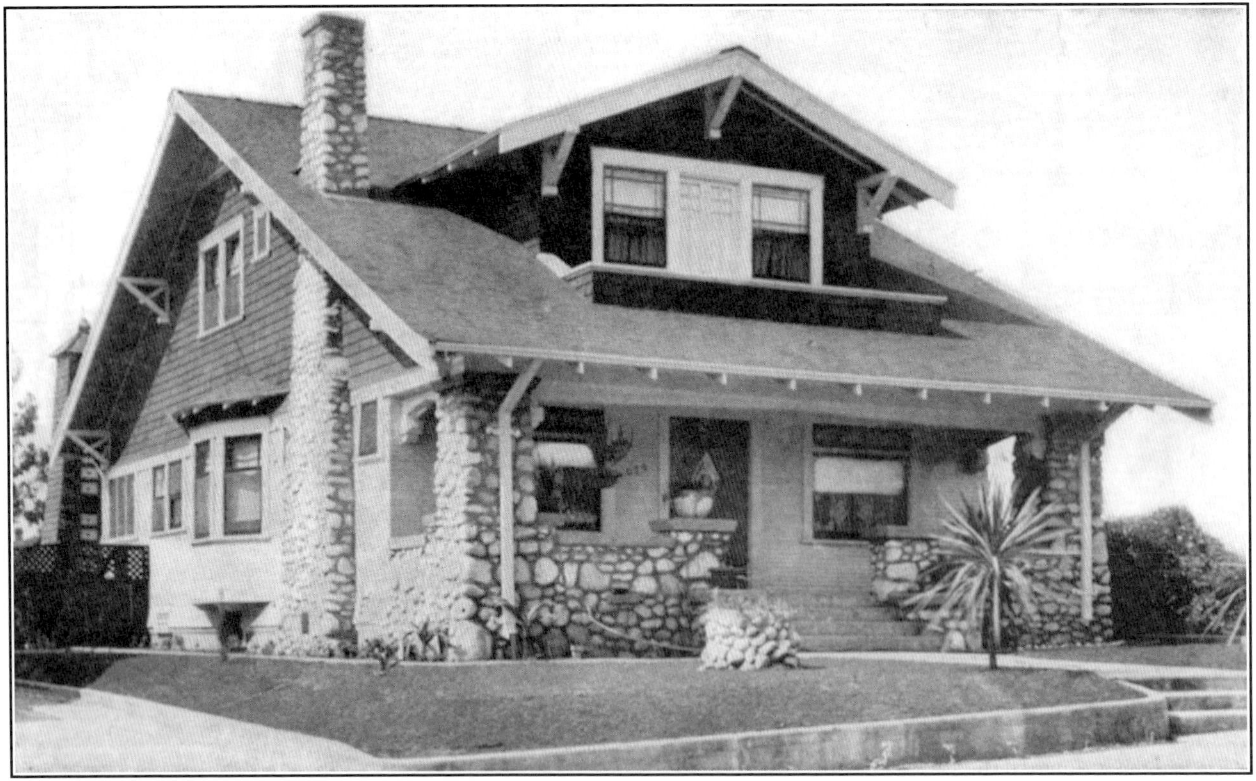

Cost $2800.00 to $3100.00.

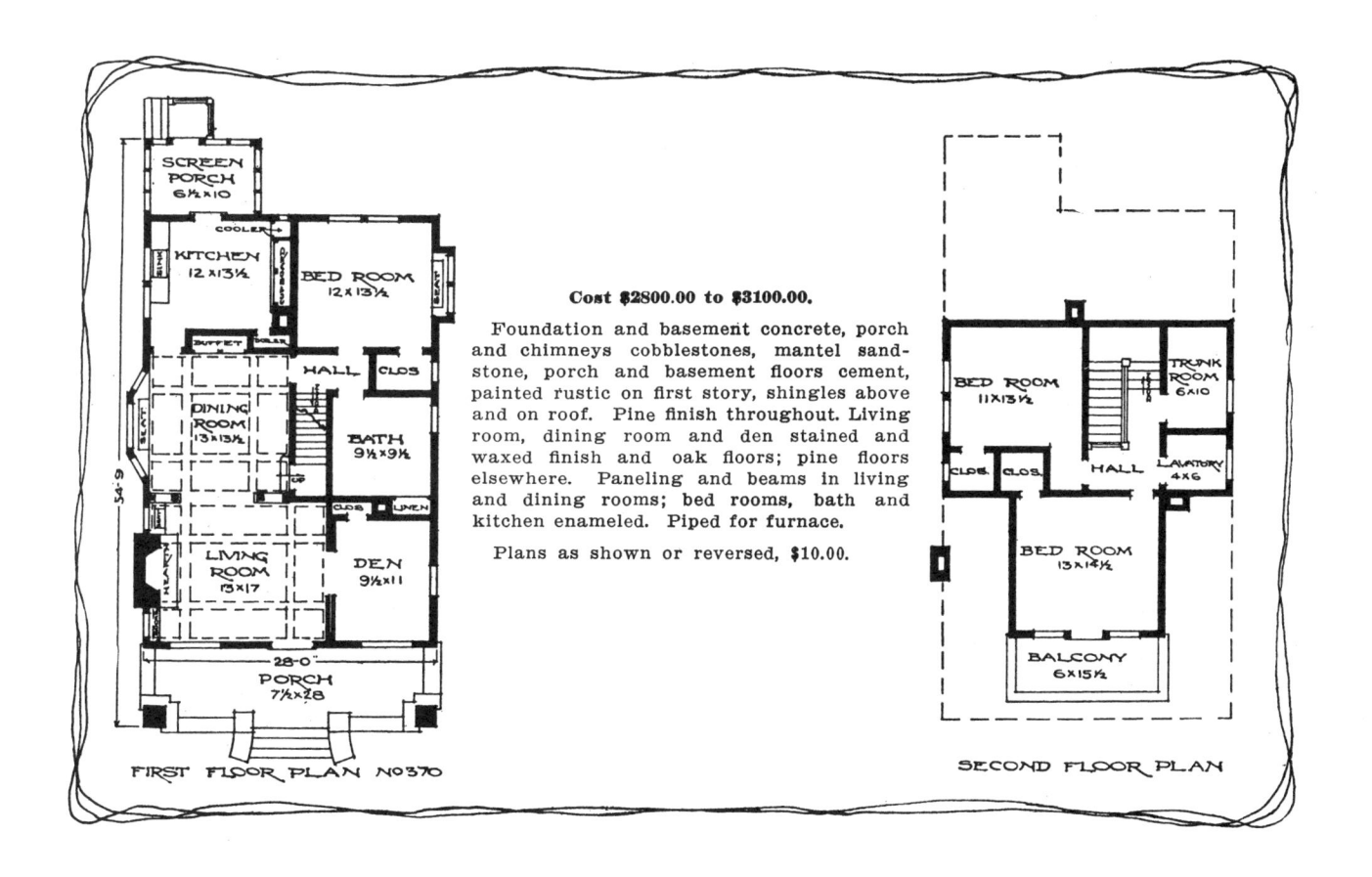

Foundation and basement concrete, porch and chimneys cobblestones, mantel sandstone, porch and basement floors cement, painted rustic on first story, shingles above and on roof. Pine finish throughout. Living room, dining room and den stained and waxed finish and oak floors; pine floors elsewhere. Paneling and beams in living and dining rooms; bed rooms, bath and kitchen enameled. Piped for furnace.

Plans as shown or reversed, $10.00.

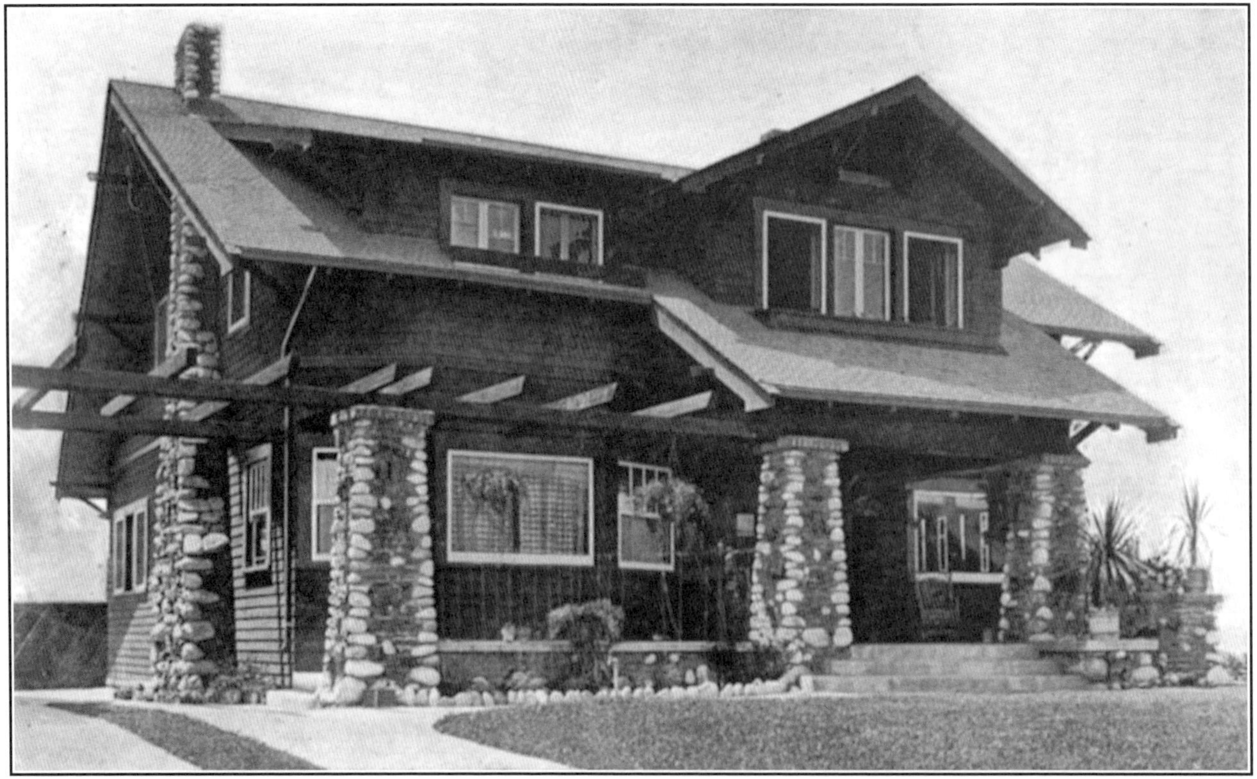

Cost $3800.00 to $4200.00.

Concrete foundation and basement, front porch brick and cobblestones with brick floor and steps. Cement floor in basement and patio. Mantels pressed brick. Plaster base on walls with shingles above and on roof. Pine finish throughout. Oak floors in living and dining rooms, den, reception and stair halls. Other floors pine. Beamed ceiling in living room, paneling in reception and stair halls, dining room and den, stained and waxed finish downstairs, except kitchen varnished. **Other finish and kitchen and bath** room wainscot enameled. Pipes for furnace included.

Plans as shown or reversed, $10.00

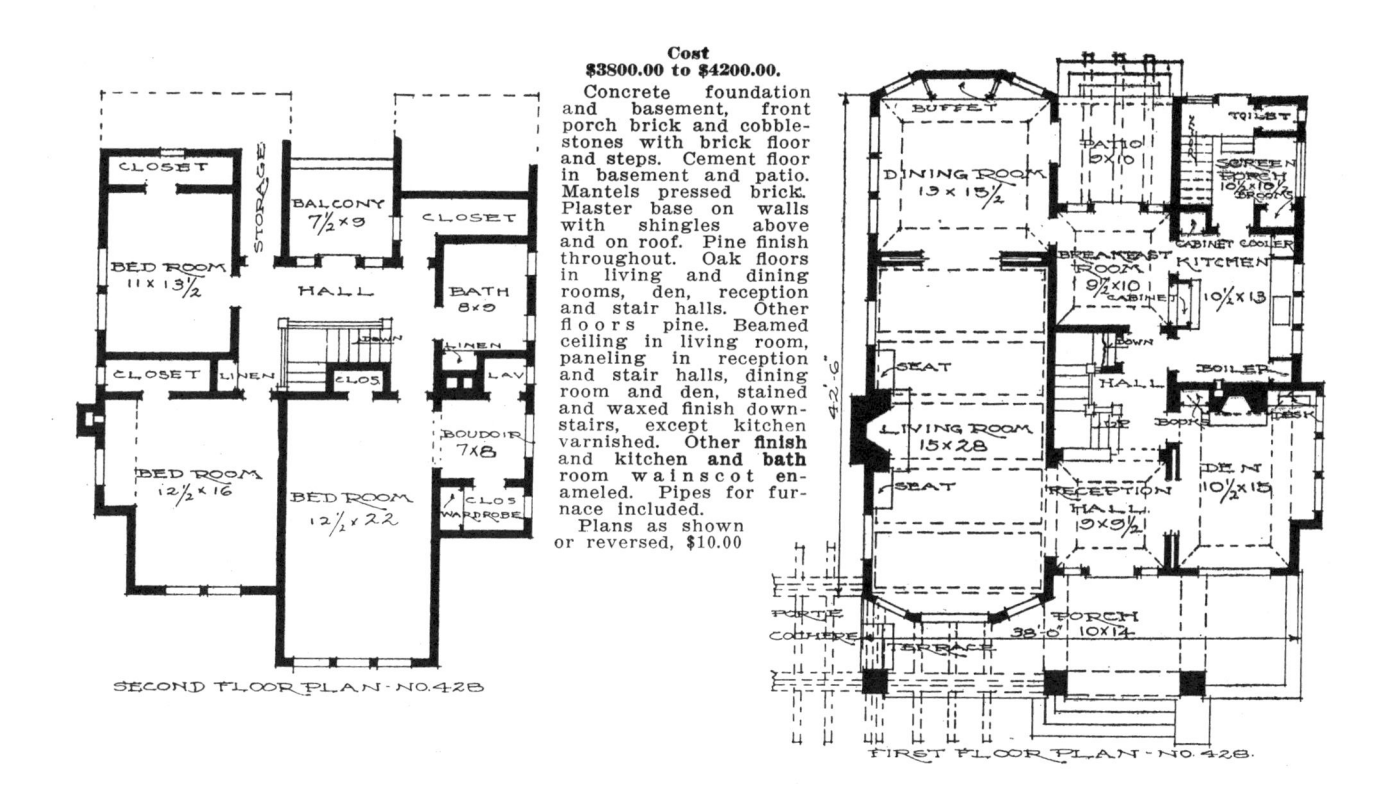

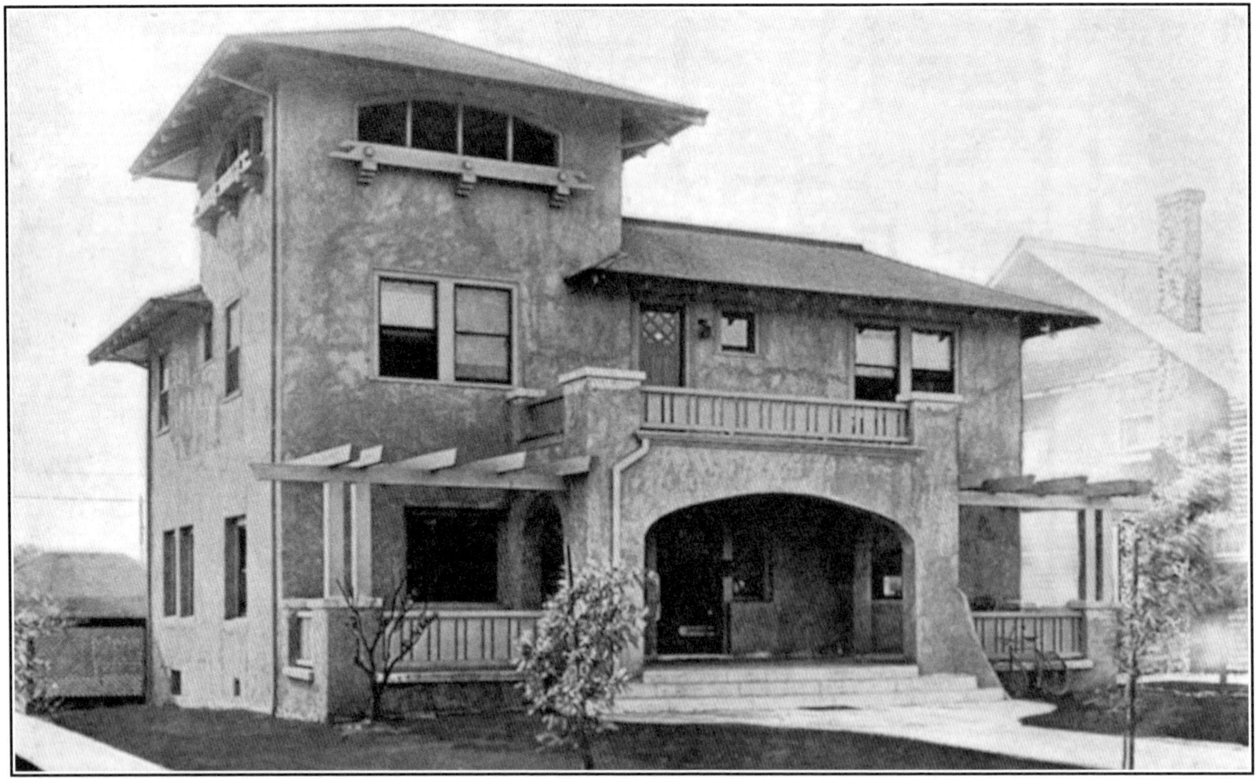

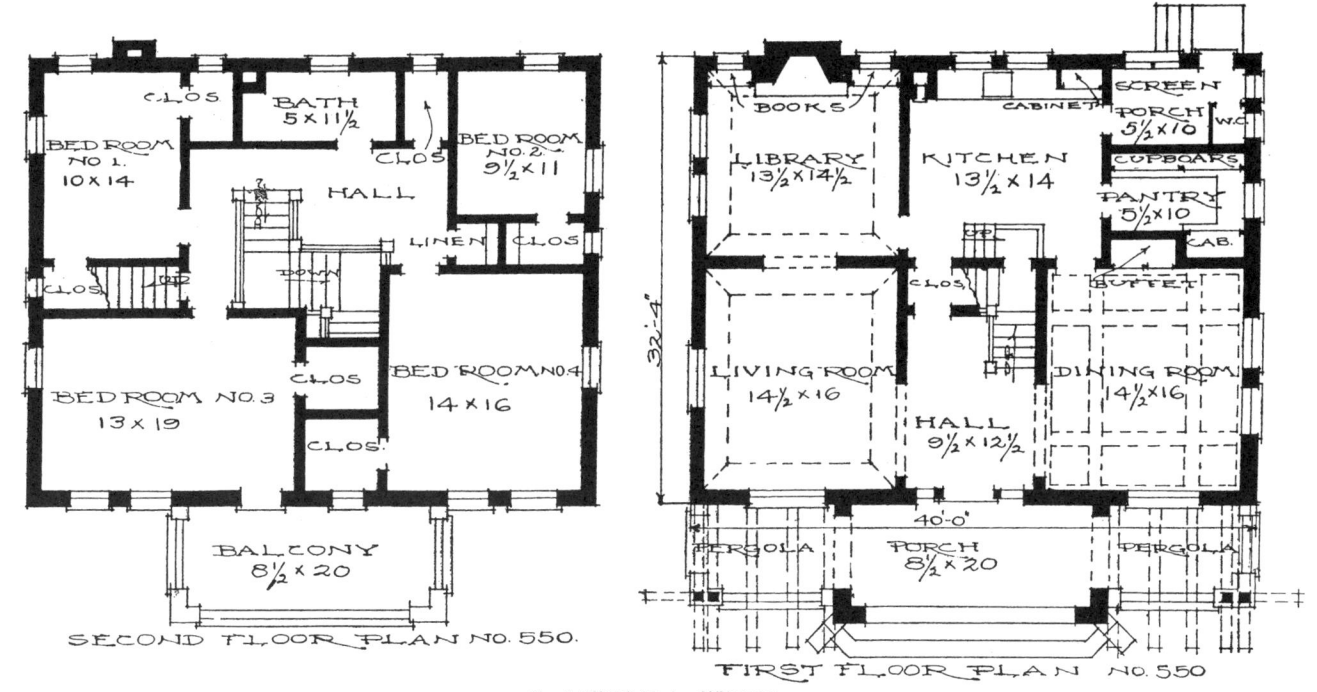

Cost $5000.00 to $5500.00.

Foundation, basement and all exterior walls of building concrete. Porch and basement floors cement. Mantel pressed brick, rough plaster on walls, tile or shingles on roof. Oak floors on first story, except kitchen and pantry, other floors pine. Paneled wainscot and beamed ceiling in dining room. Pine finish throughout, stained and waxed in living and dining rooms, library and tower. Other finish and wainscot in kitchen, bath room and toilet room enameled. Furnace included.

Plans as shown or reversed, $10.00.

No 334
Done At
"Ye Planry"

Stairway

No 334
Done At
"Ye Planry"

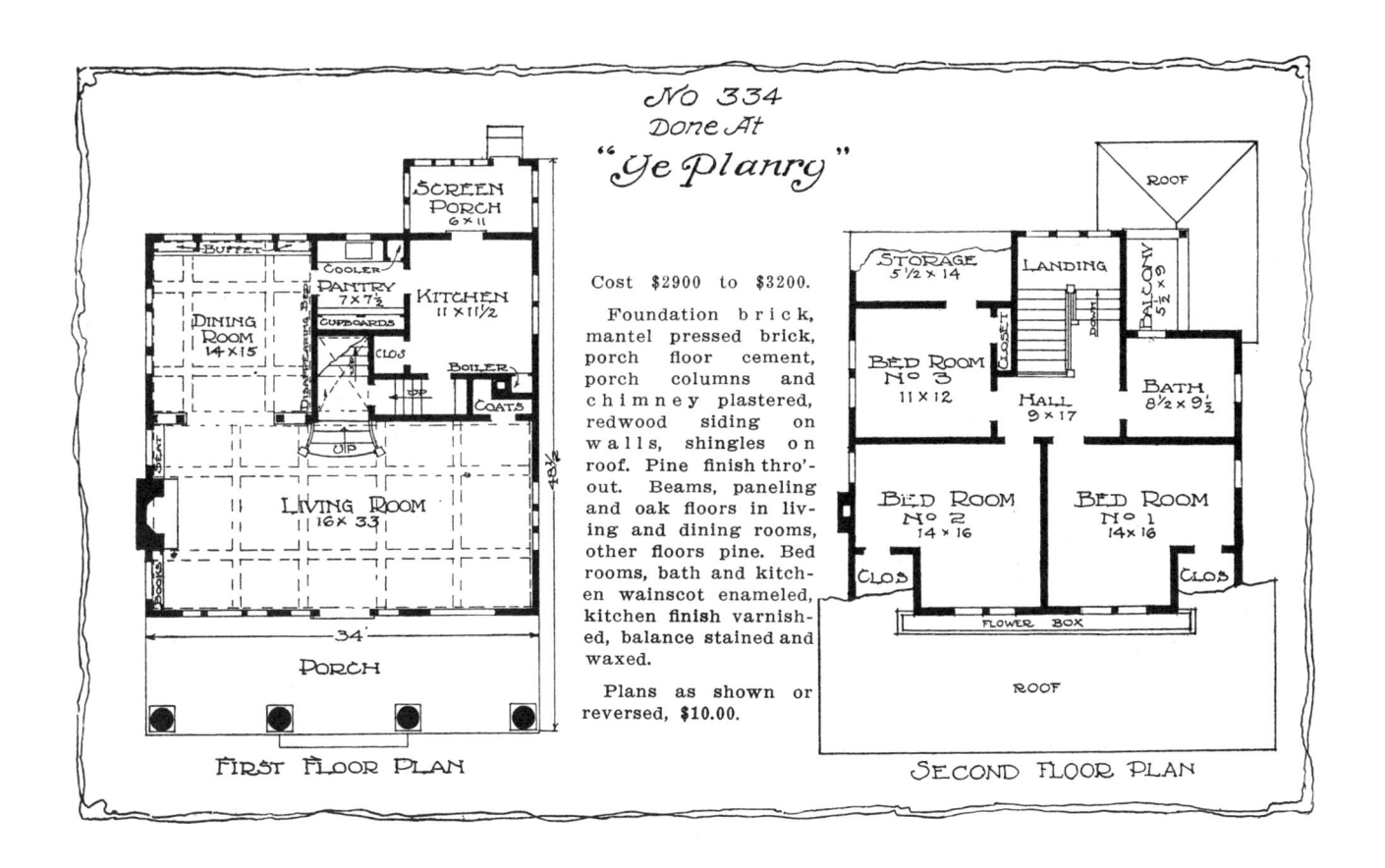

Cost $2900 to $3200.

Foundation brick, mantel pressed brick, porch floor cement, porch columns and chimney plastered, redwood siding on walls, shingles on roof. Pine finish thro'out. Beams, paneling and oak floors in living and dining rooms, other floors pine. Bed rooms, bath and kitchen wainscot enameled, kitchen finish varnished, balance stained and waxed.

Plans as shown or reversed, $10.00.

FIRST FLOOR PLAN

SECOND FLOOR PLAN

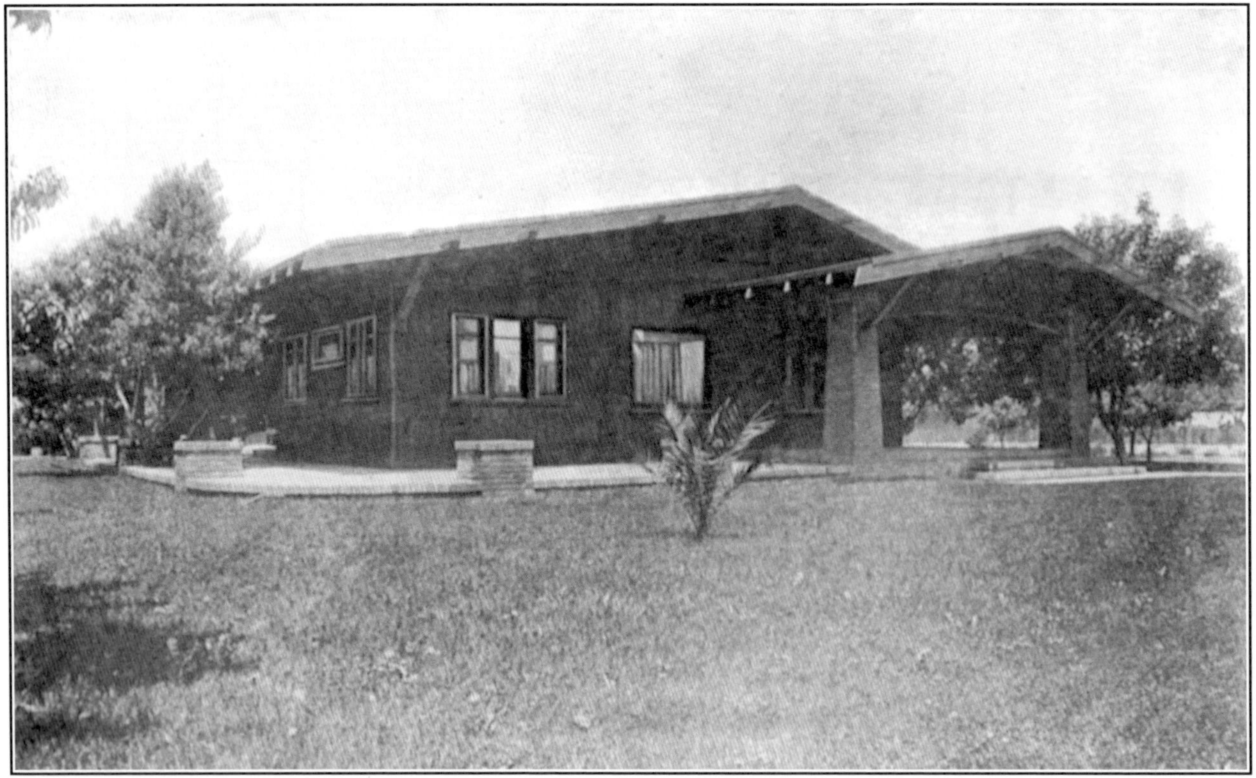

Cost $5000.00 to $5500.00.

Basement and foundation concrete to grade line. Porch, chimneys and foundation above grade, brick. Mantel pressed brick or tile, basement floor cement, porch and pergola floors tile. Shakes on walls and composition roof. Pine finish, stained and waxed in living and dining rooms, music room and library. Other finish enameled yellow pine, oak floors throughout, except tile in bath and pine in kitchen. Paneling and beamed ceiling in living and dining rooms and music room. Imitation leather panels in library, and enameled wainscot in kitchen and bath room.

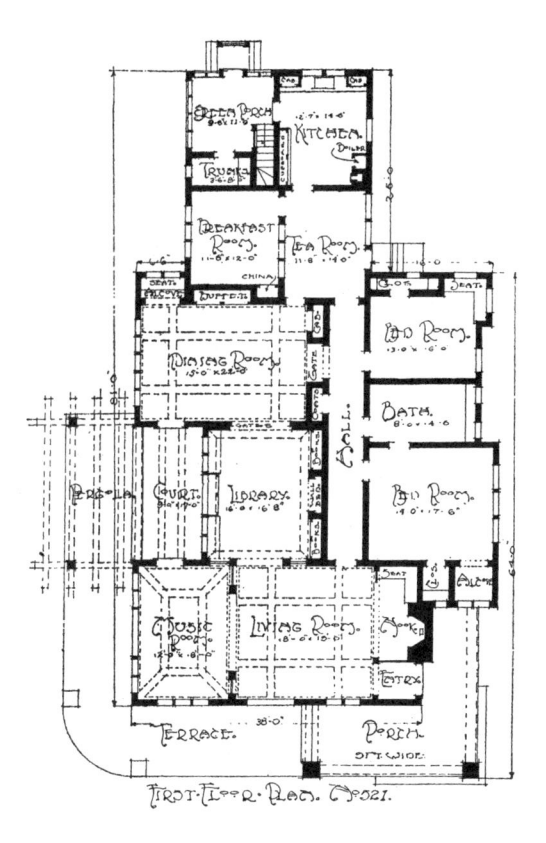

Plans as shown or reversed, $10.00.

NO. 800
DONE AT
"Ye Planry"

Cost $6000.00 to $6500.00.

Foundation and basement, concrete. Porches, pergola and terrace cobblestones with brick floors. Basement floor cement, mantels tile. Shakes on walls and composition roofing. Tower rough plaster with tile roof. Oak floors throughout except pine in kitchen, servant's room and bath, and tile in up-stairs bath room. Stained and waxed pine finish in reception hall and book alcove, living and dining rooms and den. Balance of finish and kitchen and bath room wainscots enameled. Leather paneling in den, beamed ceilings and plaster paneling in living and dining rooms. Wood paneled ceiling in book alcove.

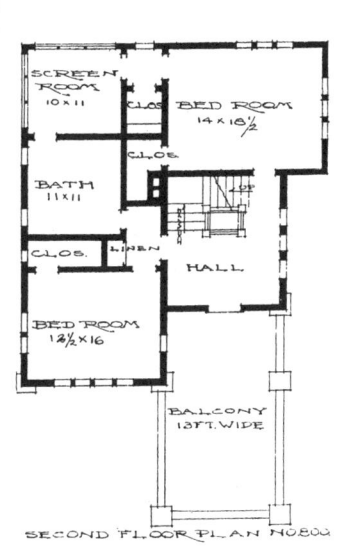

Plans as shown or reversed, $10.00.

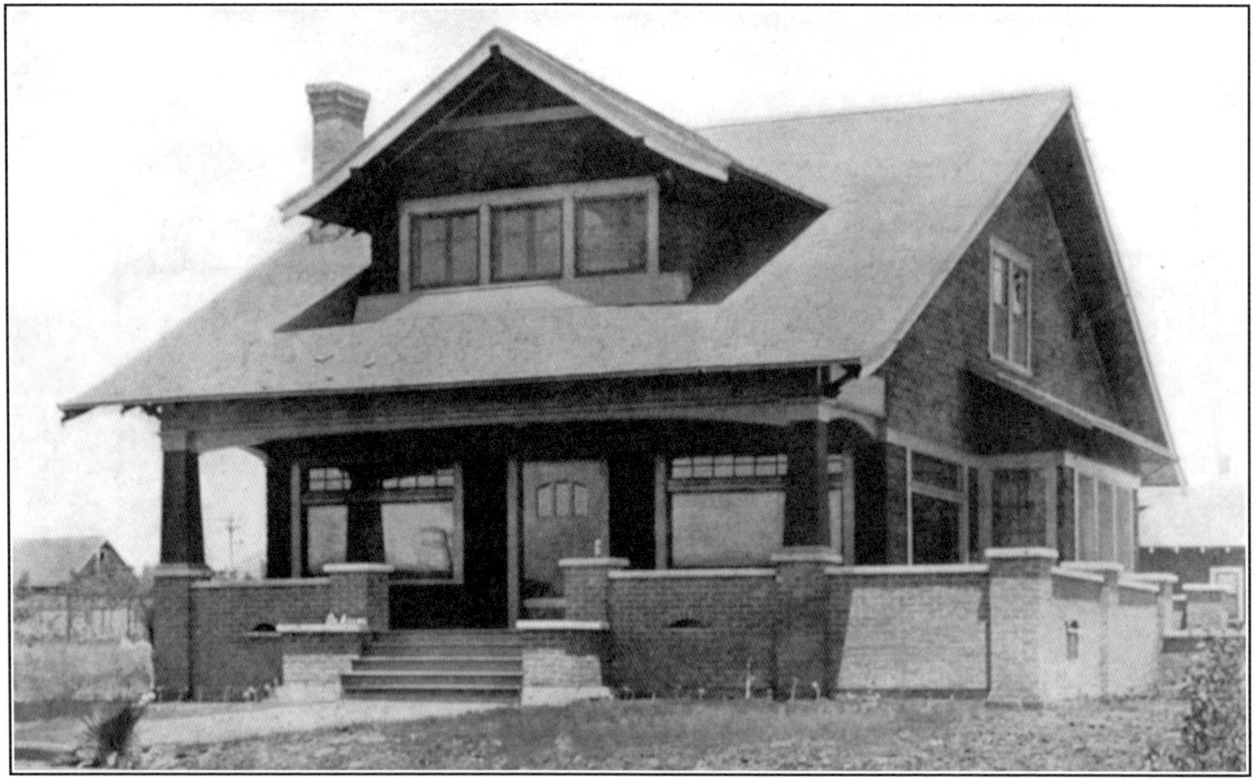

Cost $2700.00 to $3000.00

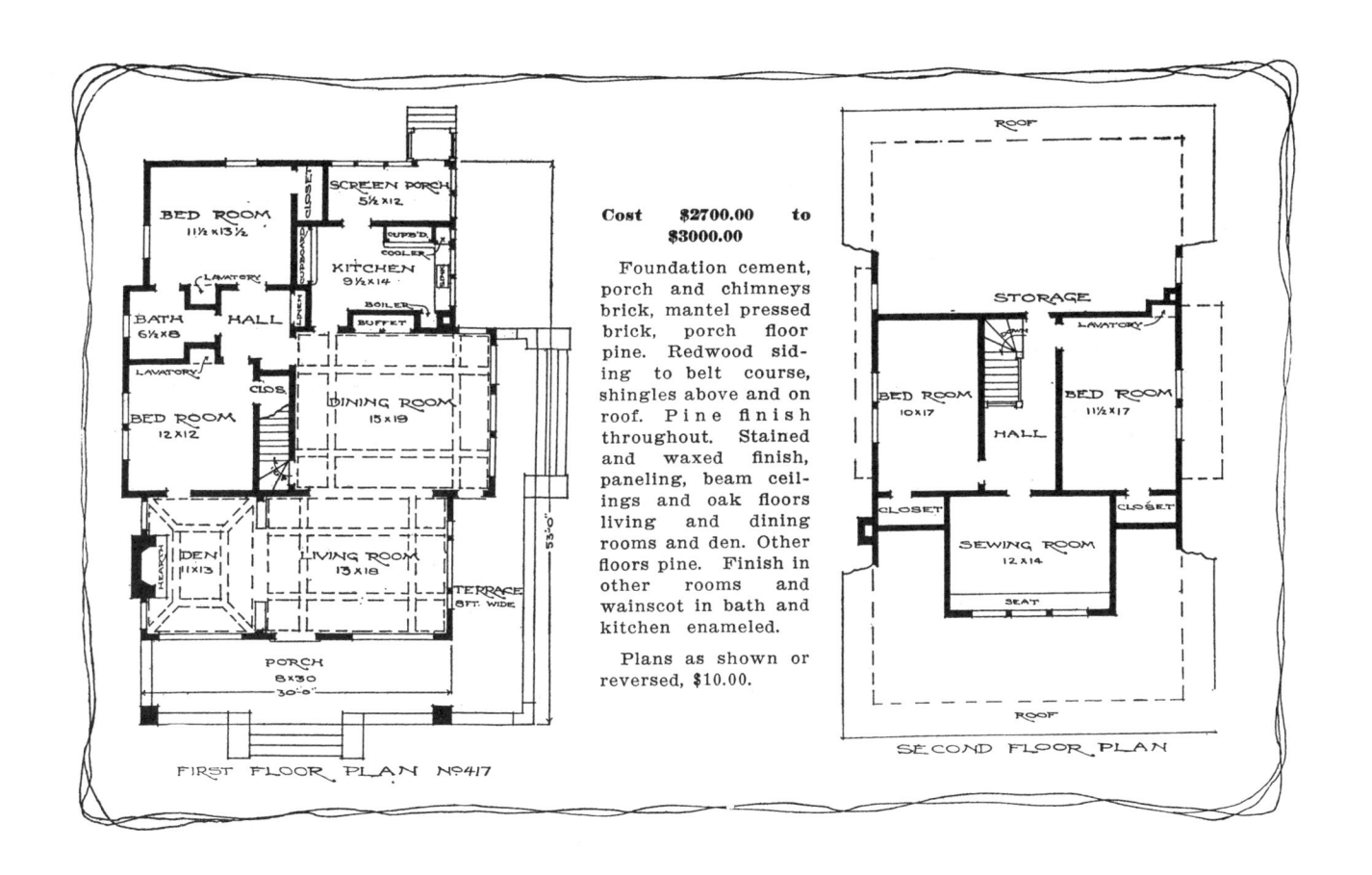

Foundation cement, porch and chimneys brick, mantel pressed brick, porch floor pine. Redwood siding to belt course, shingles above and on roof. Pine finish throughout. Stained and waxed finish, paneling, beam ceilings and oak floors living and dining rooms and den. Other floors pine. Finish in other rooms and wainscot in bath and kitchen enameled.

Plans as shown or reversed, $10.00.

FIRST FLOOR PLAN No. 417

SECOND FLOOR PLAN

Cost $2200.00 to $2400.00.

Foundation and porch brick, porch floor cement, mantels tile, rustic siding on walls, roof shingled, oak floors in living and dining rooms, balance pine. Pine finish throughout. Paneling and plate rail in dining room, rough finish in attic den, bath room and plaster wainscot in kitchen enameled, woodwork in bed rooms and kitchen varnished and rubbed to dull gloss.

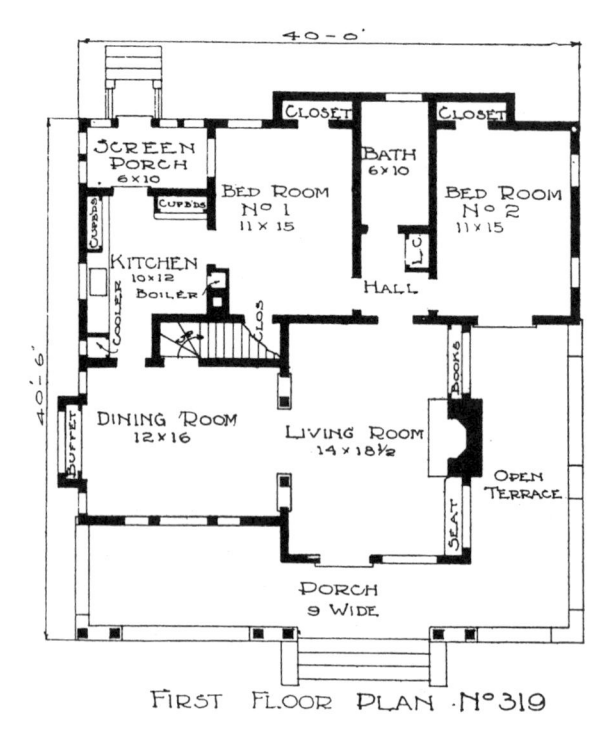

Plans as shown or reversed, $10.00.

FIRST FLOOR PLAN · N° 319

Cost $2500.00 to $2750.00.

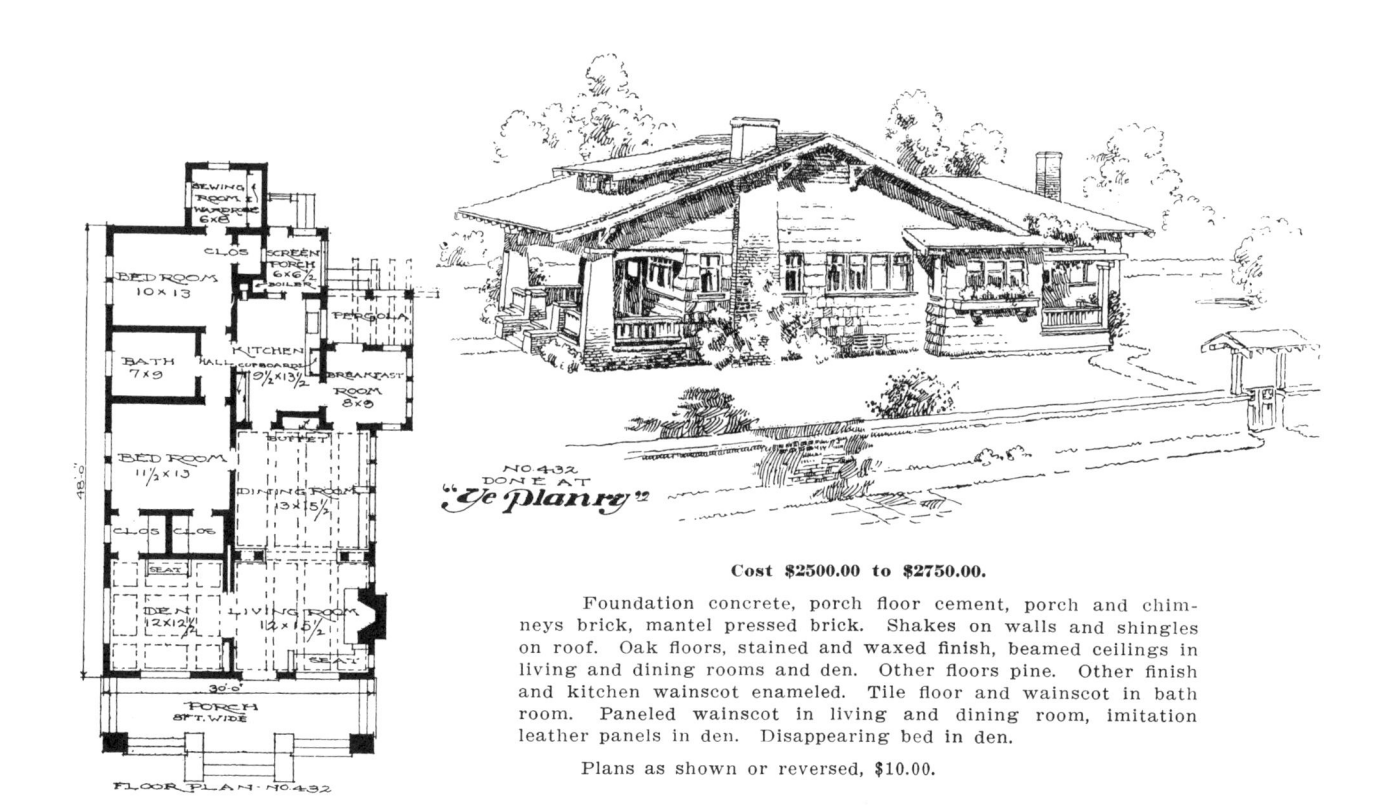

Foundation concrete, porch floor cement, porch and chimneys brick, mantel pressed brick. Shakes on walls and shingles on roof. Oak floors, stained and waxed finish, beamed ceilings in living and dining rooms and den. Other floors pine. Other finish and kitchen wainscot enameled. Tile floor and wainscot in bath room. Paneled wainscot in living and dining room, imitation leather panels in den. Disappearing bed in den.

Plans as shown or reversed, $10.00.

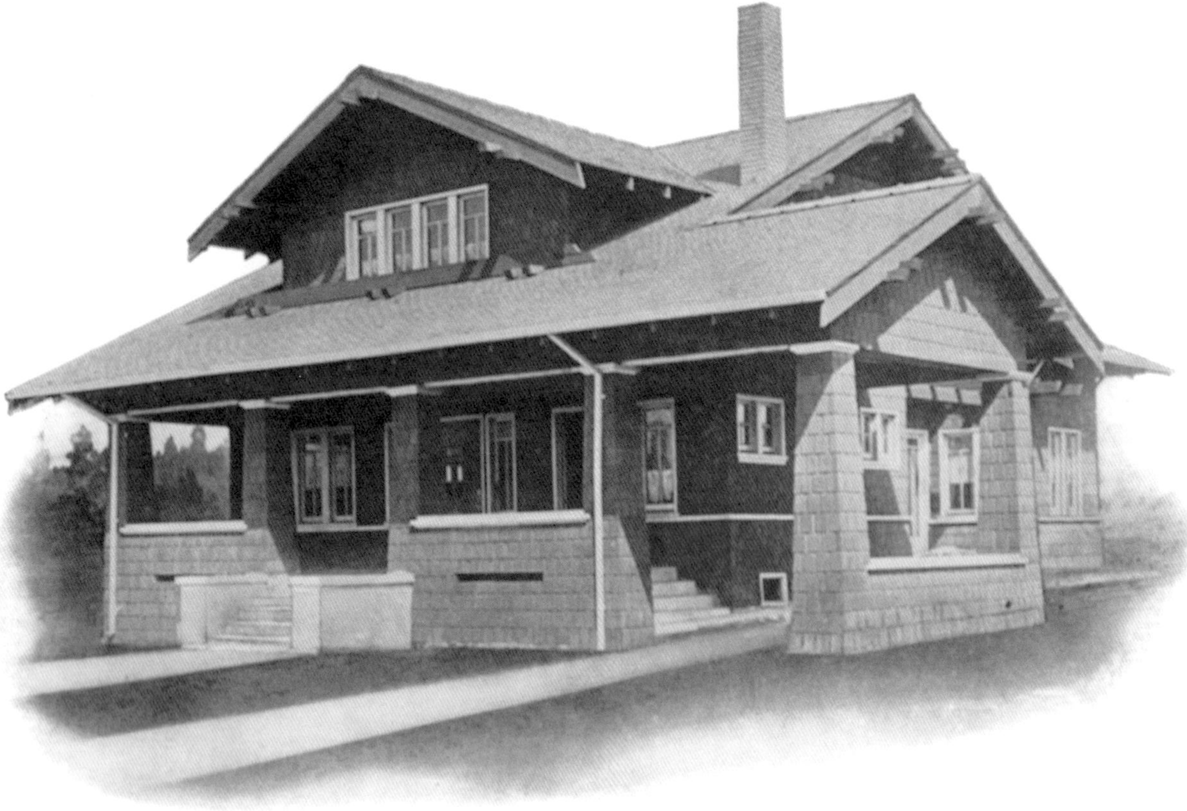

Cost
$3300.00 to $3600.00

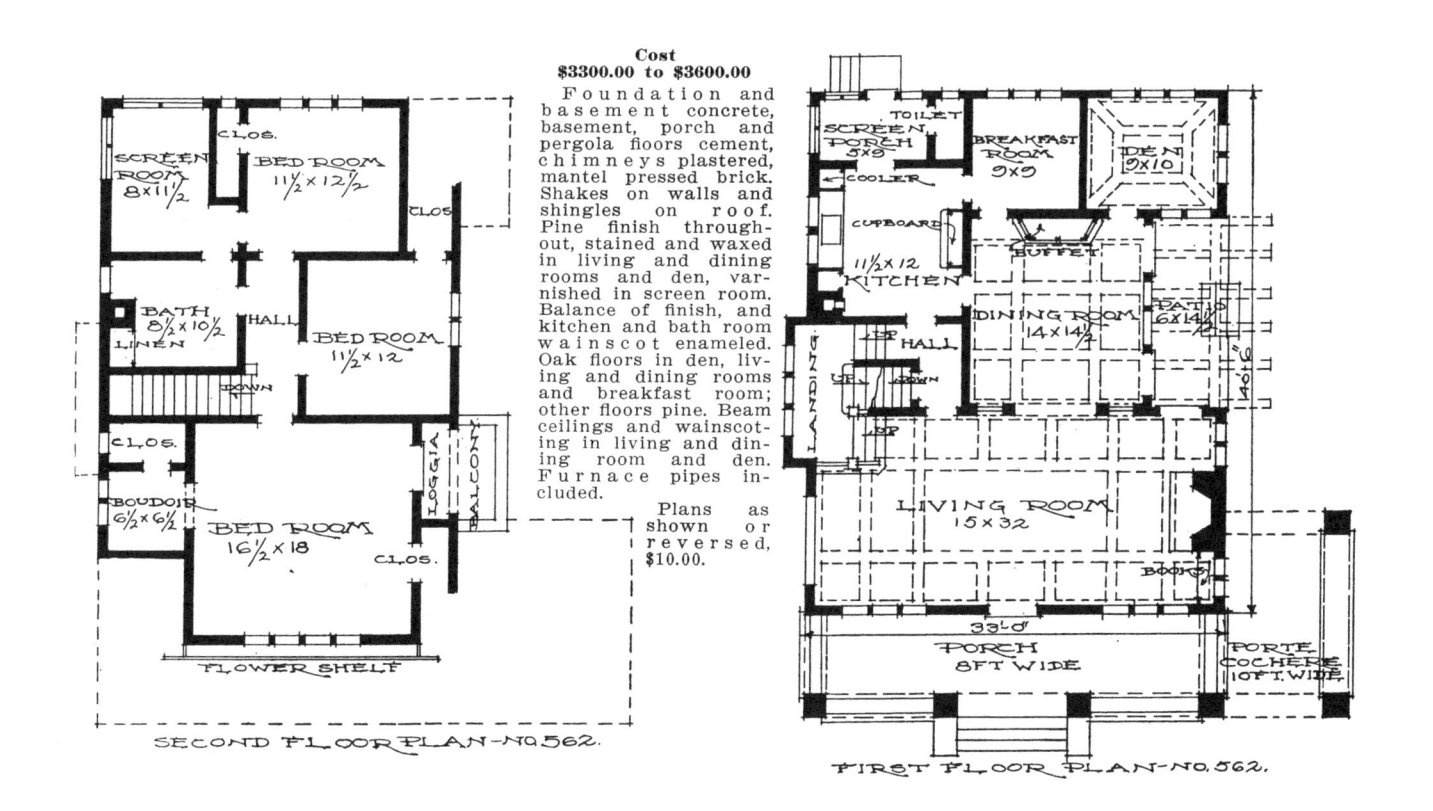

Foundation and basement concrete, basement, porch and pergola floors cement, chimneys plastered, mantel pressed brick. Shakes on walls and shingles on roof. Pine finish throughout, stained and waxed in living and dining rooms and den, varnished in screen room. Balance of finish, and kitchen and bath room wainscot enameled. Oak floors in den, living and dining rooms and breakfast room; other floors pine. Beam ceilings and wainscoting in living and dining room and den. Furnace pipes included.

Plans as shown or reversed, $10.00.

SECOND FLOOR PLAN—No. 562.

FIRST FLOOR PLAN—No. 562.

115

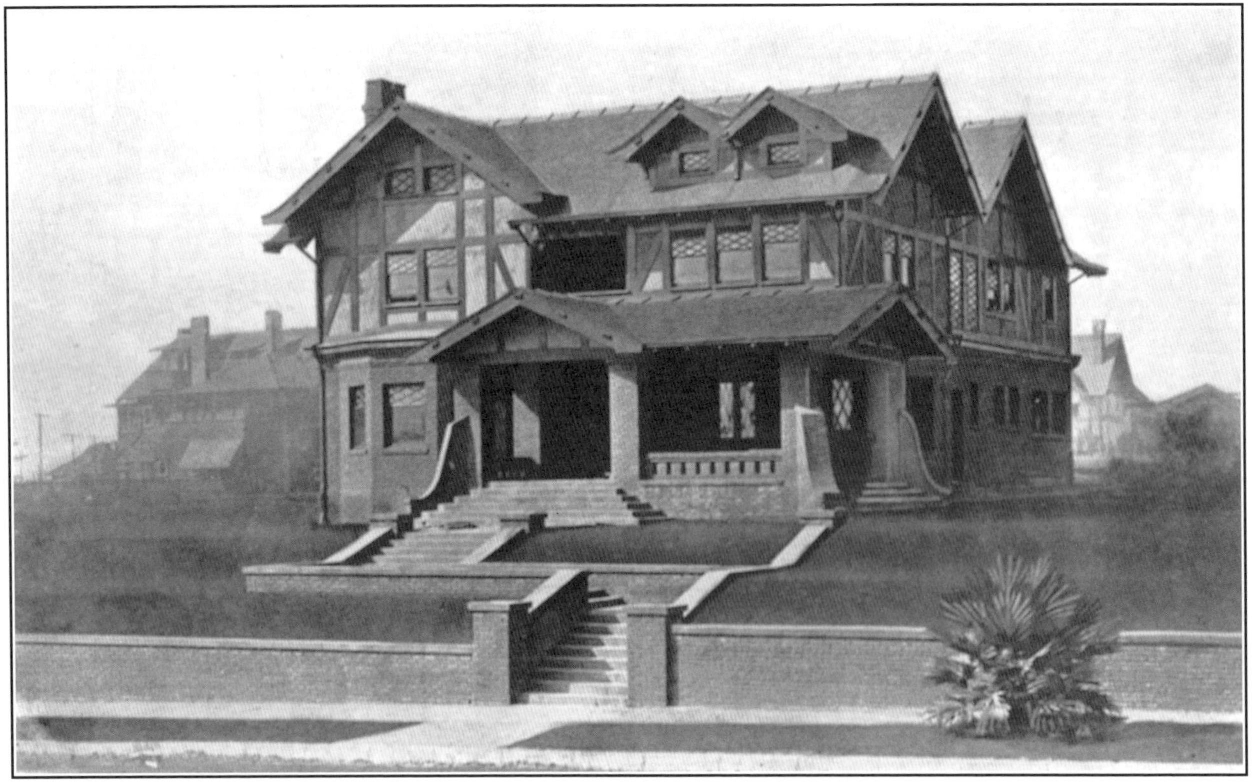

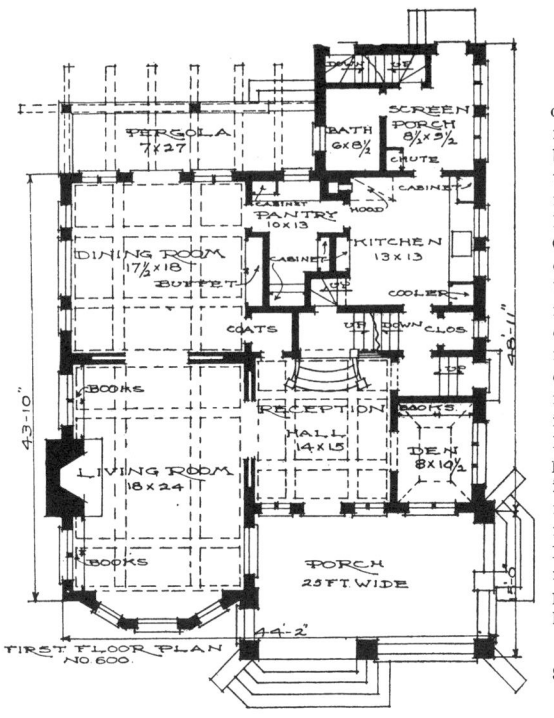

Cost $11000.00 to $12000.00.

Foundation and basement concrete. Porch, pergola and basement floors cement. First story brick veneered, second story half timber and plaster; shingles on roof. Pressed brick mantel in living room, tile in bed room. Oak floors throughout first story, except pine in kitchen, pantry, bath and screen porch. Maple floors throughout second floor, except tile in bath room. Pine finish on first story, white cedar on second story. Downstairs finish stained and waxed except in kitchen, bath and pantry. Balance of finish and kitchen, pantry and bath room wainscoting, enameled. Beam ceilings in reception hall, living and dining rooms, indirect lighting in den. Paneled wainscot in dining room, plaster or imitation leather panels in living room, reception hall and den. Furnace included.

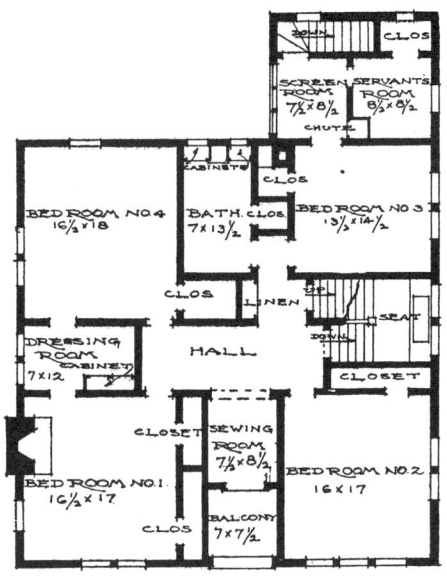

Plans as shown or reversed, $10.00.

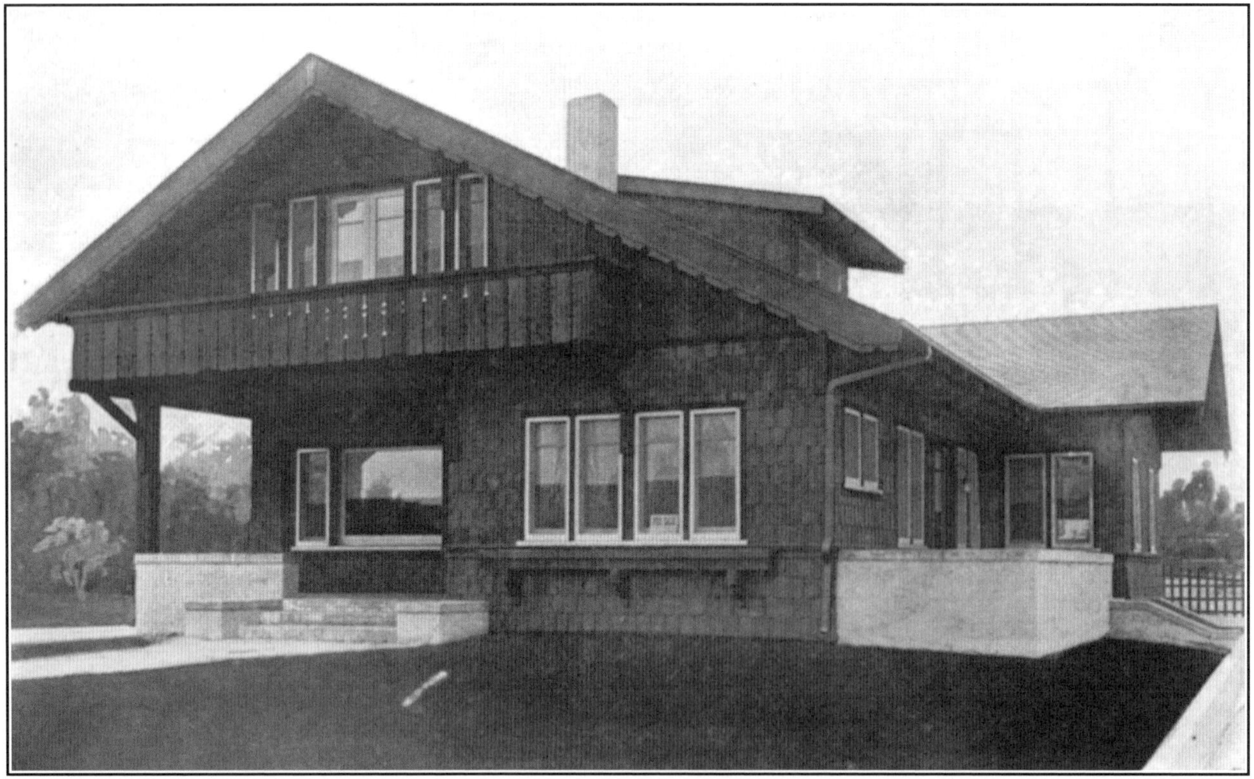

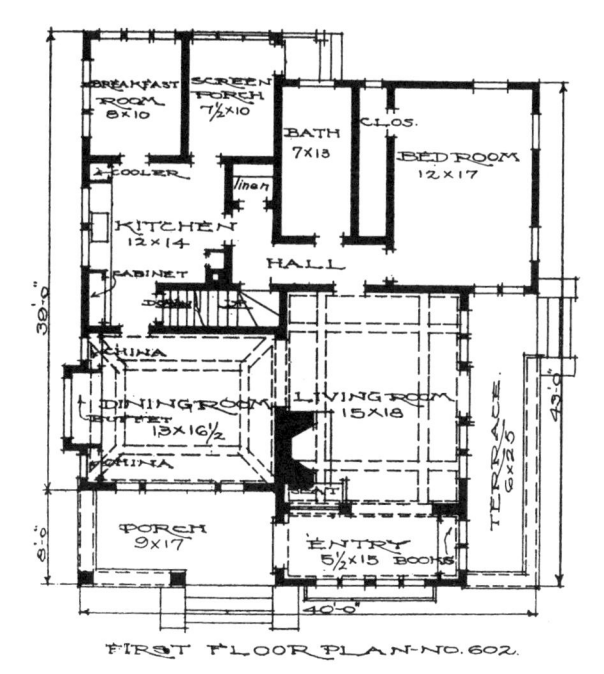

Cost $3100.00 to $3400.00.

Foundation and basement concrete; porch, terrace and basement floors cement; porch, terrace and chimney plastered; shakes on walls and shingles on roof. Mantel tile. Pine finish throughout. Oak floors on first story, except kitchen, breakfast room and bath. Other floors pine. Paneled wainscot in dining room, beam ceilings and stained and waxed finish in living and dining rooms. Balance of finish and kitchen and bathroom wainscot enameled. Furnace pipes included.

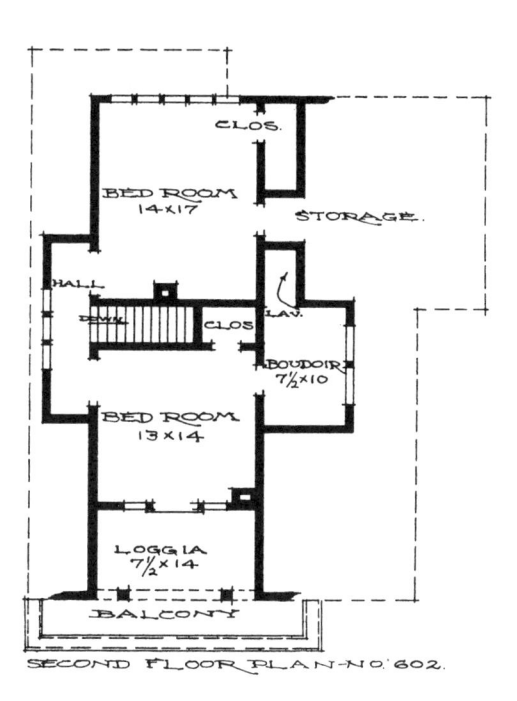

Plans as shown or reversed, $10.00.

No. 770
DONE AT
"Ye Planry"

FIRST FLOOR PLAN NO. 770

SECOND FLOOR PLAN - NO. 770

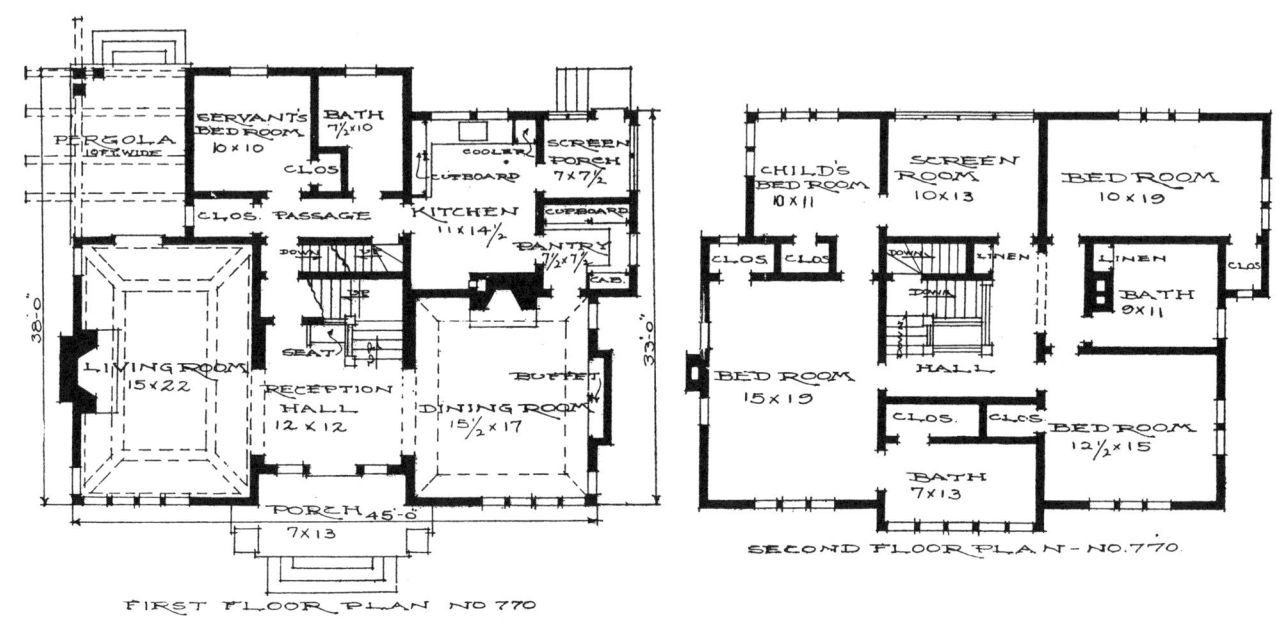

Cost $5000.00 to $5500.00.

Foundation, porch, pergola and chimneys brick. Basement floor cement, pergola and porch floors tile. Shakes on walls and shingles on roof. Mantel, tile in dining room and pressed brick in living room. Oak floors and stained and waxed finish in reception hall, living and dining room and up-stairs hall. Maple floors in up-stairs bed rooms; balance of floors pine. Varnished finish in servant's room and bath, and screen room. Balance of finish and kitchen and bath room wainscots enameled. Indirect lighting and plaster paneling in dining room, beamed ceiling and paneled wainscot in living room. Furnace included.

Plans as shown or reversed, $10.00.

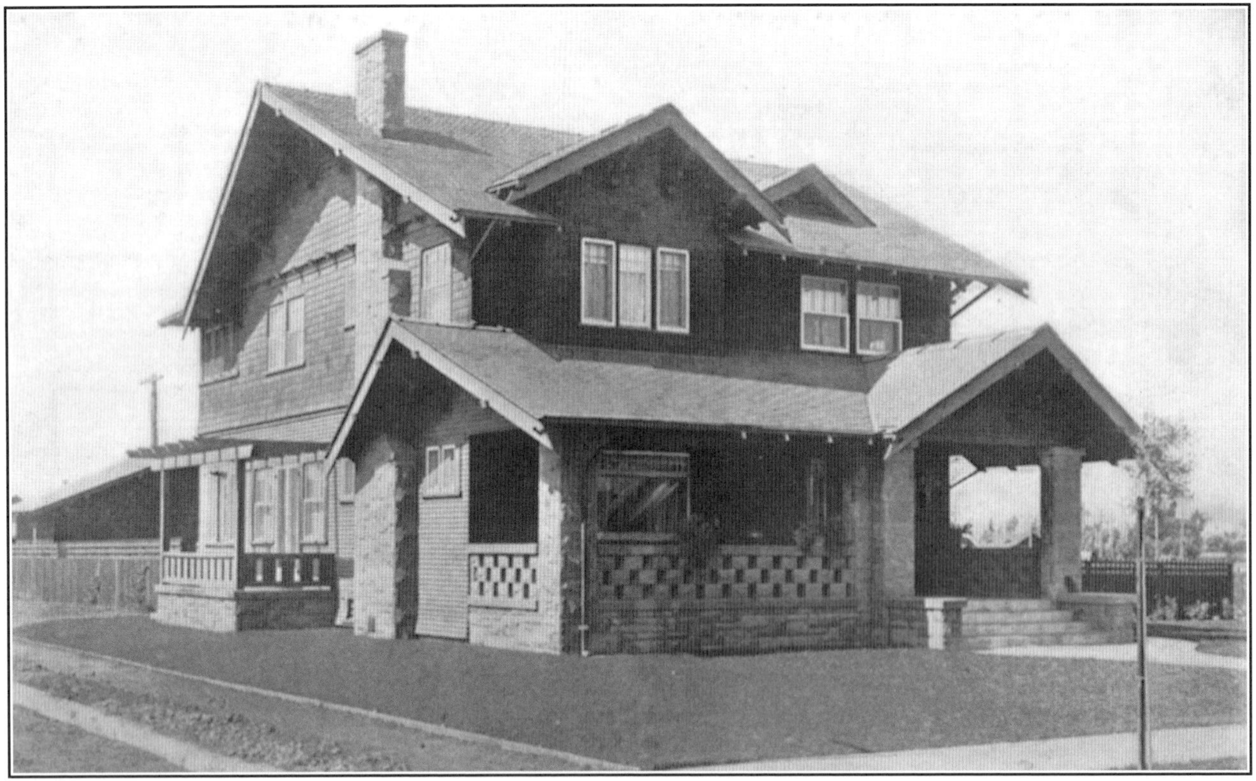

FIRST FLOOR PLAN - NO. 524.

SECOND FLOOR PLAN - NO. 524.

Cost $4000.00 to $4400.00.

Foundation and basement concrete, porch, basement and pergola floors cement. Porch and chimneys cement stone, mantel sandstone. Redwood siding on first story, shingles above and on roof. Pine finish throughout. Oak floors throughout, except pine in kitchen and bath. Stained and waxed finish and beamed ceilings in entry, living room and dining room and den, balance of finish, kitchen and bath room wainscot enameled. Panel wainscot in dining room and den. Furnace included. Plans as shown or reversed, $10.00.

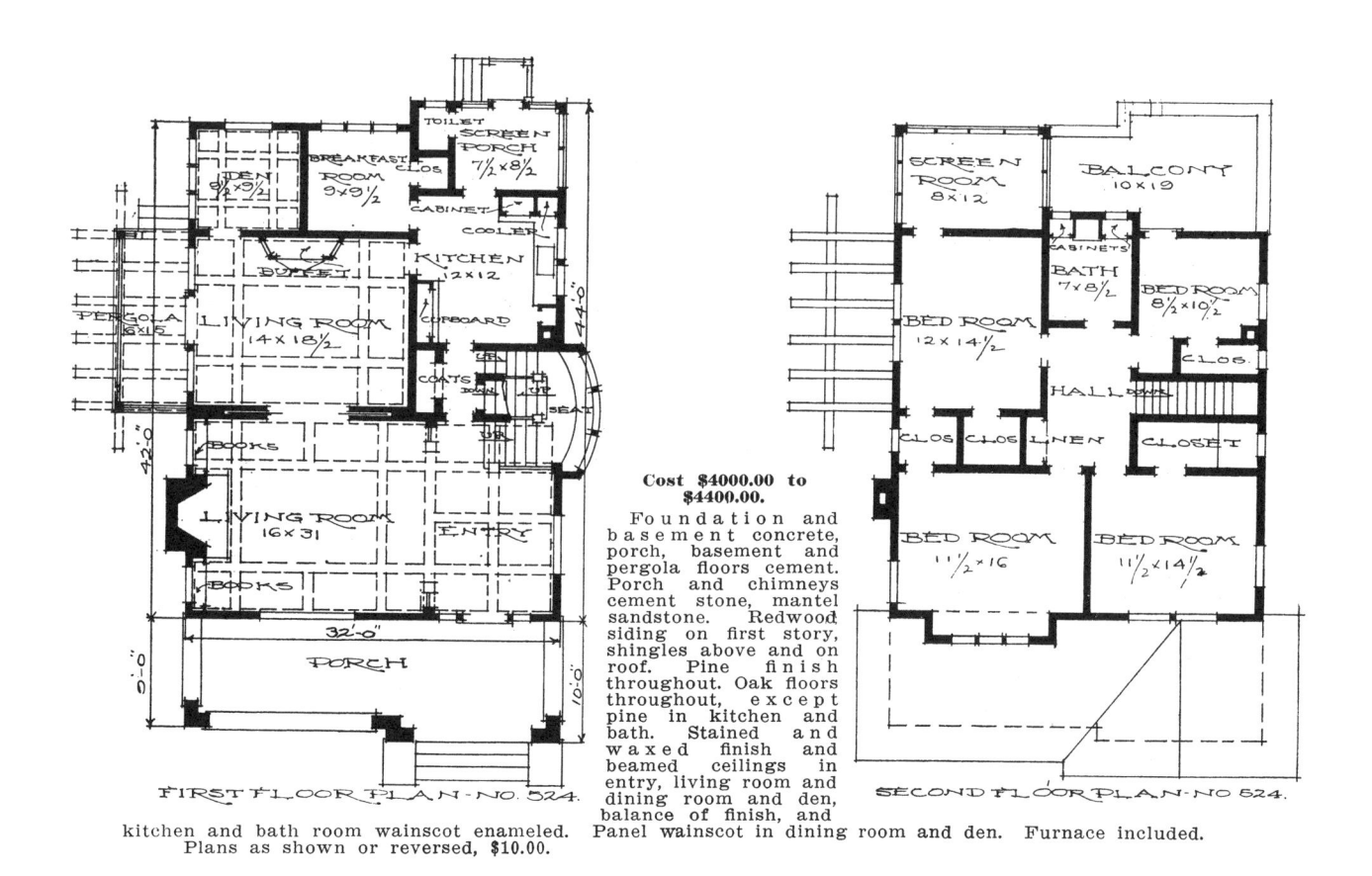

123

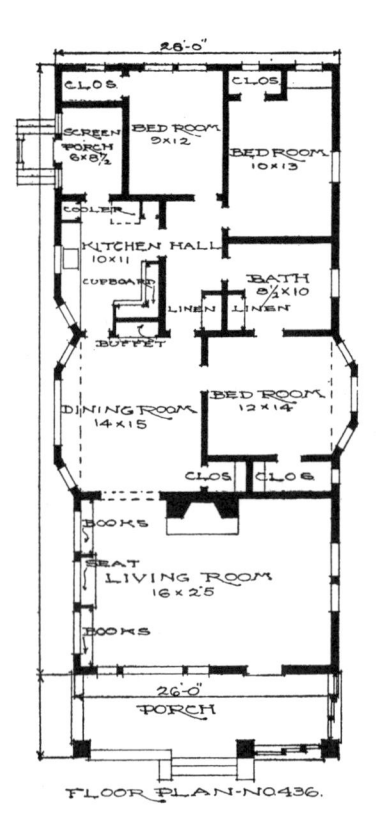

Cost $2300.00 to $2500.00.

Foundation and chimneys brick, porch floor cement, mantel pressed brick. Redwood siding on walls and shingles on roof. Pine finish throughout, stained and waxed in living and dining rooms. Enameled in bath room, varnished elsewhere. Enameled wainscot in kitchen and bath room. Oak floors and paneled wainscot in living and dining rooms.

Plans as shown or reversed, $10.00.

Cost $2300.00 to $2550.00.

Foundation concrete; porch, chimney and mantel plastered. Porch floors cement, shakes on walls and shingles on roof. Pine finish throughout. Oak floors, stained and waxed finish in living and dining rooms; balance of finish, and kitchen and bath room wainscot enameled. Beam ceiling and paneled wainscot in dining room, indirect lighting and plaster paneling in living room. Screen room walls and ceiling paneled in redwood.

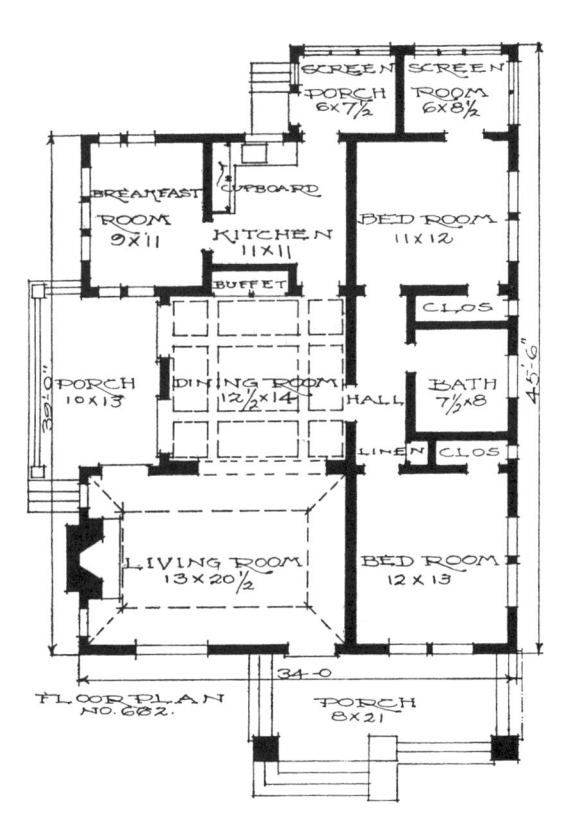

Plans as shown or reversed, $10.00.

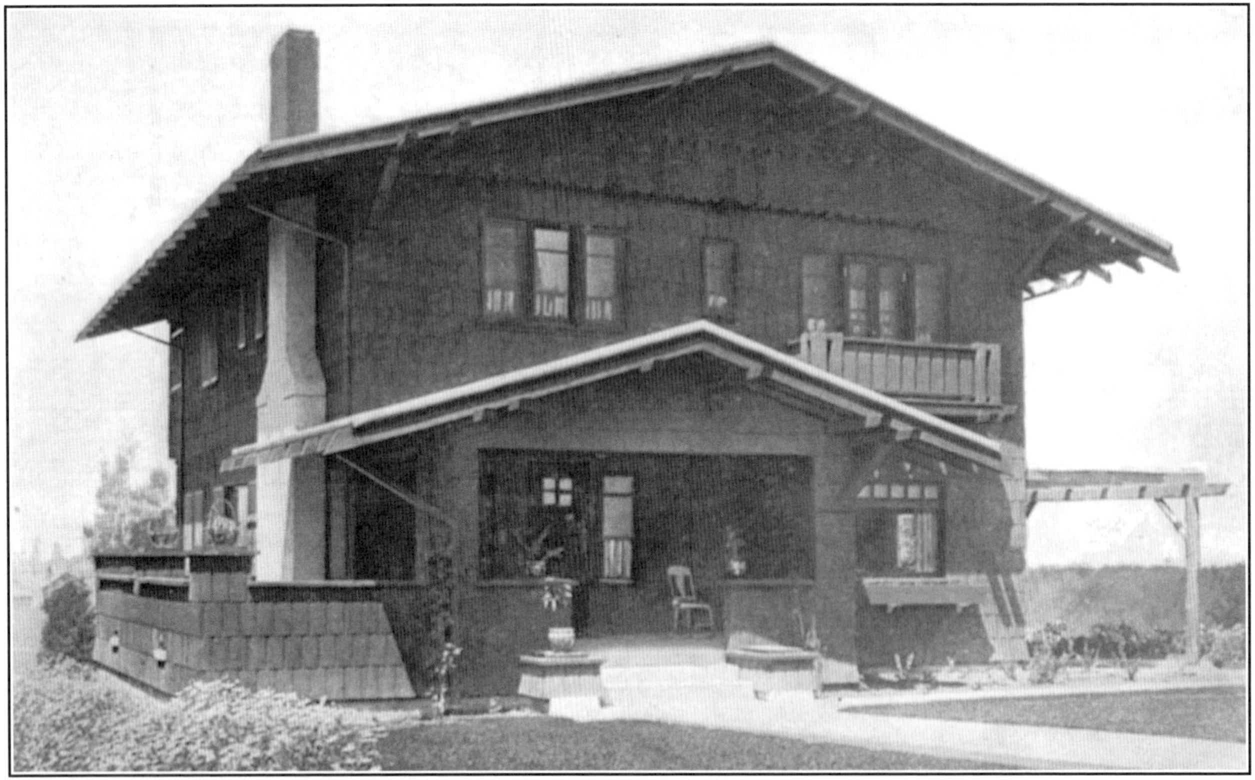

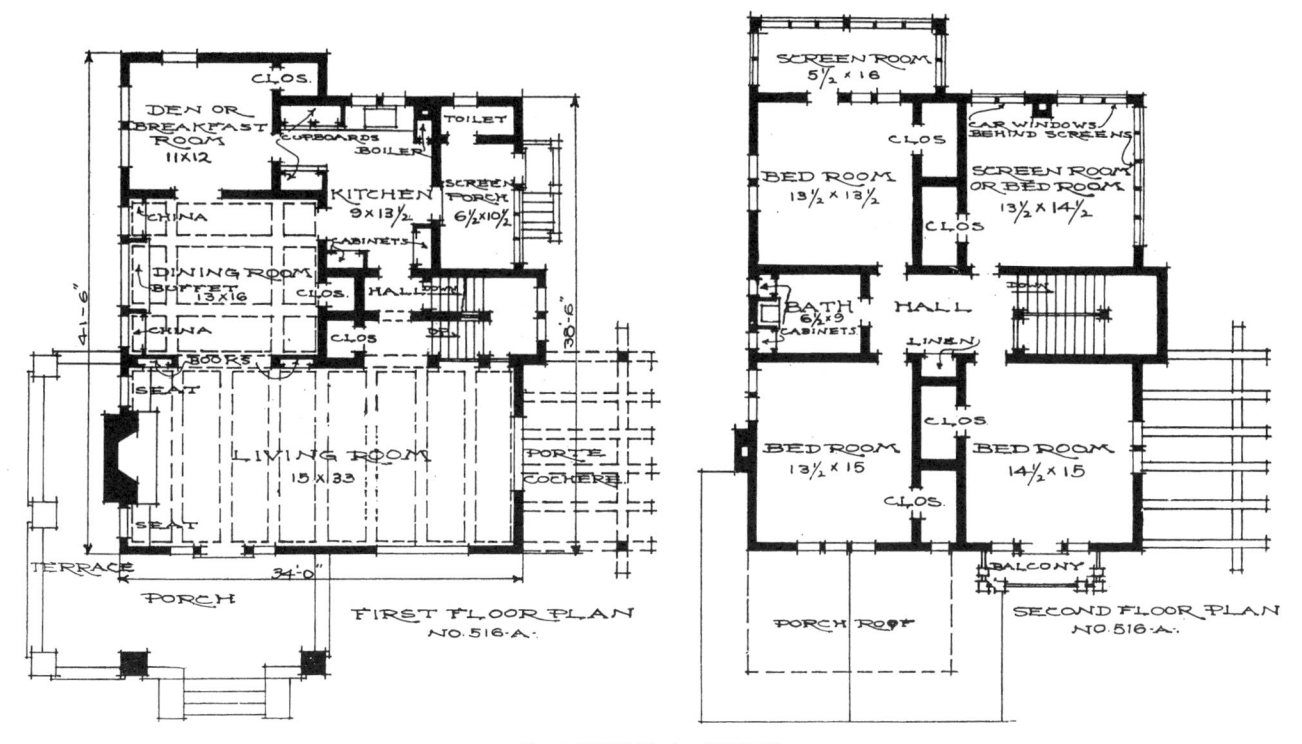

Cost $3800.00 to $4200.00.

Foundation and basement concrete, basement and porch floors cement, chimneys plastered. Shakes on walls and composition roof. Pressed brick mantel. Pine finish throughout. Oak floors except pine in kitchen and screen room. Paneled wainscot in dining room. Beamed ceiling in living and dining rooms. Living and dining rooms and den stained, and waxed finish; screen room finish stained; balance of finish, kitchen and bath room wainscot enameled. Furnace included.

Plans as shown or reversed, $10.00.

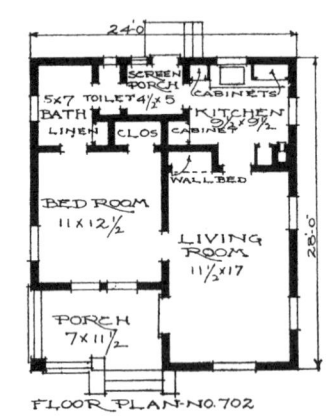

Cost $725.00 to $775.00.

Foundations concrete, rustic siding on walls of 702, shakes on 703, roofs shingled. Pine floors and finish throughout, stained and waxed in living rooms and varnished elsewhere. Plaster paneling and wall-bed in living rooms. Enameled wainscot in baths and kitchens. The exteriors of these houses are interchangeable.

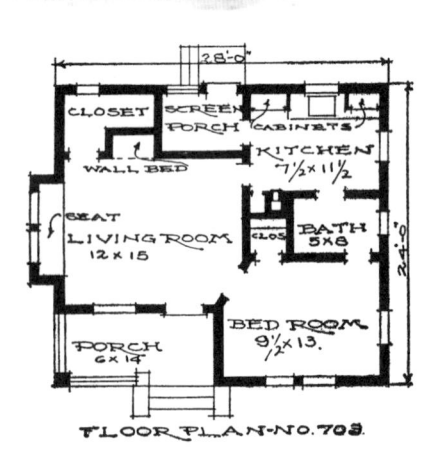

Plans as shown or reversed, $500.

Cost $1900.00 to $2100.00.

Foundation concrete, porch and chimneys brick, porch floor cement, mantel pressed brick. Redwood siding to top of windows, shingles above and on roof. Oak floors, paneled wainscot and beamed ceilings in living and dining rooms. Other floors pine. Stained and waxed finish in living and dining rooms and den. Other finish and kitchen and bath room wainscot enameled. Wall bed in den.

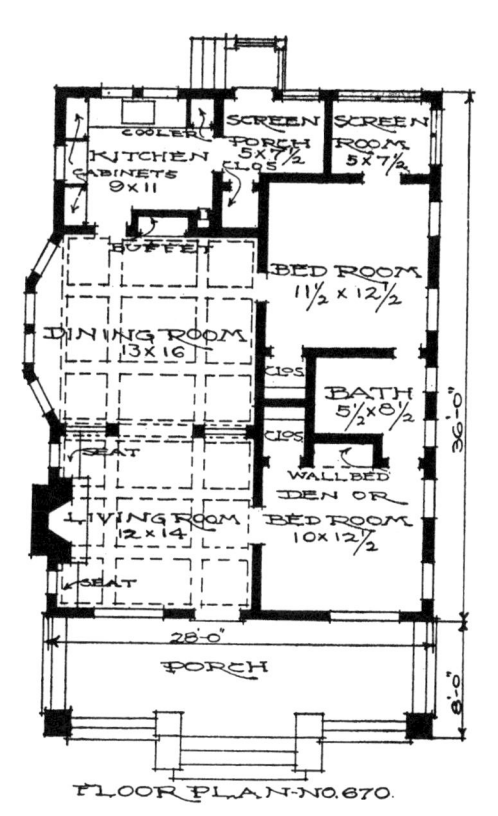

Plans as shown or reversed, $10.00.

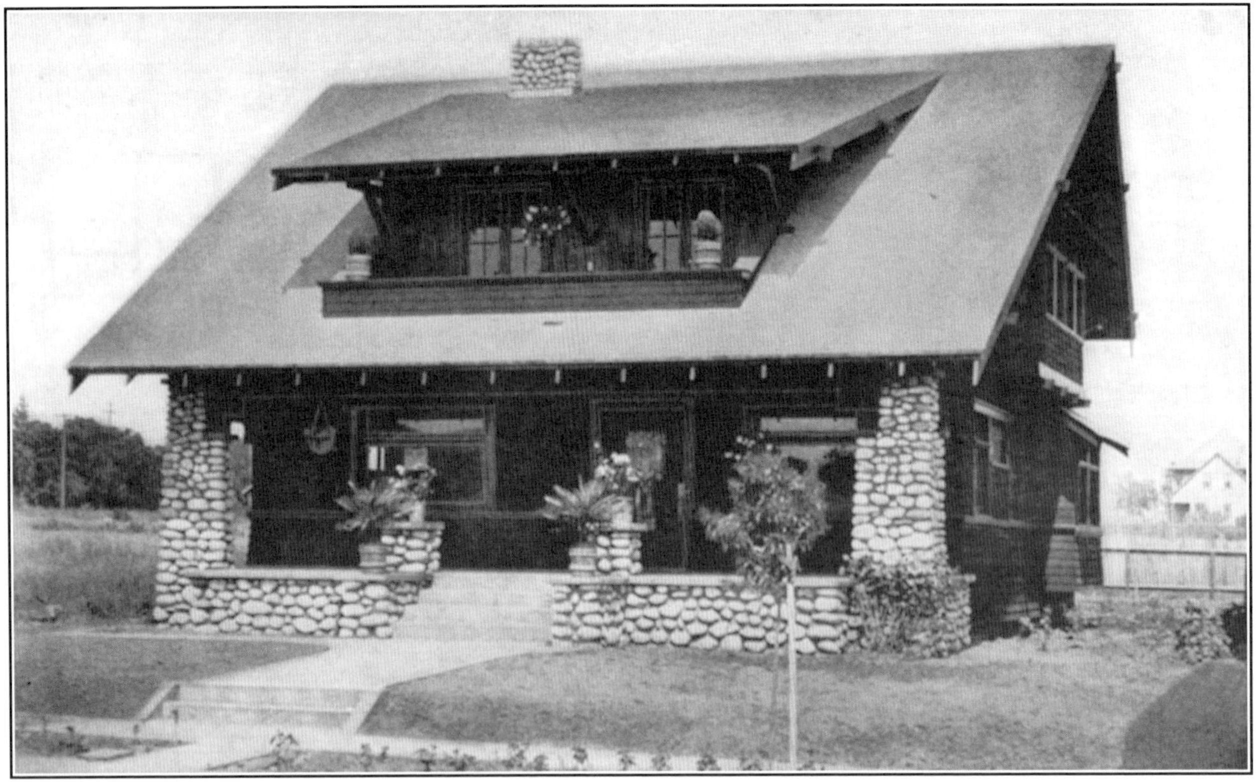

Cost $3000.00 to $3300.00

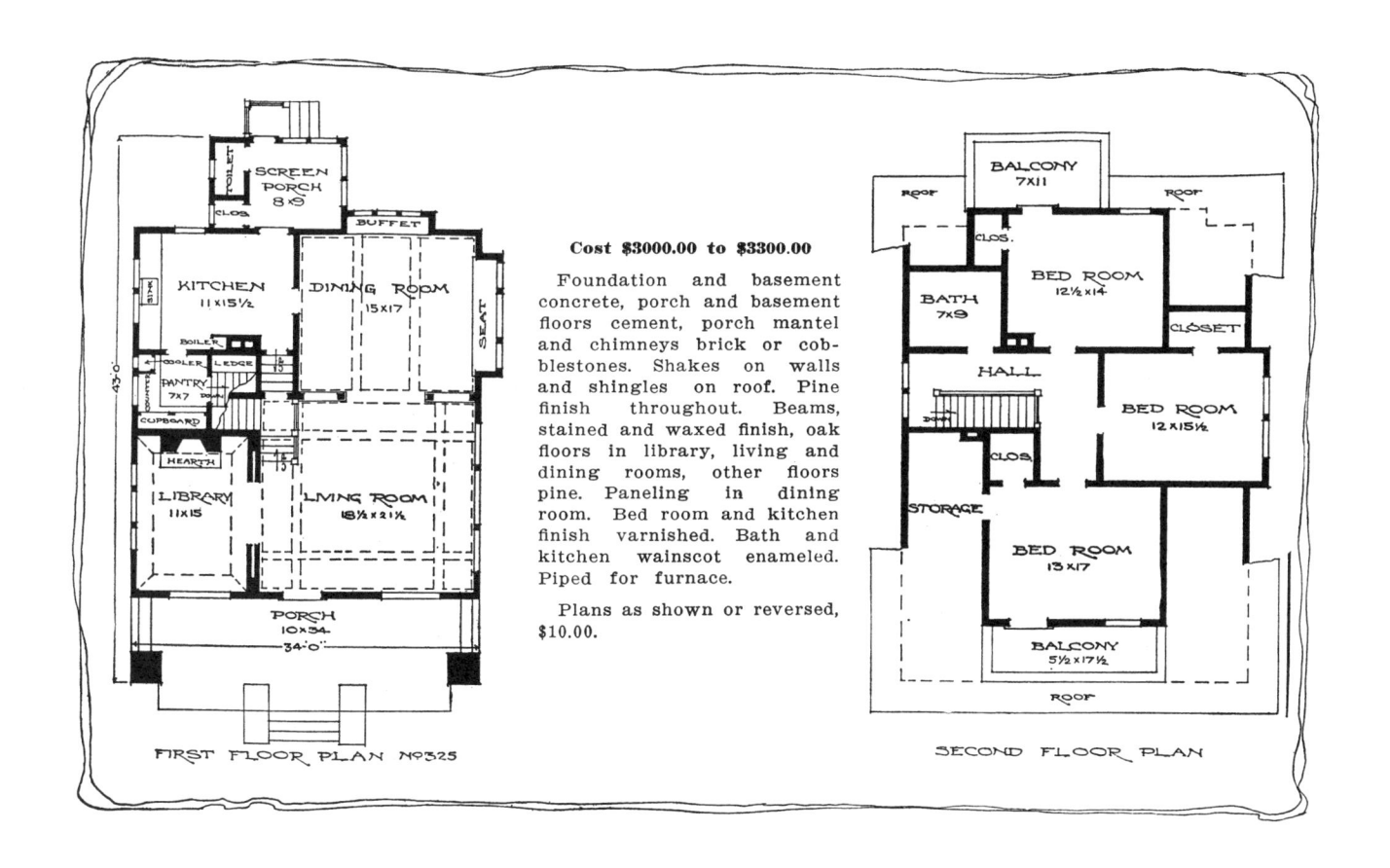

Foundation and basement concrete, porch and basement floors cement, porch mantel and chimneys brick or cobblestones. Shakes on walls and shingles on roof. Pine finish throughout. Beams, stained and waxed finish, oak floors in library, living and dining rooms, other floors pine. Paneling in dining room. Bed room and kitchen finish varnished. Bath and kitchen wainscot enameled. Piped for furnace.

Plans as shown or reversed, $10.00.

NO. 674.
DONE AT
"Ye Planry"

FIRST FLOOR PLAN
NO.-674

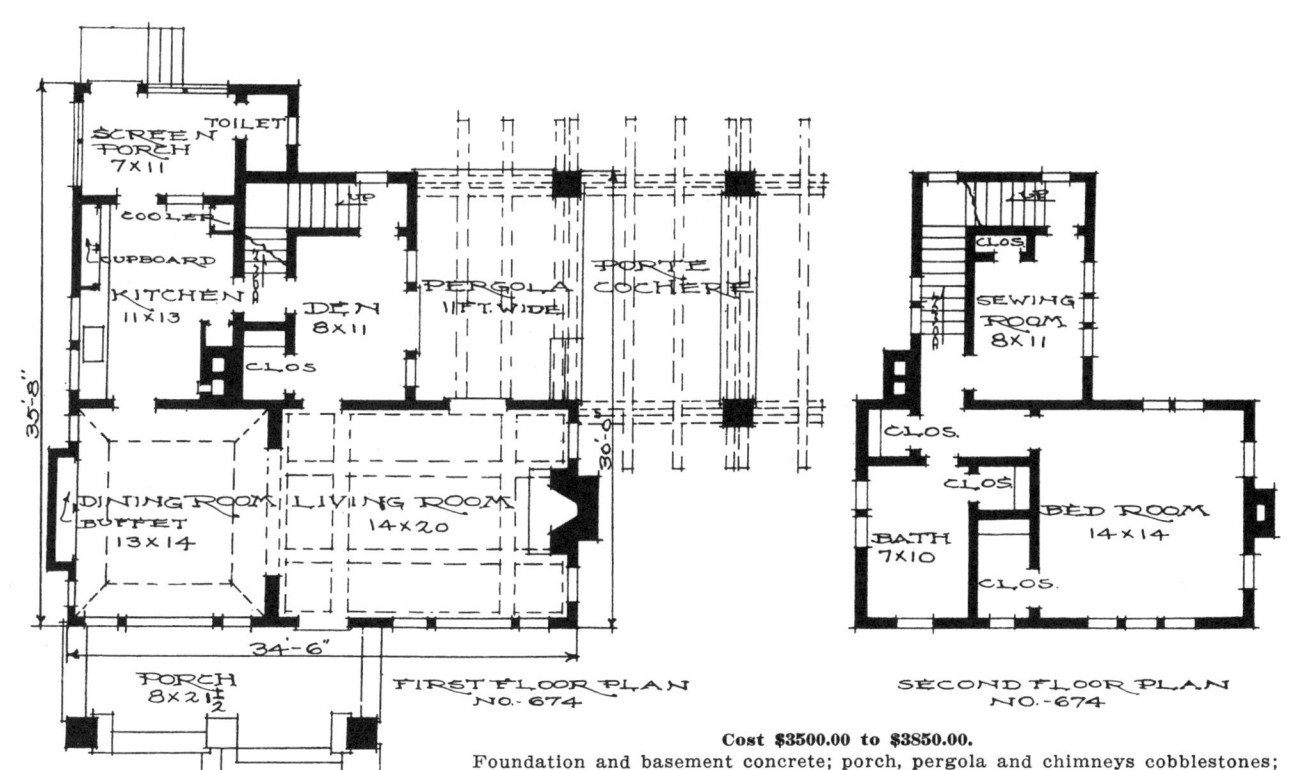

SECOND FLOOR PLAN
NO.-674

Cost $3500.00 to $3850.00.

Foundation and basement concrete; porch, pergola and chimneys cobblestones; pergola and porch floors brick. Basement floor cement. Tower rough plaster with tile roof, shakes on walls and composition roof. White cedar enameled in **kitchen and second story.** Oak floors, stained and waxed, and pine finish in living and dining rooms and den; other floors pine; kitchen and bath room wainscot enameled. Plaster paneling and indirect lighting in dining room, beamed ceiling in living room. Furnace included. Two more bed rooms may be added if desired.

Plans as shown or reversed, $10.00.

Frequent demands are made upon us for other than residence buildings and shown herewith is what has been described as the "Ne Plus Ultra of garages" and "the handsomest garage in the West," built from our plans—a brick building with glazed white tile facing, plate-glass windows, tile floor in the show-room, cement floors elsewhere, and every appointment of a modern garage.

On the page following are shown suggestions for different structures which may be incorporated in special plans. The apartment-house shown is a stock plan, having two four-room apartments on each floor.

City Residence on an Elevated Lot

Sketch of a Garage

Done At "Ye Planry"

Suggestion for a Park Entrance

A Four Suite Apartment House

NO. 673
DONE AT
"Ye Planry"

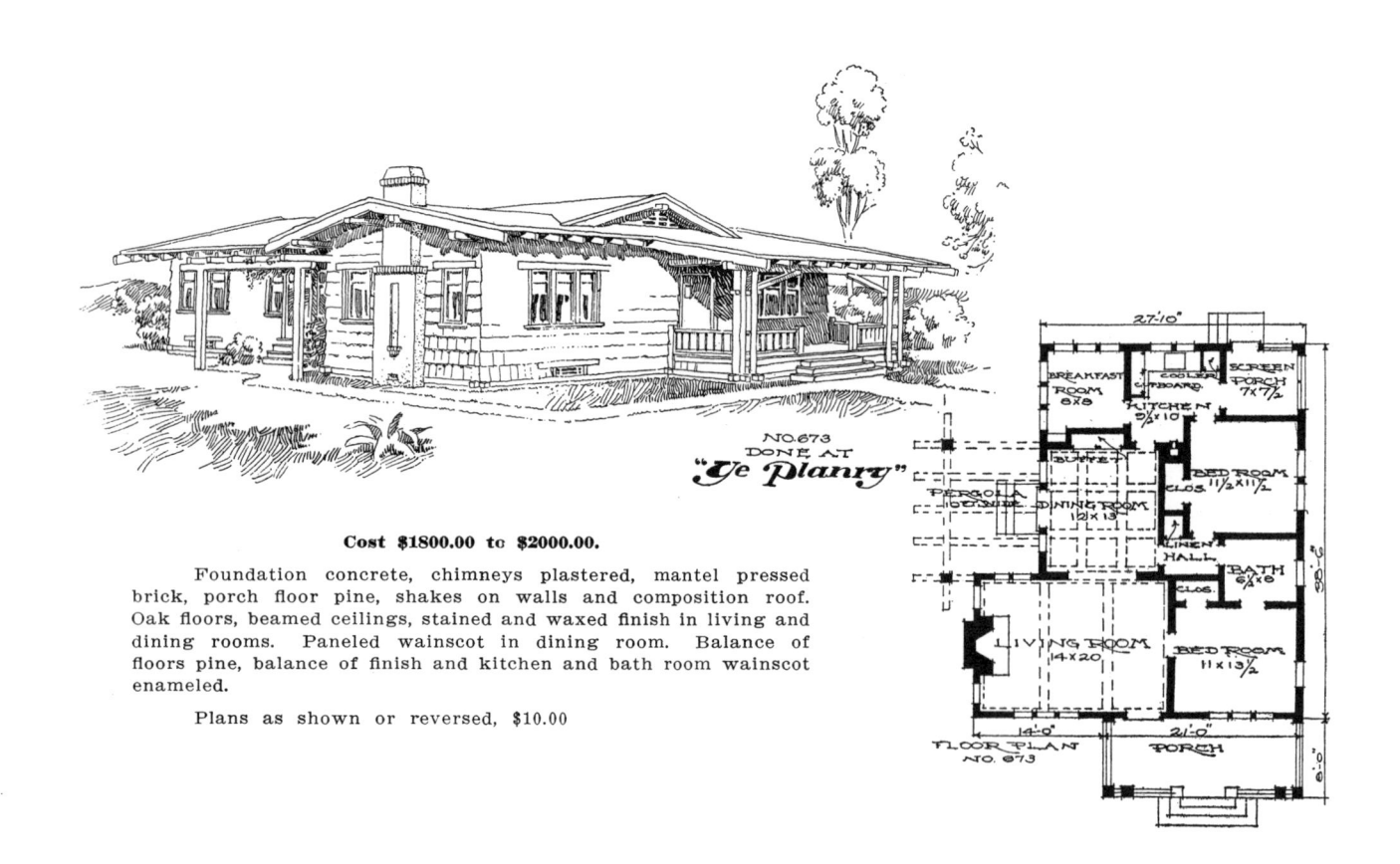

Cost $1800.00 to $2000.00.

Foundation concrete, chimneys plastered, mantel pressed brick, porch floor pine, shakes on walls and composition roof. Oak floors, beamed ceilings, stained and waxed finish in living and dining rooms. Paneled wainscot in dining room. Balance of floors pine, balance of finish and kitchen and bath room wainscot enameled.

Plans as shown or reversed, $10.00

Cost $3200.00 to $3500.00.

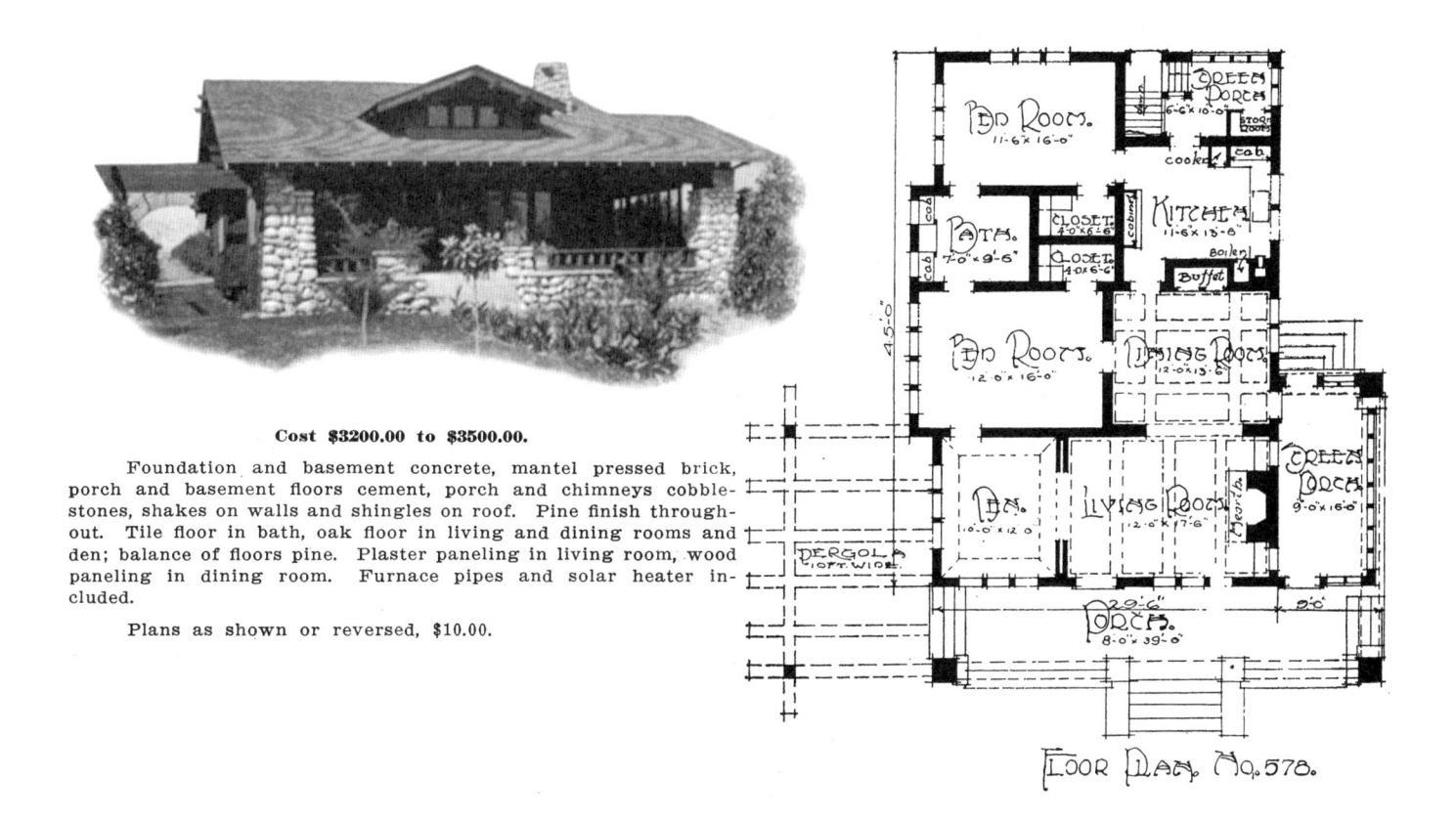

Foundation and basement concrete, mantel pressed brick, porch and basement floors cement, porch and chimneys cobblestones, shakes on walls and shingles on roof. Pine finish throughout. Tile floor in bath, oak floor in living and dining rooms and den; balance of floors pine. Plaster paneling in living room, wood paneling in dining room. Furnace pipes and solar heater included.

Plans as shown or reversed, $10.00.

NO. 811.
DONE AT
"Ye Planry"

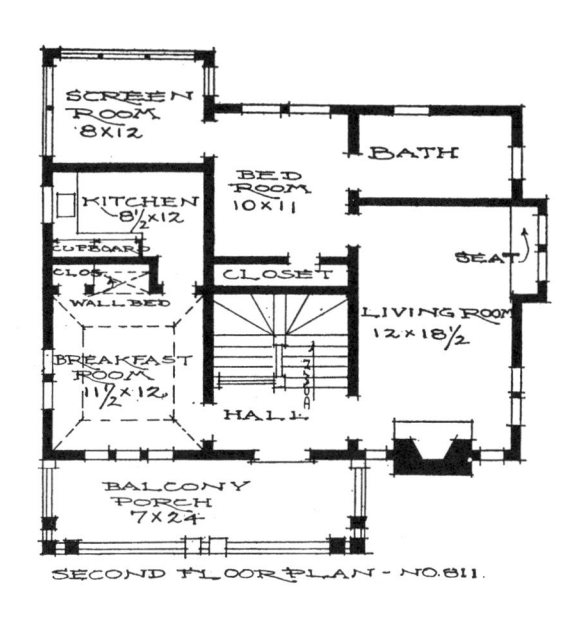

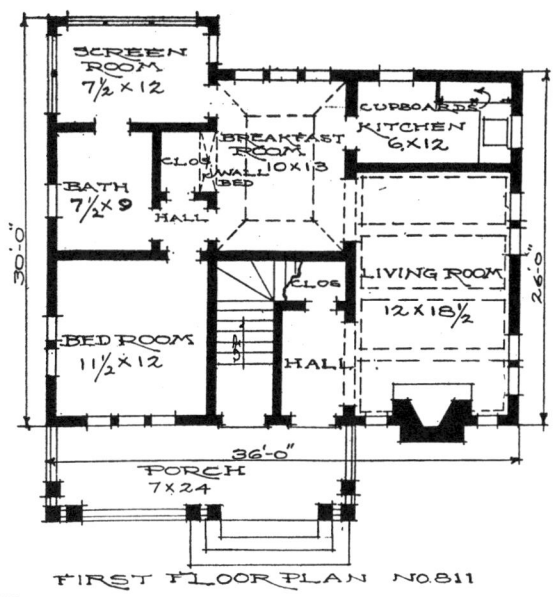

Cost $3600.00 to $4000.00.

"Bungalo Flats" designed primarily as an adjunct to a hotel or summer resort, where light housekeeping may be done, and the principal meals taken at the main dining room. With enlarged kitchen facilities such a building would be a profitable investment in any locality.

Foundation concrete, cobblestone chimney, tile mantels, shakes on walls and composition roofing. Oak floors, stained and waxed finish and panel wainscot in living and breakfast rooms and dens. Other floors pine; other finish and bath room and kitchen wainscots enameled. Beam ceiling in living rooms, and indirect lighting in breakfast rooms.

Plans as shown or reversed, $10.00.

139

Cost $725.00 to $775.00.

Foundation concrete, shingles on walls of No. 704, shakes on walls of No. 705. Shingled roofs. Pine floors throughout, pine finish, stained and waxed in living rooms, and varnished elsewhere. Plaster paneling and wall-beds in living rooms. Enameled wainscot in baths and kitchens. The exterior of these houses may be exchanged.

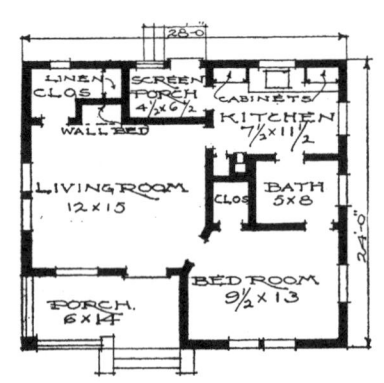

Plans as shown or reversed, $5.00.

FLOOR PLAN - NO. 704 & 705

Cost $2250.00 to $2500.00.

Foundation concrete, porch and chimney cobblestones, porch floor cement. Shakes on walls and composition roof. Plastered mantel. Oak floors, except pine in kitchen and bath. Pine finish throughout. Indirect lighting and stained and waxed finish in living and dining rooms. Balance of finish and kitchen and bath room wainscot enameled. Imitation leather panels in dining room and plaster panels in living room.

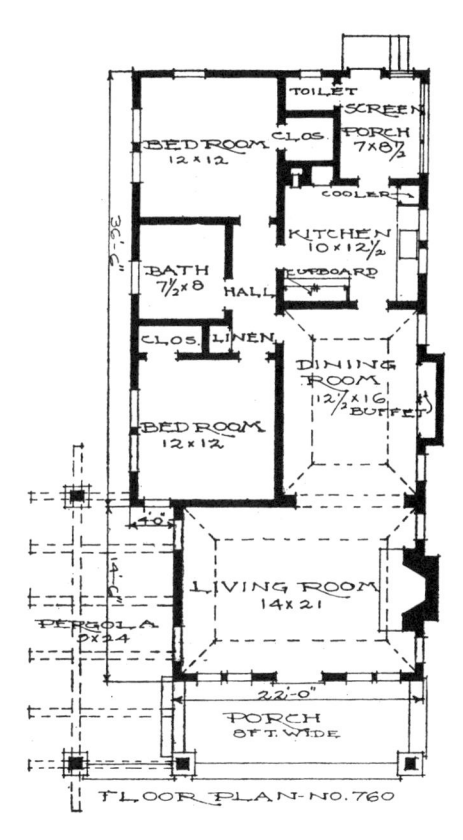

Plans as shown or reversed, $10.00.

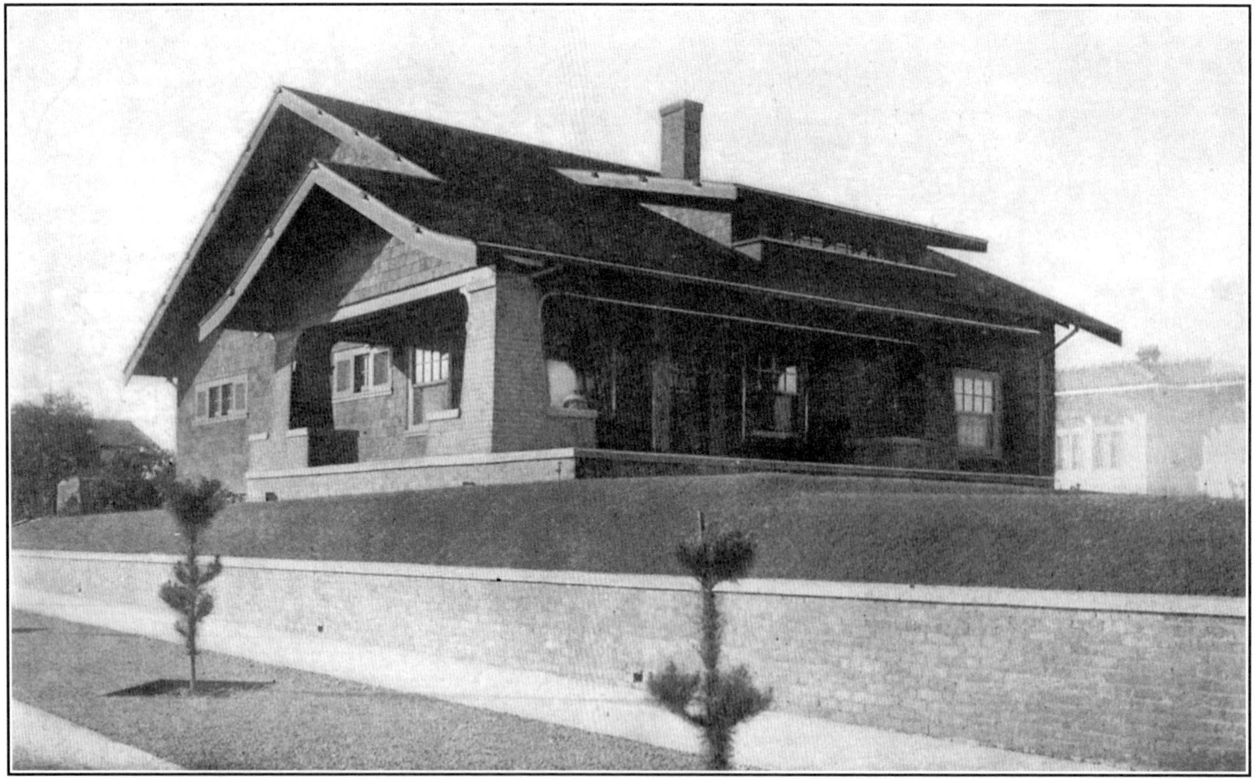

FLOOR PLAN

No. 251 Done At "Ye Planry"

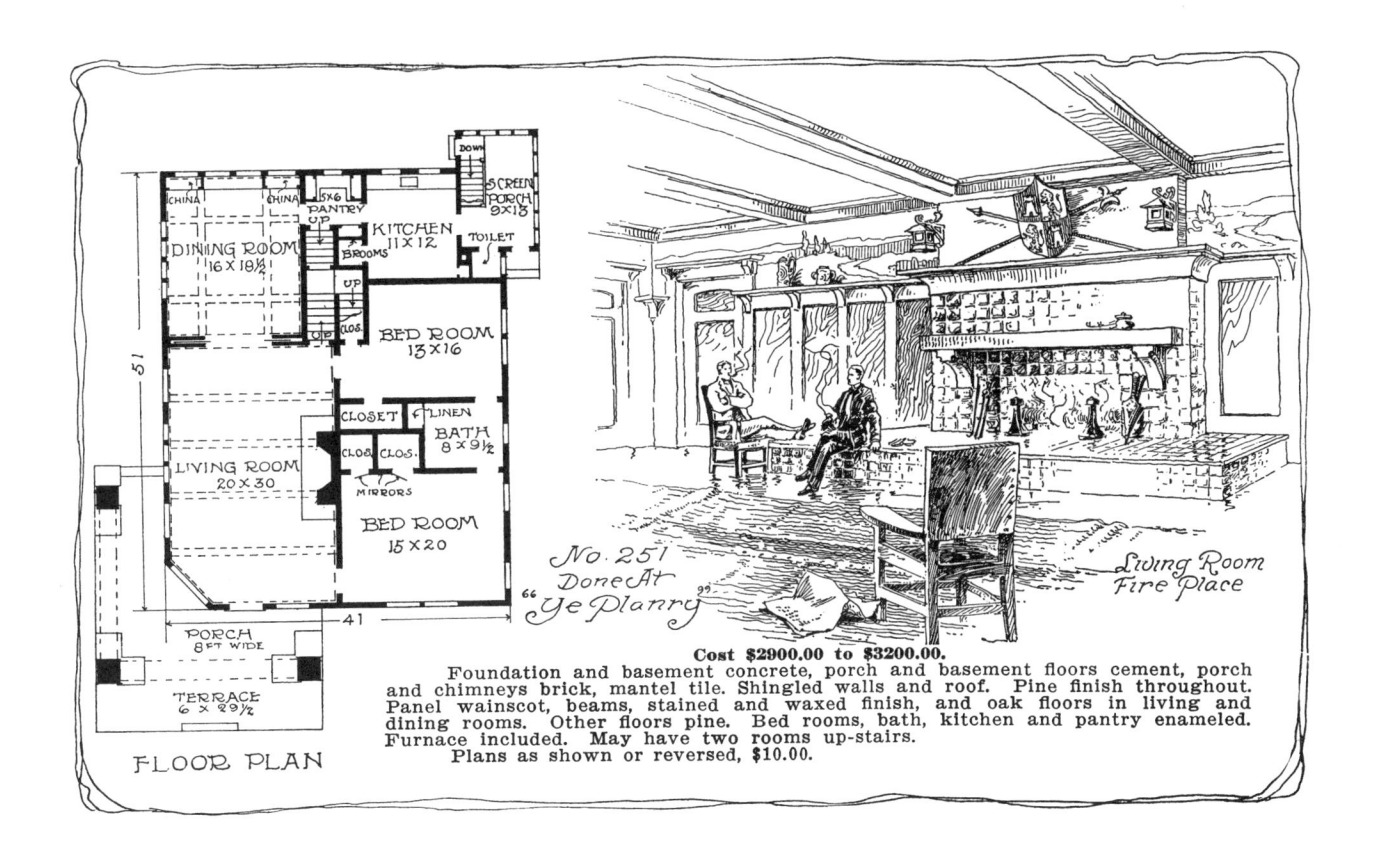

Living Room Fire Place

Cost $2900.00 to $3200.00.

Foundation and basement concrete, porch and basement floors cement, porch and chimneys brick, mantel tile. Shingled walls and roof. Pine finish throughout. Panel wainscot, beams, stained and waxed finish, and oak floors in living and dining rooms. Other floors pine. Bed rooms, bath, kitchen and pantry enameled. Furnace included. May have two rooms up-stairs.

Plans as shown or reversed, $10.00.

Living Room — Looking Towards
— Inglenook —

No. 525
Done at
"Ye Planry"

FIRST FLOOR PLAN N° 525

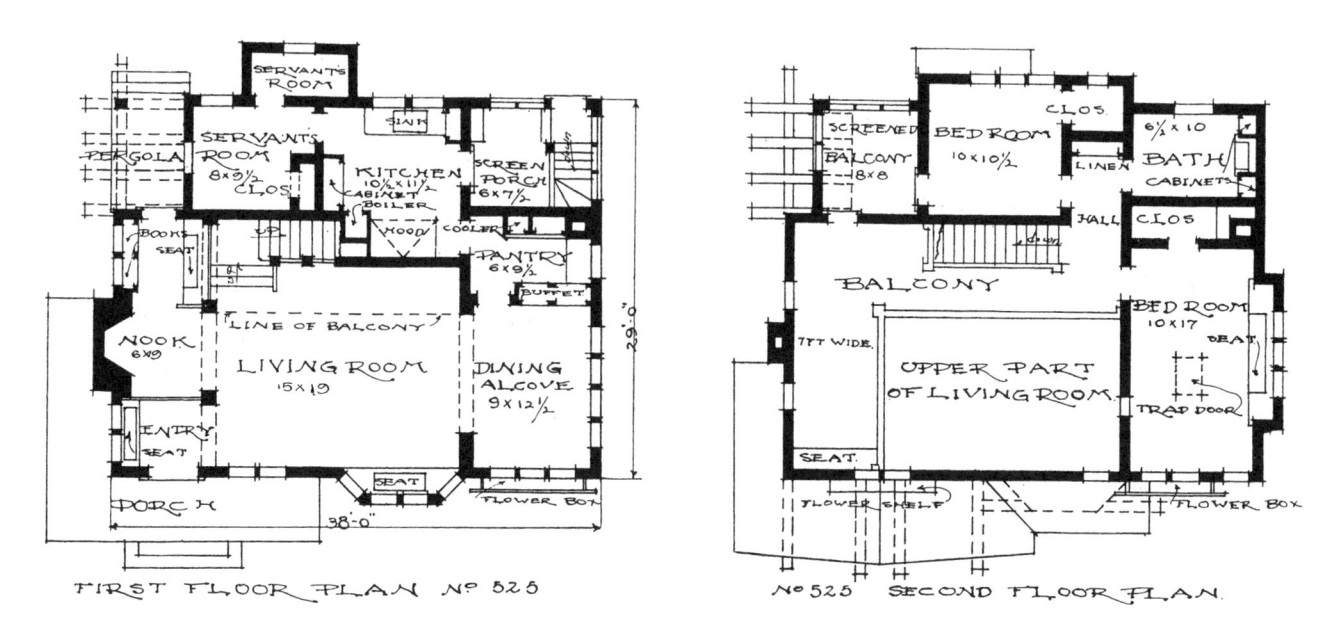

N° 525 SECOND FLOOR PLAN

Cost $3000.00 to $3300.00.

Foundation and basement concrete, basement floor cement, porch floor brick, mantel pressed brick, shakes on walls and shingles on roof. Pine finish throughout. Oak floors in living room and dining alcove and nook. Plaster paneling, living room walls and ceiling, and walls of nook. Wood paneling walls and ceiling of dining alcove and ceiling of nook. Down-stairs finish stained and waxed, except pantry, kitchen and servant's room finish varnished. Finish on second story and bath room and kitchen wainscot enameled. Furnace included.

Plans as shown or reversed, $10.00.

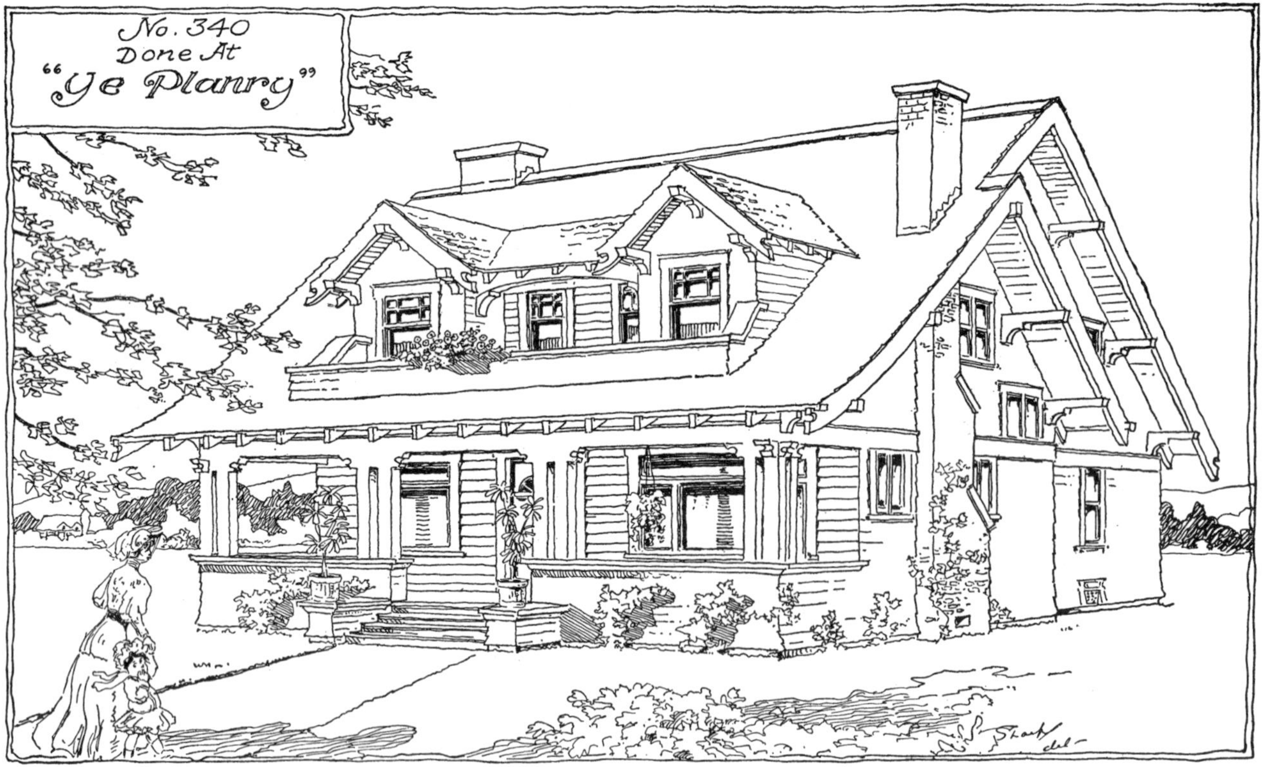
No. 340
Done At
"Ye Planry"

Cost $2900.00 to $3200.00

Foundation and basement concrete, basement floor cement. Porch floor pine. Chimneys brick, mantel pressed brick. Redwood siding to top of windows, shingles above and on roof. Pine finish throughout. Beamed ceilings, stained and waxed finish and oak floors in living and dining rooms. Other floors pine. Paneled wainscot in dining room. Kitchen and bed room finish varnished. Kitchen wainscot and bath room enameled. Furnace included.

Plans as shown or reversed, $10.00.

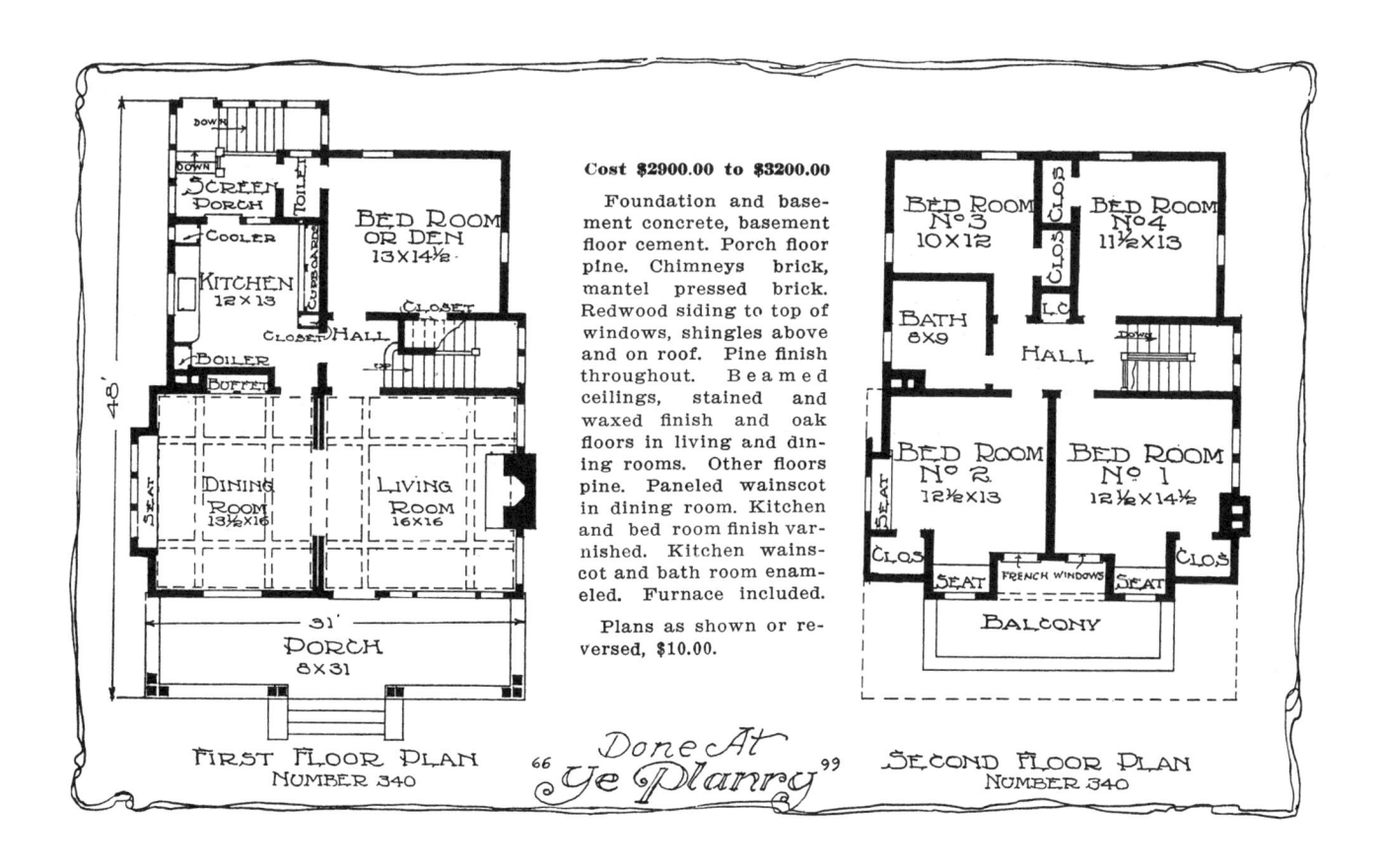

First Floor Plan
Number 340

"Done At Ye Planry"

Second Floor Plan
Number 340

147

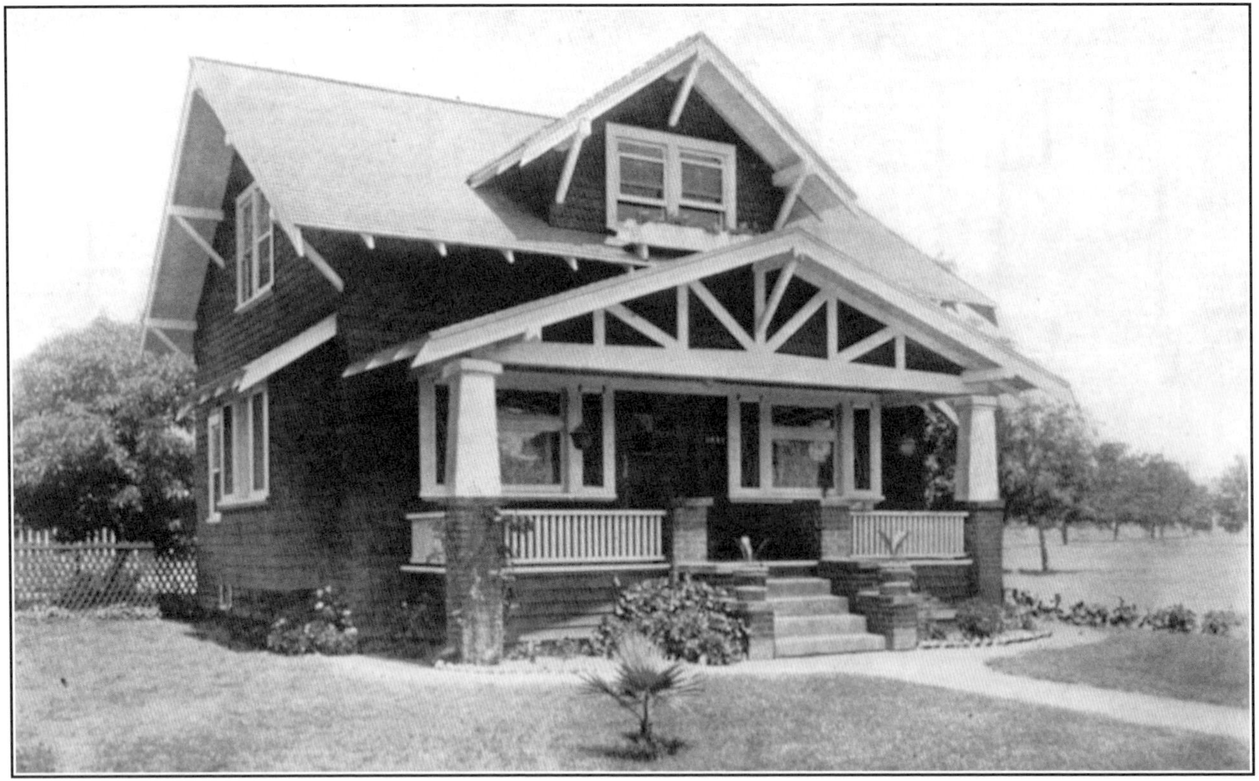

Cost $1850 to $2050.

Foundation, chimney and porch columns brick, mantel pressed brick, redwood siding on walls and shingles on roof. Porch floor pine. Pine finish throughout. Ceiling beams, stained and waxed finish and oak floors in living and dining rooms, other floors pine. Panel wainscoting and plate rail in dining room. Bath and kitchen wainscot enameled, balance of finish varnished.

Plans as shown or reversed, $10.00.

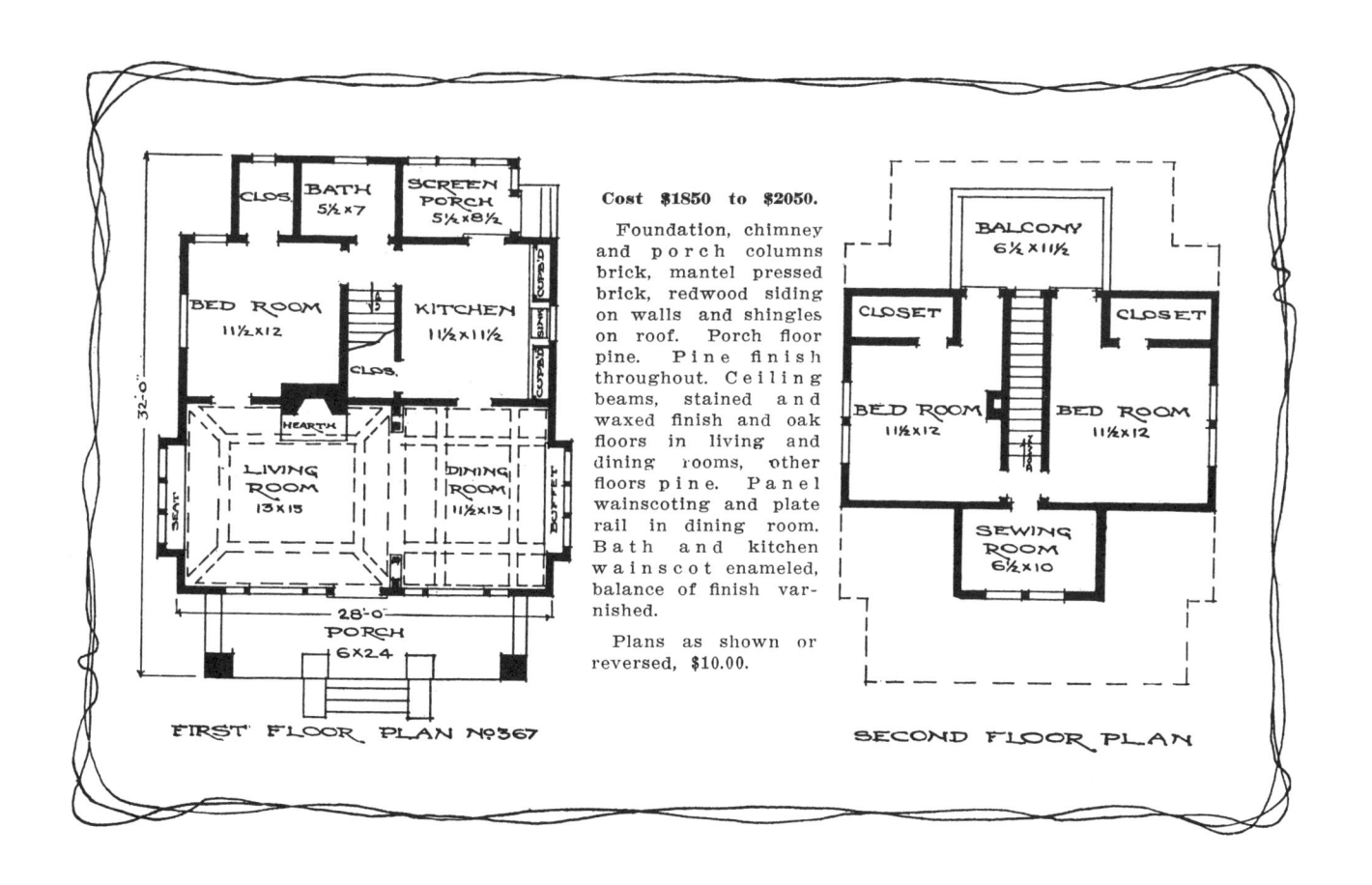

No. 350
Done At
"Ye Planry"

FIRST FLOOR PLAN
NO. 350.

Dining Room Buffet & Stairway

Cost $2200.00 to $2500.00

Designed for 30 ft. lot. Foundation and chimneys brick, mantel pressed brick, porch floor pine. Redwood siding on walls and shingles on roof. Pine finish throughout. Stained and waxed finish and oak floors in living and dining rooms. Other floors pine. Kitchen and bed room finish varnished. Kitchen wainscot and bath room enameled.

Plans as shown or reversed, $10.00.

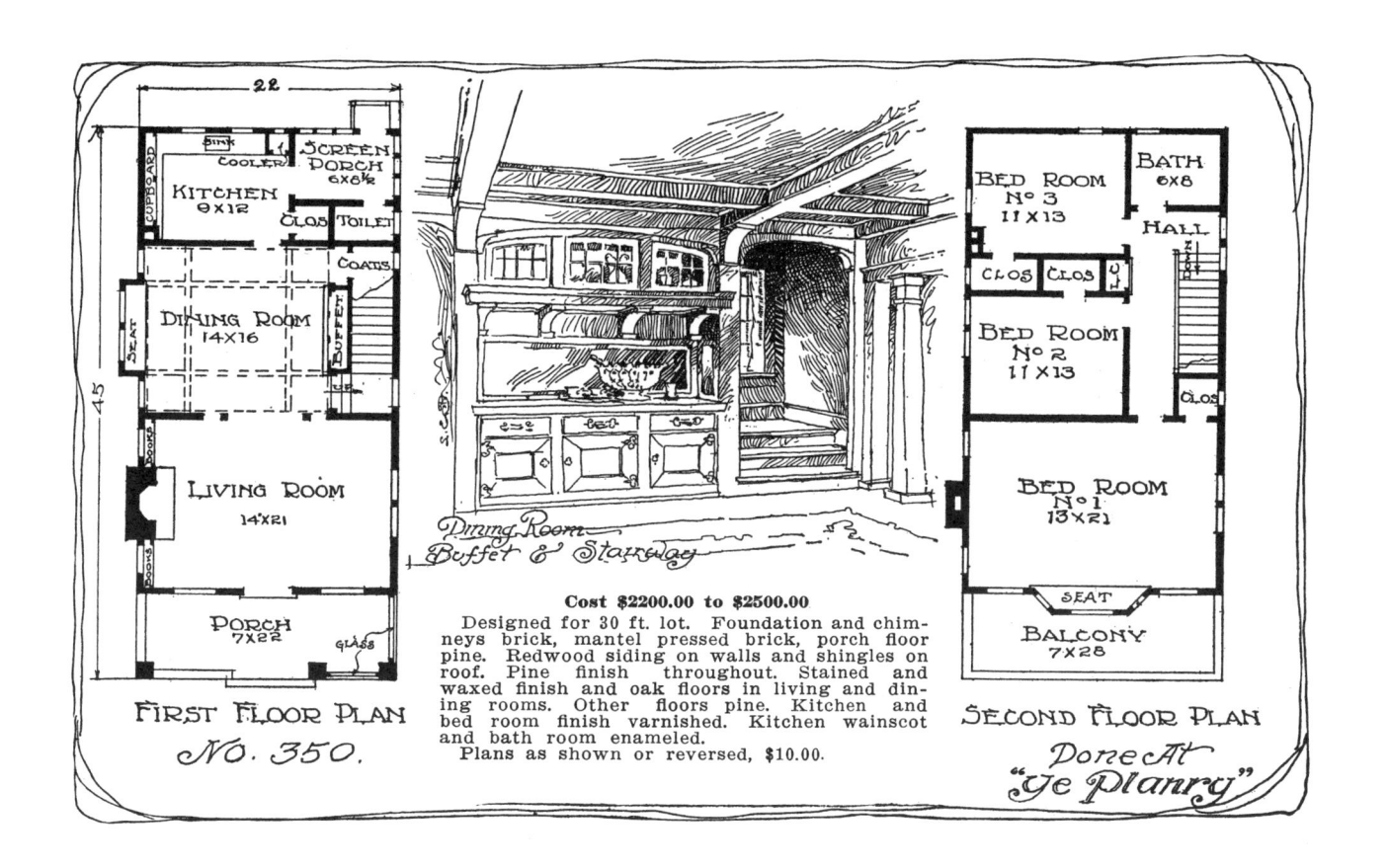

SECOND FLOOR PLAN

Done At "Ye Planry"

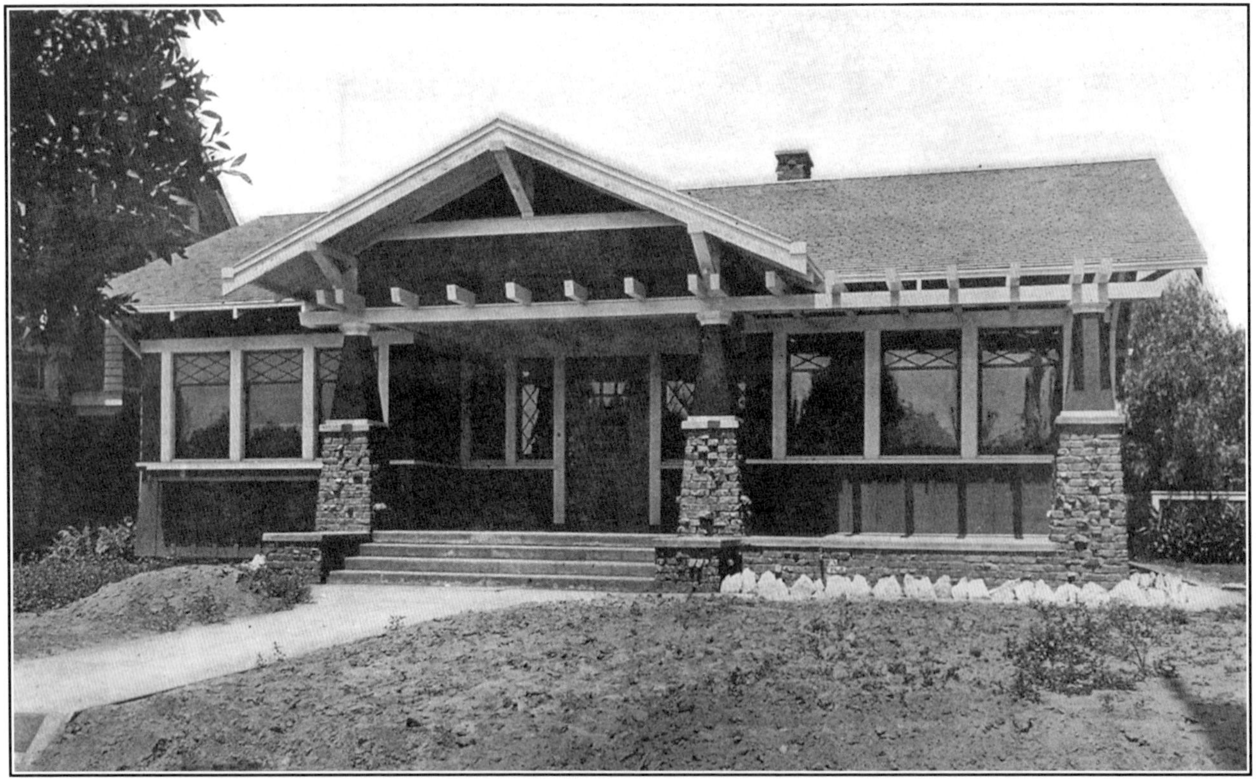

Living Room Towards Pergola.

No 328 Done At "Ye Planry"

FLOOR PLAN

Cost $2000.00 to $2300.00.
Foundation concrete, porch, chimney and mantel clinker brick, porch and pergola floors cement, roof shingles, 1" x12" vertical boards to window sills and shingles above. Pine finish throughout. Oak floors in living and dining rooms, pine elsewhere. Beam ceilings and paneling in living and dining rooms, bath and bed rooms white enamel. Kitchen finish varnished, with enameled wainscot.
Plans as shown or reversed, $10.00.

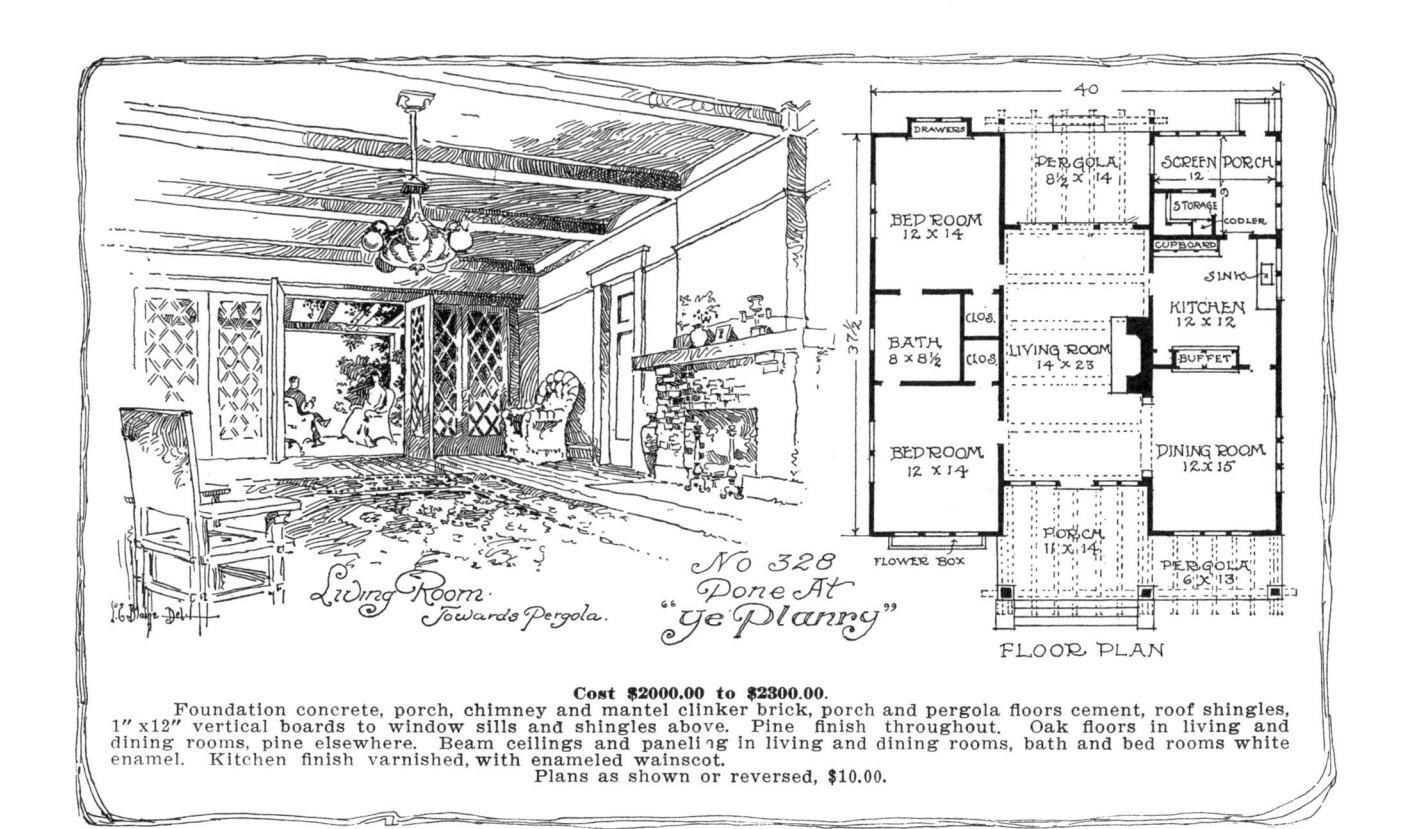

No. 224.
Done At
Ye Planry

Cost $2800.00 to $3100.00.

Foundation concrete, porch floor cement, porch and chimneys cobblestones, mantel pressed brick. First story siding, shingles above and on roof. Pine finish throughout. Stained and waxed finish, paneling, beams and oak floors in living and dining rooms, pine floors elsewhere. Bed rooms and kitchen finish varnished, kitchen wainscot and bath room enameled.

Plans as shown or reversed, $10.00.

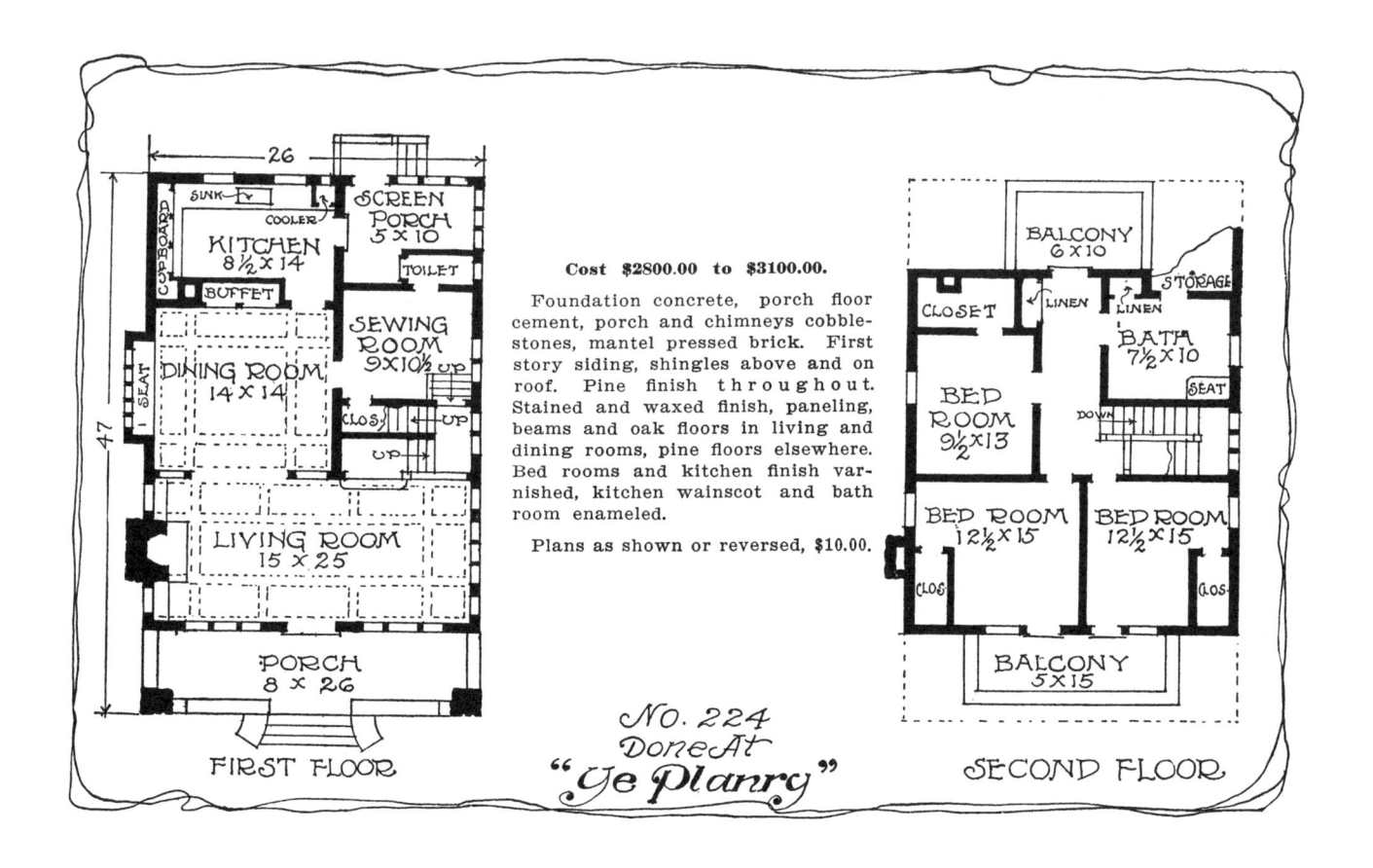

No. 224 Done At "Ye Planry"

FIRST FLOOR

SECOND FLOOR

FLOOR PLAN No 297

Sketch of Dining Room

Fireplace

DONE AT "Ye Planry"

Cost $2200.00 to $2400.00.

Foundation, porch and chimneys brick, mantel tile, porch floor cement. Redwood siding on walls, and shingles on roof. Pine finish throughout. Stained and waxed finish and oak floors in living and dining rooms and den; other floors pine. Paneling in dining room, beams in dining and living rooms. Kitchen wainscot and bath room enameled, other finish varnished.

Plans as shown or reversed, $10.00.

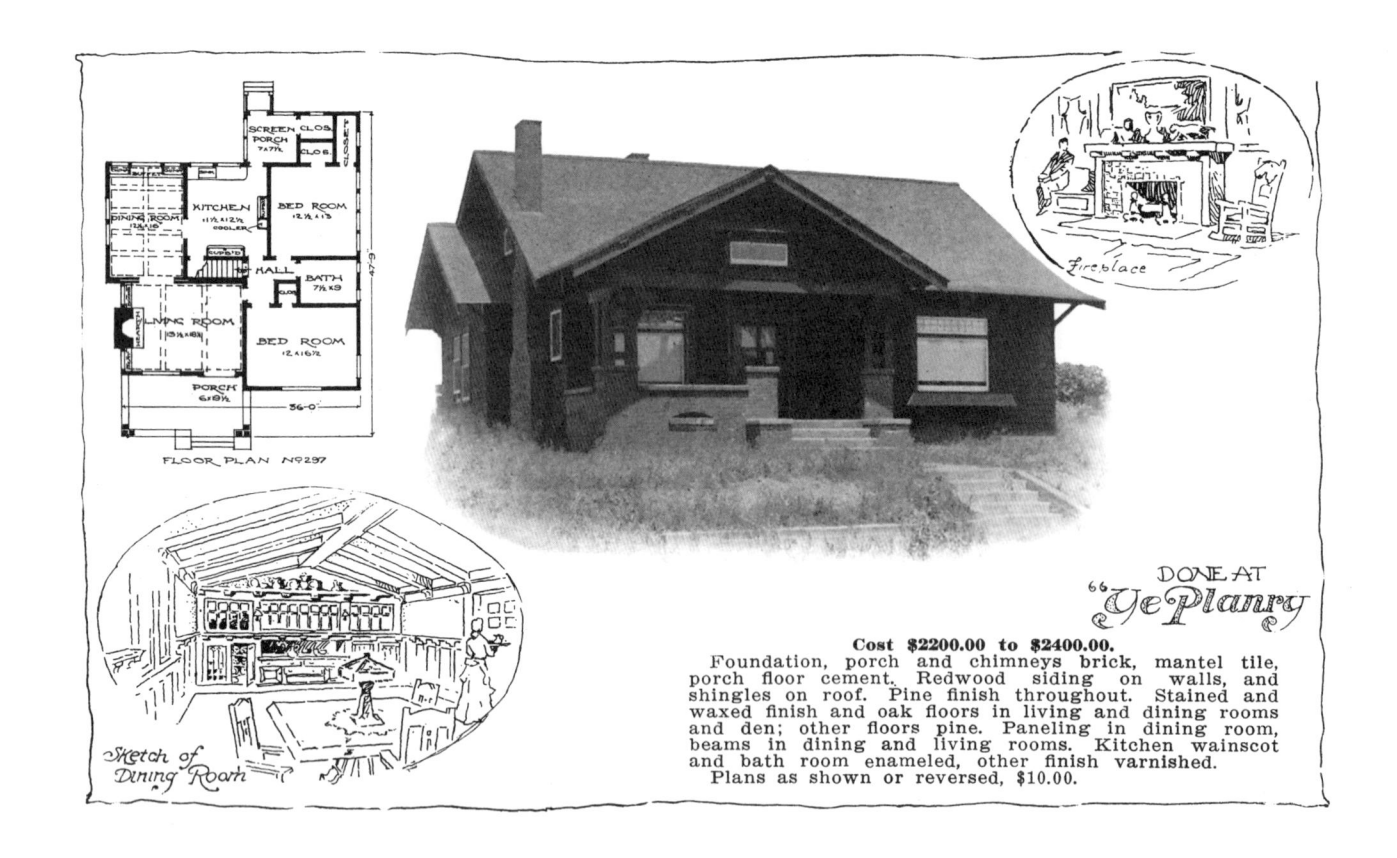

Cost $2400.00 to $2600.00.

Foundation concrete, porch floor cement; plastered porch and walls to window sills. Shakes above and shingles on roof. Plastered mantel. Oak floors except pine in kitchen and bath. Pine finish throughout. Indirect lighting and stained and waxed finish in living and dining rooms. Screen room finish varnished. Balance of finish, and kitchen and bath room wainscot enameled. Imitation leather panels in dining room and plaster panels in living room.

Plans as shown or reversed, $10.00.

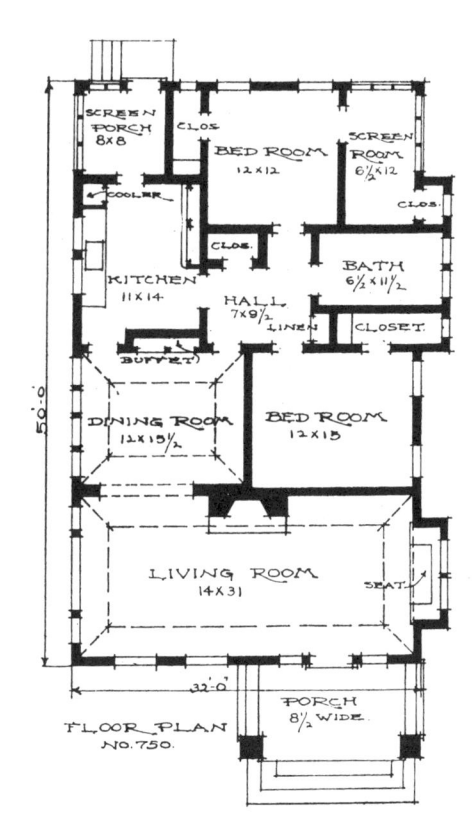

157

Cost $1950.00 to $2150.00.

Foundation concrete, chimney brick, mantel pressed brick. Porch floor pine; first story siding, shingles above and on roof. Pine finish throughout. Living and dining rooms and den stained and waxed finish, and oak floors. Other floors pine. Beam ceilings in living and dining rooms. Paneling in dining room. Bed rooms, kitchen and bath enameled. May have two rooms up-stairs.

Plans as shown or reversed, $10.00.

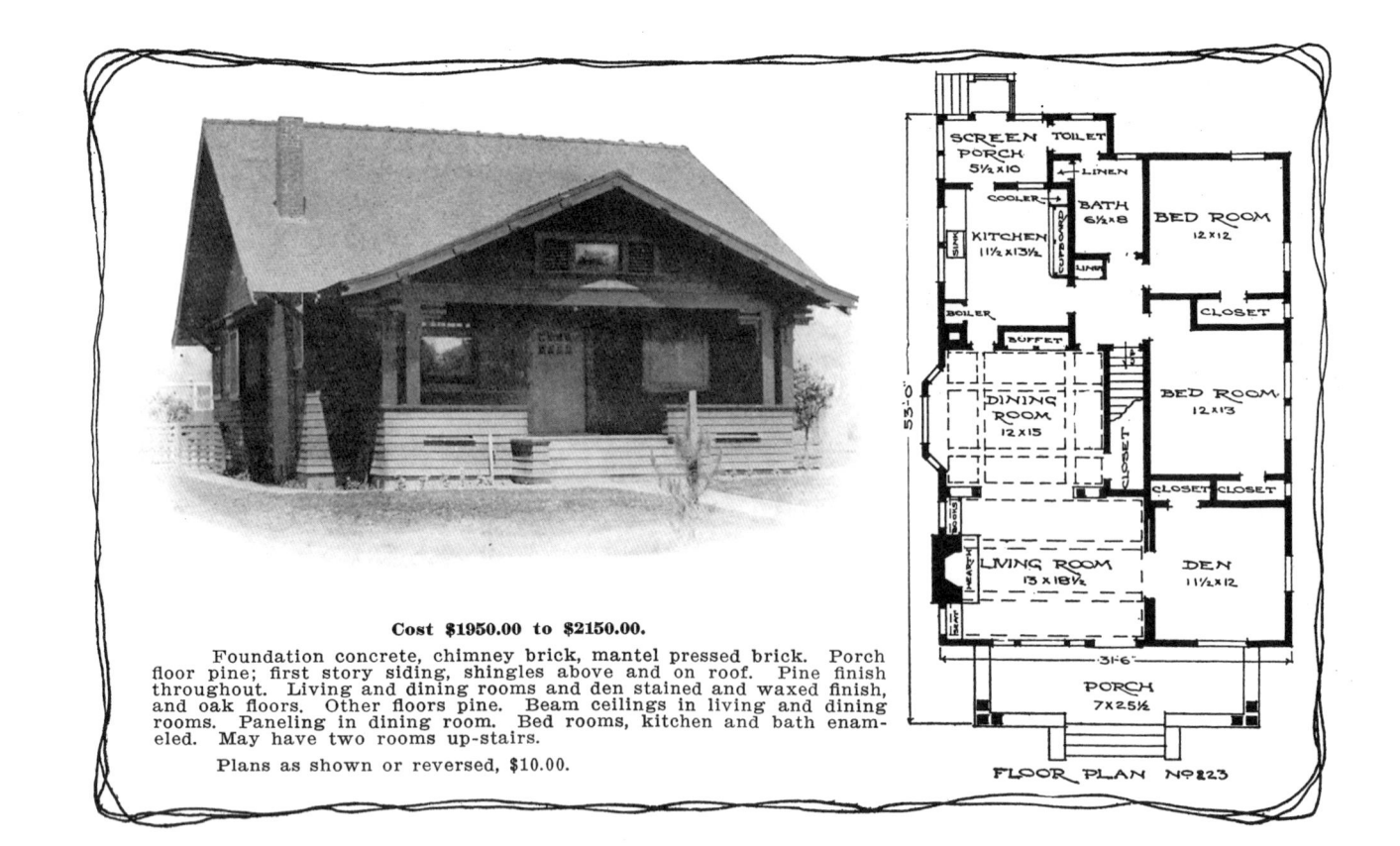

FLOOR PLAN No. 223

| We are Agents for Limbert's Arts and Crafts Furniture | **Fredericks**
You Can Depend upon Us for Quality and Low Prices | We are Agents for Garland Stoves and Ranges |

We invite you to visit our

Modern Furnished Bungalow

Situated on the second floor. It will offer you many good ideas for furnishing your new home.

Furniture, Carpets, Draperies, Gas Stoves and Ranges, Refrigerators, Picture Framing

| Investigate Our Charge Account and Credit System | **Los Angeles Furniture Co.**
420-24 So. Spring St. | Free Delivery
Of all goods to nearby towns in our own Auto Trucks. You surely will appreciate getting your purchases in bright, new, first-class condition. |

FLOOR PLAN No 212

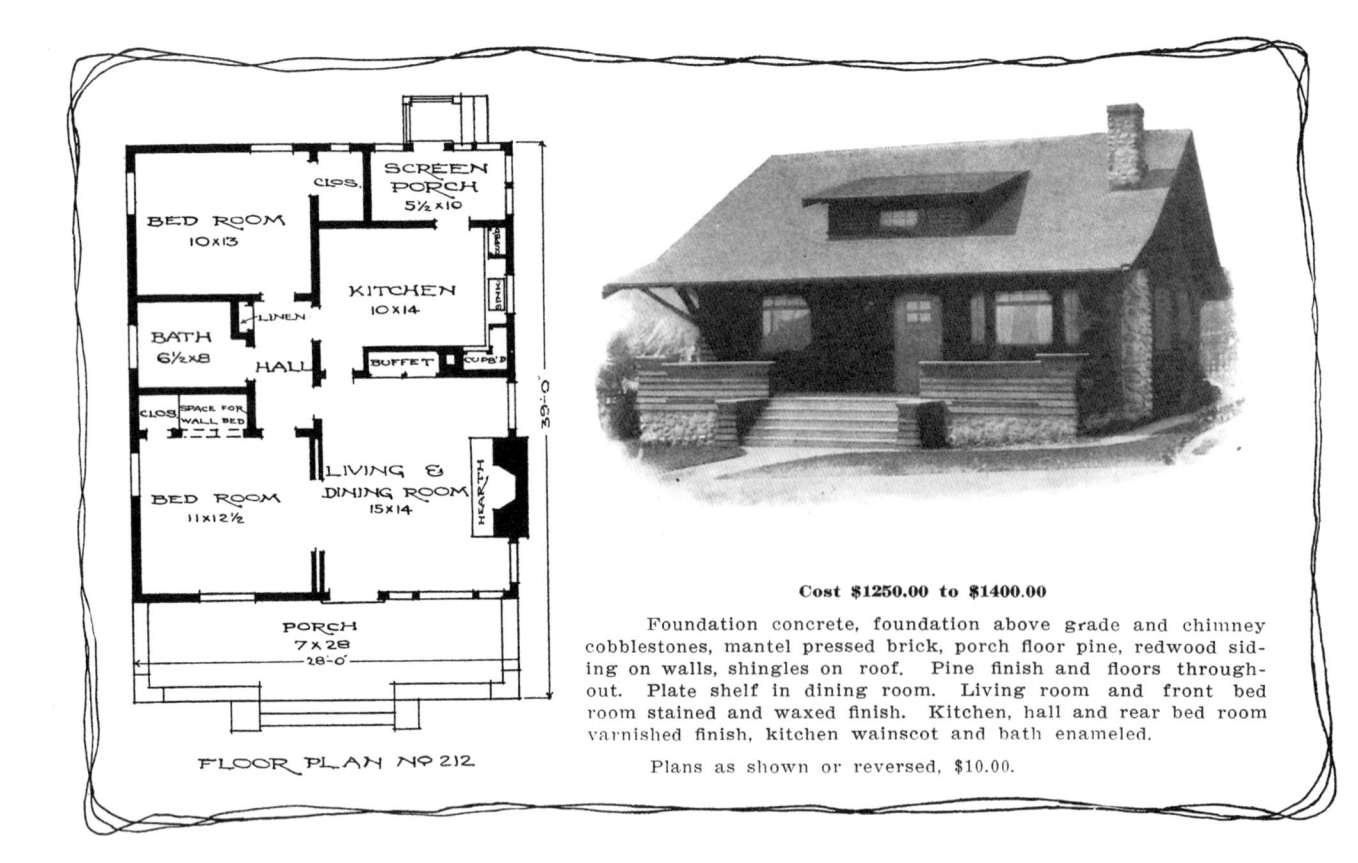

Cost $1250.00 to $1400.00

Foundation concrete, foundation above grade and chimney cobblestones, mantel pressed brick, porch floor pine, redwood siding on walls, shingles on roof. Pine finish and floors throughout. Plate shelf in dining room. Living room and front bed room stained and waxed finish. Kitchen, hall and rear bed room varnished finish, kitchen wainscot and bath enameled.

Plans as shown or reversed, $10.00.

Just try and see if it's true

That our paint is more durable than the ordinary kind. You'll be convinced of its superiority then.

We carry the largest stock of paints, oils, varnishes, brushes, wall finish, etc., in the city. Call or write for color cards.

H. R. TIBBETTS PAINT CO.

THIRD AND SAN PEDRO STREETS

Phones: Main 1929; Home F 3381

LOS ANGELES, CALIFORNIA

No. 324 "Done At Ye Planry"

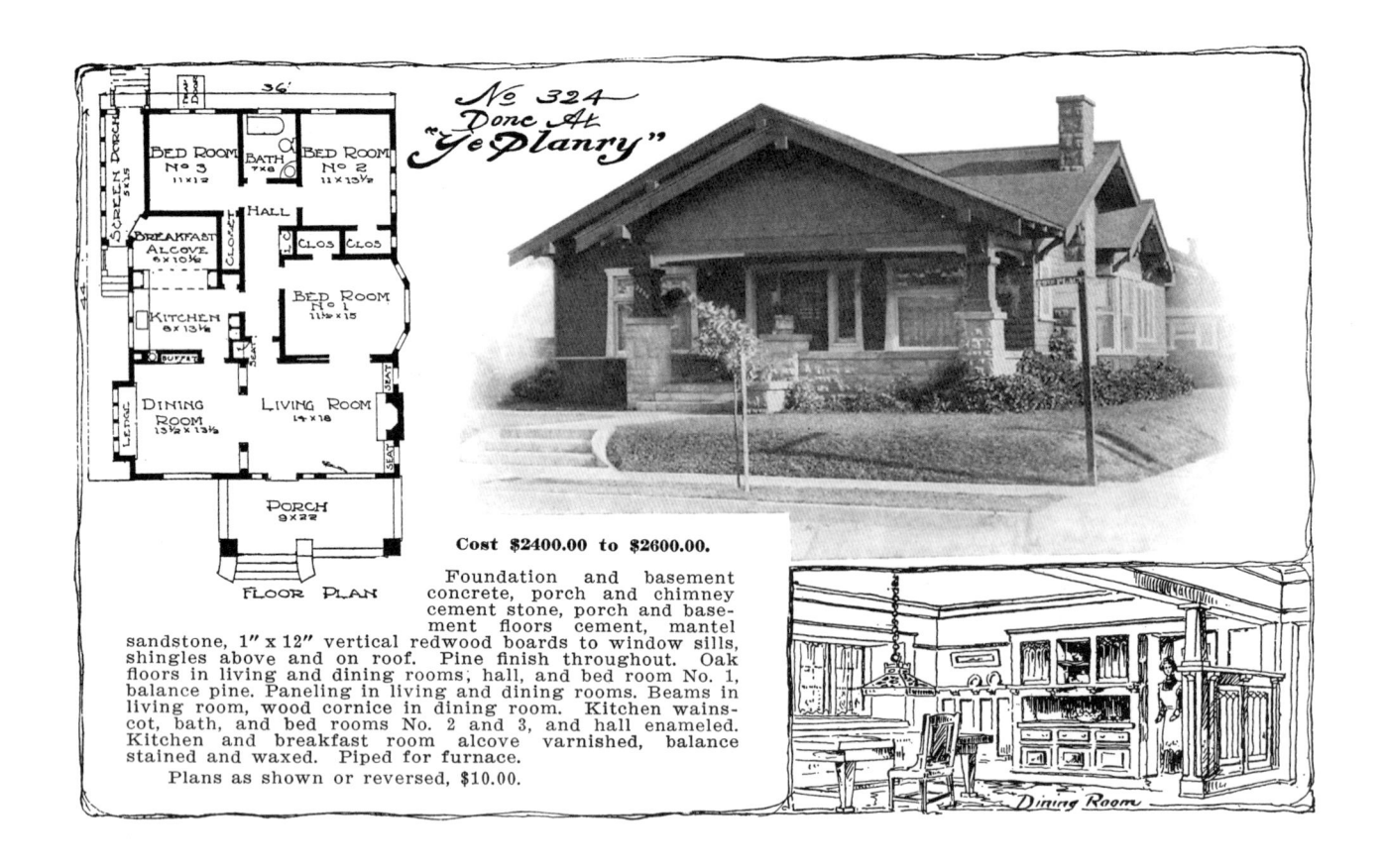

Cost $2400.00 to $2600.00.

Foundation and basement concrete, porch and chimney cement stone, porch and basement floors cement, mantel sandstone, 1" x 12" vertical redwood boards to window sills, shingles above and on roof. Pine finish throughout. Oak floors in living and dining rooms, hall, and bed room No. 1, balance pine. Paneling in living and dining rooms. Beams in living room, wood cornice in dining room. Kitchen wainscot, bath, and bed rooms No. 2 and 3, and hall enameled. Kitchen and breakfast room alcove varnished, balance stained and waxed. Piped for furnace.

Plans as shown or reversed, $10.00.

ABSOLUTELY WEATHER PROOF · ABSOLUTELY FIRE PROOF

The Bexhill Patent Casement Window

Is the MOST SIMPLE and UP-TO-DATE window on the market. No racks, wheels, pulleys, cords or weights; and well adapted for any kind of structure.

An old English window, recently patented in the United States, and rapidly growing in popularity. Made complete with frame, sash and hardware, before leaving our factory. Catalogue and prices upon application.

SOUTHERN CALIFORNIA CASEMENT WINDOW CO.

W. P. STORY BLDG., LOS ANGELES, CAL. — Exclusive Manufacturers for Southern California

---

MORTGAGES! BUILDING LOANS!

We Do a Mortgage Business Exclusively

F 7121
Main 2715

CHANDLER & GORE
611 DELTA BUILDING, LOS ANGELES

Perspective Sketch No. 229 Done At "Ye Planry"

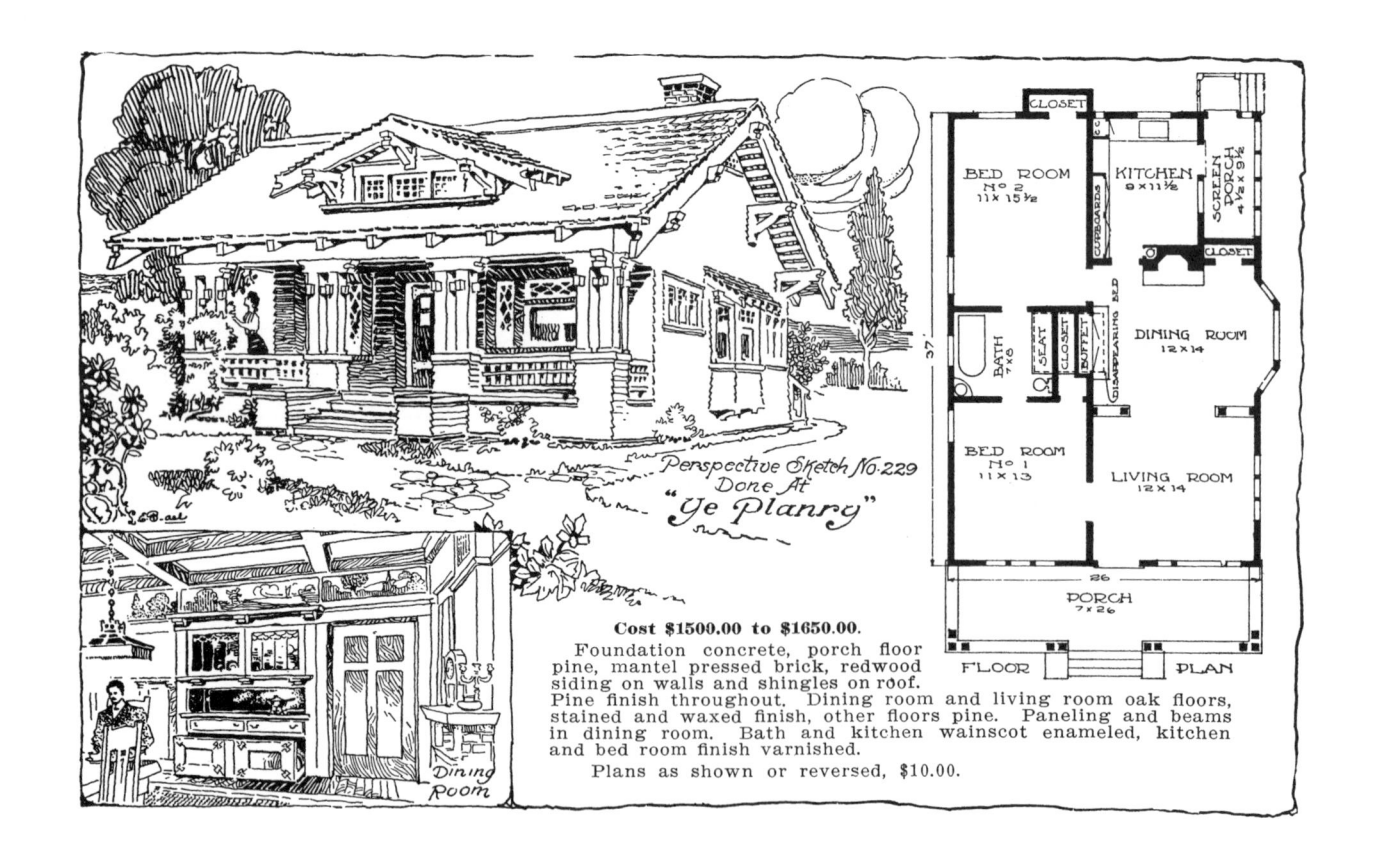

Cost $1500.00 to $1650.00.

Foundation concrete, porch floor pine, mantel pressed brick, redwood siding on walls and shingles on roof. Pine finish throughout. Dining room and living room oak floors, stained and waxed finish, other floors pine. Paneling and beams in dining room. Bath and kitchen wainscot enameled, kitchen and bed room finish varnished.

Plans as shown or reversed, $10.00.

See Our "Colonial" and "Hammered Fixture" Rooms

Specialists in Lighting Devices

THE MISSION FIXTURE CO.

Designers and Manufacturers of

Artistic Lighting Fixtures of Every Style

We are displaying in our show-rooms fixtures especially adapted to

Bungalows and Residences in the Mission Style

We install *more* fixtures, take out *more* permits than
ANY OTHER FIRM IN SOUTHERN CALIFORNIA
WHY?

113-115 WEST NINTH STREET
LOS ANGELES, CALIFORNIA

PHONES: HOME F 4668
MAIN 4668

FLOOR PLAN No 148

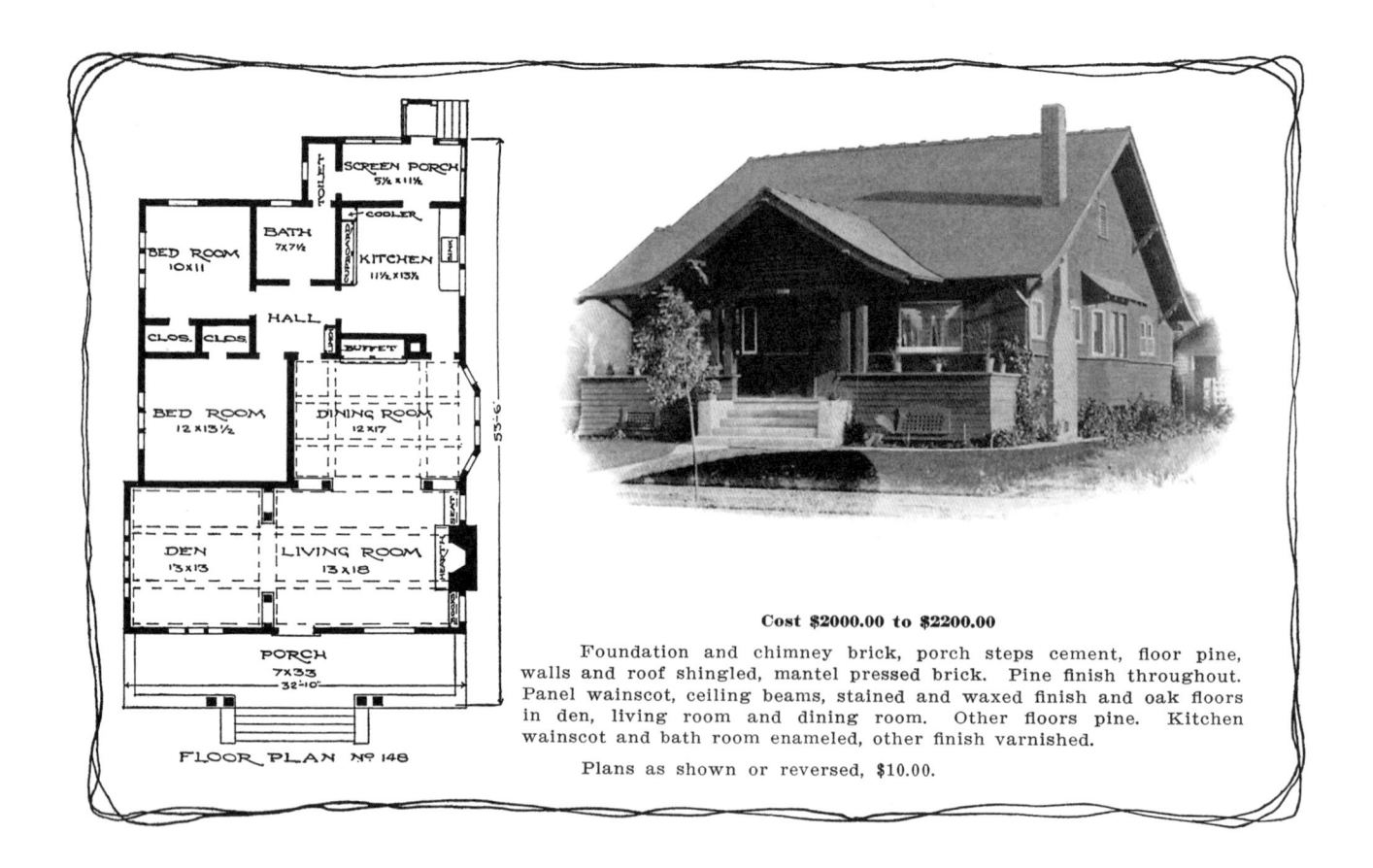

Cost $2000.00 to $2200.00

Foundation and chimney brick, porch steps cement, floor pine, walls and roof shingled, mantel pressed brick. Pine finish throughout. Panel wainscot, ceiling beams, stained and waxed finish and oak floors in den, living room and dining room. Other floors pine. Kitchen wainscot and bath room enameled, other finish varnished.

Plans as shown or reversed, $10.00.

Main 1924 Home A1639

NATIONAL HARDWOOD COMPANY

Exclusive Wholesale and Retail Dealers in All Kinds of Hardwood Flooring; Laid, Scraped and Finished

HARDWOOD FLOORING A SPECIALTY

The Housewife's Soliloquy

To clean or not to clean; that is the question.

Whether 'tis better for the wife to suffer

The sneers and grumblings of an outraged husband,

Or to give up the pleasures (?) of spring cleaning

And let the dust and dirt stay in the carpets,

Or to put in

HARDWOOD FLOORS

Old Floors Cleaned, Repaired and Polished

Agents for the **Best Felt Broom** on the market

Floor Wax, Cleaner, Brushes, etc., always on hand.

Our prices will get your orders. Our material and workmanship will keep your trade.

The best of stock, skilled workmen, and our entire attention devoted to pleasing you, tells the tale of our success.

Office and Yard :: :: **634-646 Aliso Street**

PLAN NO 275
DONE AT
"Ye Planry"

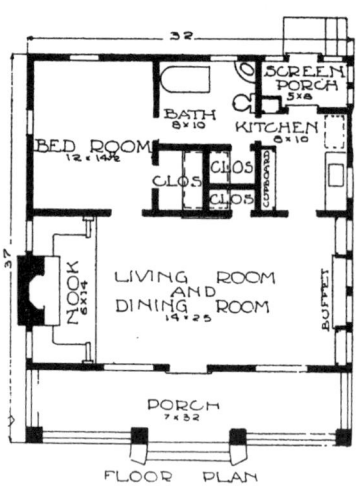

Chimney Nook

FLOOR PLAN

Cost $1300.00 to $1500.00

Foundation brick, porch walls and mantel cobblestones, porch floor pine. Redwood siding on walls, and shingles on roof. Pine finish throughout. Disappearing bed, panel wainscot, ceiling beams and oak floor in living room and nook. Other floors pine. Finish in living room and nook stained and waxed. Other finish, bath and kitchen wainscot enameled.

Plans as shown or reversed, $10.00.

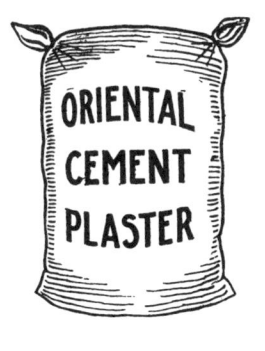

Oriental Cement-Plaster

TO THE DEALER: Oriental Cement-Plaster possesses the quality to maintain its superior strength and color, no matter how long it is stored.

TO THE ARCHITECT AND CONTRACTOR: Oriental Cement-Plaster finishes like Alabaster; it works easier, makes a harder wall and goes farther than any other Plaster.

TO THE BUILDER OF HOUSES: If ORIENTAL CEMENT-PLASTER is harder than other materials, lasts longer and is cheaper in the end, isn't it the material you want in that new building of yours? You know, and we know, that in years past the first repairs usually made on a building has been upon its walls. Not so with the walls made of ORIENTAL CEMENT-PLASTER. We have many testimonials from those who have used "ORIENTAL" to the effect that it is the **best Plaster they have ever used; that it has not its equal.** ORIENTAL has many good points which other plasters do not possess, and is superior to Hard Wall Plasters made from rock Gypsum because all Gyp Rock, when exposed to the atmosphere will melt—in other words disintegrate—while that of Gypsite, when exposed to the air, will harden. A great many old adobe buildings in New Mexico plastered fifty years ago with Gypsite just as it was taken from its natural bed, stand today with the plaster as perfect as the day it was spread on. This being the case, it demonstrates thoroughly that it makes a first-class plaster. Our headquarters are at No. 206 Severance Bldg., Cor. 6th and Main Sts.

ORIENTAL CEMENT AND PLASTER COMPANY, LOS ANGELES, CALIFORNIA

Perspective No 338
DONE AT
"Ye Planry"

Cost $1600.00 to $1800.00

Foundation and mantel brick, porch floor pine, redwood siding on walls, shingles on roof. Pine finish throughout. Paneling, ceiling beams, stained and waxed finish and oak floors in living and dining rooms. Other floors pine. Other finish varnished, except bath room and kitchen wainscot enameled.

Plans as shown or reversed, $10.00.

HOFFMAN-MARKS COMPANY

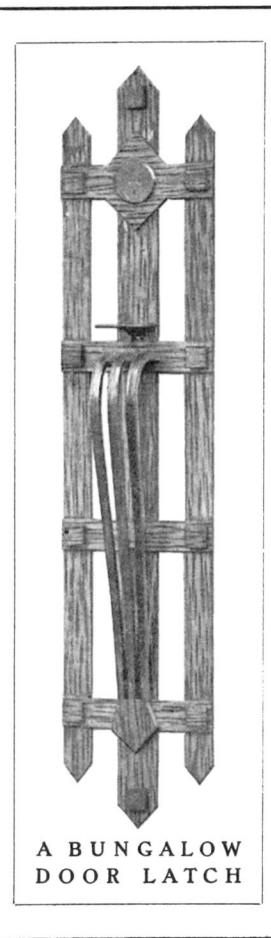

OUR SPECIALTY IS BUILDERS' HARDWARE

A very complete line of factory goods carried in open stock at all times. We will draft for your inspection special designs embodying your own ideas for trimmings to correspond with the symmetry of your Bungalow and have it carried out in hand work if desired. If you build we want to see you.

226 South Main Street :: Los Angeles, California

Phones: Main 1499; Home 1499

A BUNGALOW DOOR LATCH

Design No. 243
Done at
"Ye Planry"

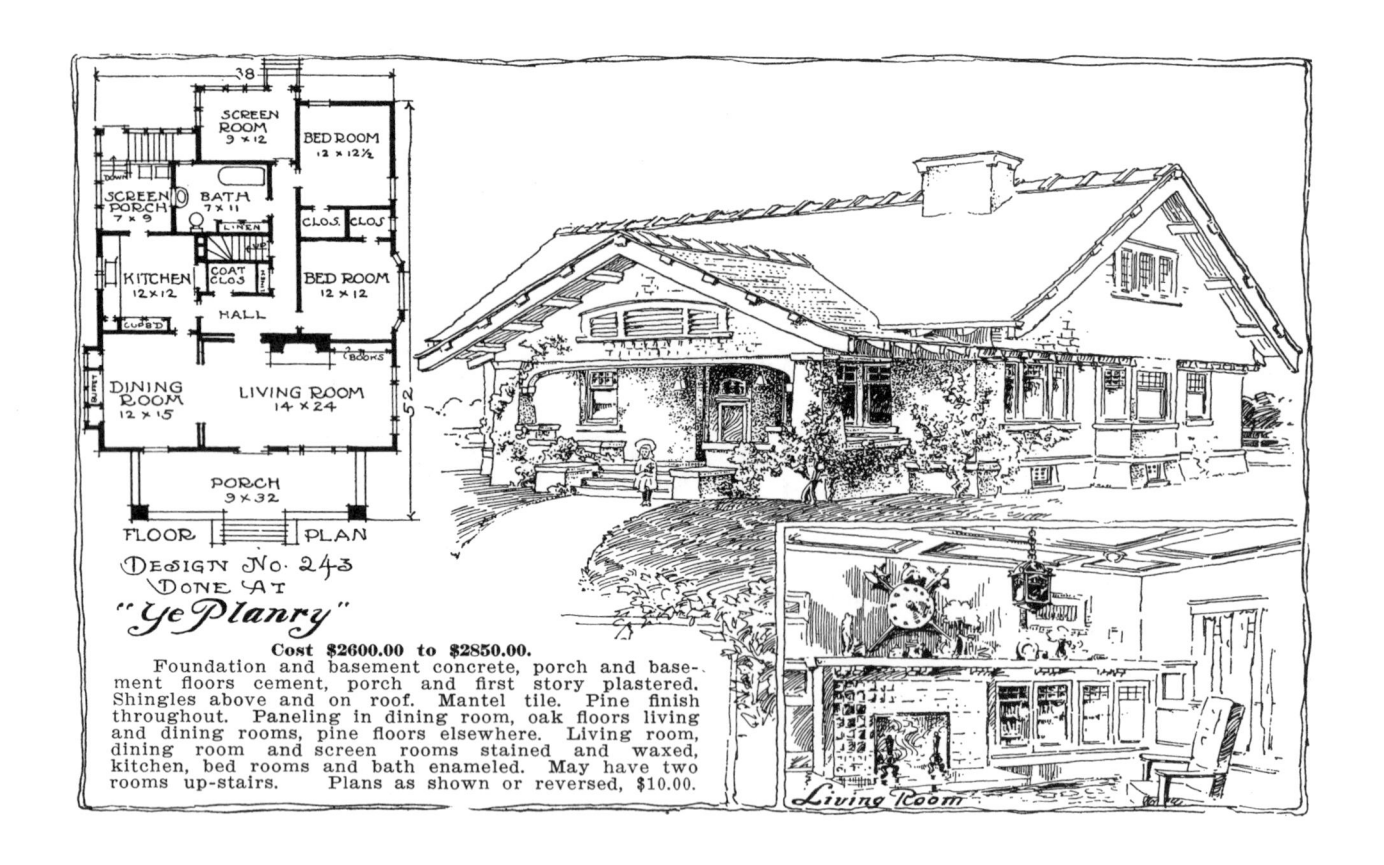

Cost $2600.00 to $2850.00.

Foundation and basement concrete, porch and basement floors cement, porch and first story plastered. Shingles above and on roof. Mantel tile. Pine finish throughout. Paneling in dining room, oak floors living and dining rooms, pine floors elsewhere. Living room, dining room and screen rooms stained and waxed, kitchen, bed rooms and bath enameled. May have two rooms up-stairs. Plans as shown or reversed, $10.00.

The California Door Co.

Dealers in

Doors, Sash, Blinds,
Plate and Window Glass

Leaded and Ornamental
Glass and Mirrors

Telephones
Home A 6560 :: Sunset Main 584

237-239-241 CENTRAL AVENUE

LOS ANGELES, CALIFORNIA

A. Blomberg, Phone Home 22737   C. Eck, Phone Main 8029

UNIVERSAL SCREEN & MILL CO.   BLOMBERG & ECK

Manufacturers of the Patent

Universal IMPROVED Removable Screen

Screen Doors Made to Order on Short Notice

OFFICE	YARD
1358 SAN JULIAN STREET	1359 SAN PEDRO STREET

LOS ANGELES, CALIFORNIA

Phones: Home 24498; Main 2763

PERSPECTIVE NO 258
DONE AT
"Ye Planry"

Fireplace

Cost $1200.00 to $1400.00.

Foundation brick, mantel cobblestones, porch floors pine, rustic siding on walls, roof shingled. Interior finish and floors pine throughout. No ceiling beams or paneling, living and dining rooms finish stained and waxed, other finish varnished and rubbed.

Plans as shown or reversed, $10.00.

WE ARE designers and workers in stained and leaded glass for churches and the home.

Los Angeles Art Glass Co.

120-122 EAST NINTH STREET
LOS ANGELES, CALIFORNIA
Home F 1177   Main 1177

Malthoid Roofing

"Cheerful Homes"

is the name of a new booklet about Malthoid Roofing. This booklet illustrates the most beautiful bungalows in California all covered with Malthoid Roofing. Some of these bungalows cost upwards of $50,000. Malthoid Roofing has made a wonderful reputation in Southern California where more of it is used than all other brands of roofing combined. Send for the new and beautiful bungalow book—"Cheerful Homes." its free.

Have you seen our green, red, white and other colored Roofings?

The Paraffine Paint Co.

MANUFACTURERS

516-518 Security Building, Los Angeles, Cal.

E. G. JUDAH, General Representative

See pages 26, 38, 48, 50, 56, 66, 74, 84, 106, 126, 132, for Houses Roofed with Malthoid

FLOOR PLAN

Living Room Fire Place

PERSPECTIVE NO 242
DONE AT
"Ye Planry"

Cost $2400.00 to $2650.00.

Foundation and basement concrete, porch and basement floors cement. Porch and exposed foundation cobbles, mantel brick, walls and roof shingles. Pine finish throughout. Panels, stained and waxed finish, and oak floors in living rooms and library, pine floors elsewhere. Beams in living room and library. Kitchen and pantry varnished. Bed rooms, bath and kitchen wainscot enameled. Plans as shown or reversed, $10.00.

South 1591 Home 10757

NATIONAL LUMBER CO.

21st and Alameda Streets :: Los Angeles, California

LUMBER :: MILL WORK
SASH AND DOORS
BUILDERS' HARDWARE

We carry the most complete line of Building Material in Southern California

Get Our Figures

WHOLESALE YARD: TERMINAL ISLAND

No. 235
Done At
"Ye Planry"

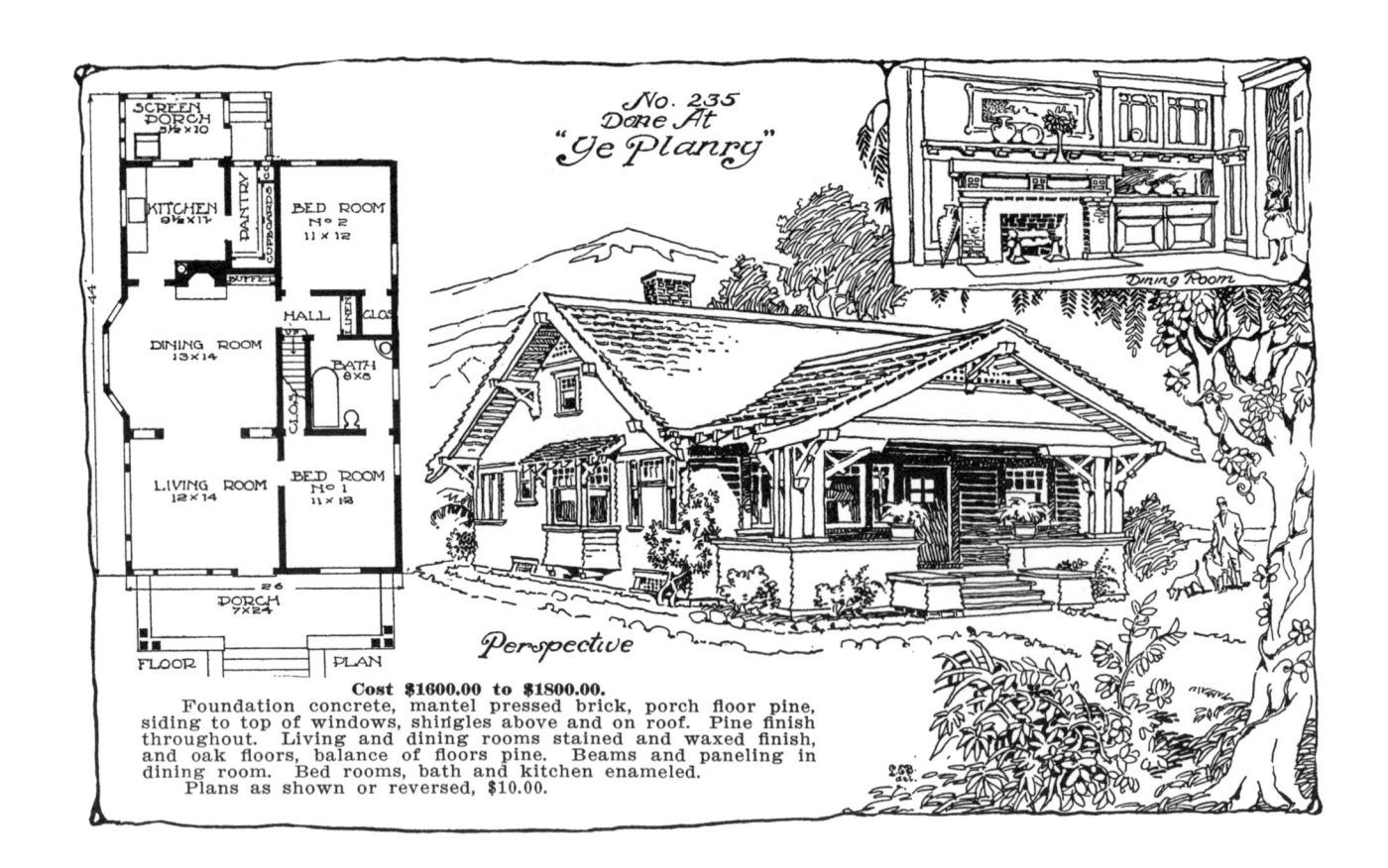

Perspective

FLOOR PLAN

Cost $1600.00 to $1800.00.

Foundation concrete, mantel pressed brick, porch floor pine, siding to top of windows, shingles above and on roof. Pine finish throughout. Living and dining rooms stained and waxed finish, and oak floors, balance of floors pine. Beams and paneling in dining room. Bed rooms, bath and kitchen enameled.

Plans as shown or reversed, $10.00.

Bungalow Wall Papers

The Best, Most Sanitary, Economical and Popular Wall Covering

WE CARRY A SPECIAL LINE IN PERMANENT COLORS FOR BUNGALOWS

DISTRIBUTORS

Mission Shingle Stains

A New Creosote Stain in Beautiful Clear Colors

We have everything for the BUNGALOW BUILDER and the HOME PAINTER. Get our samples and prices before closing your contract

Los Angeles Wall Paper & Paint Company, Inc.

529 SOUTH MAIN STREET, LOS ANGELES, CALIFORNIA

Main 724 :: Home F 8702

View From Pergola
NO 331
Done At
"Ye Planry"
Suggestion For
Lighting
Fixture
Perspective

FLOOR PLAN

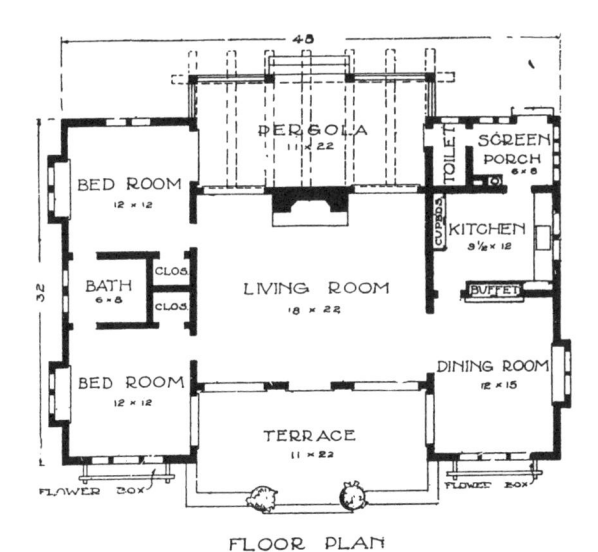

Cost $3300.00 to $3600.00.

if exterior plastered, and with genuine tile roof. $2500.00 to $2750.00 if shingled. Foundation concrete, porch and pergola floors cement, mantel boulders, walls plaster or shakes, roof tile or shingles. Pine finish throughout. Paneled wainscoting, beams, stained and waxed finish and oak floors in living and dining rooms, other floors pine. Wood ceiling in living room. Bed rooms, bath and kitchen wainscot enameled.

Plans as shown or reversed, $10.00.

The Hughes Wall Bed

A Money Saver

Manufactured by Hughes Mfg. & Lumber Co., Los Angeles

No. 284 Done At "Ye Planry"

FLOOR PLAN

- Screen Porch 7×7
- Kitchen 9×11½
- Bath 3½×9
- Buffet
- Dining Room 12×14
- Bed Room No. 2 11×12
- Closet / Closet
- Living Room 12½×12½
- Bed Room No. 1 11×11
- Porch 6×24
- 24 × 34

Cost $1300.00 to $1500.00.

Foundation, chimney and mantel brick, porch floor and steps pine, redwood siding on walls, shingles on roof. Pine floors and pine finish throughout. Living and dining rooms stained and waxed. Kitchen and bed room finish varnished and rubbed. Kitchen wainscot and bath room enameled.

Plans as shown or reversed, $10.00.

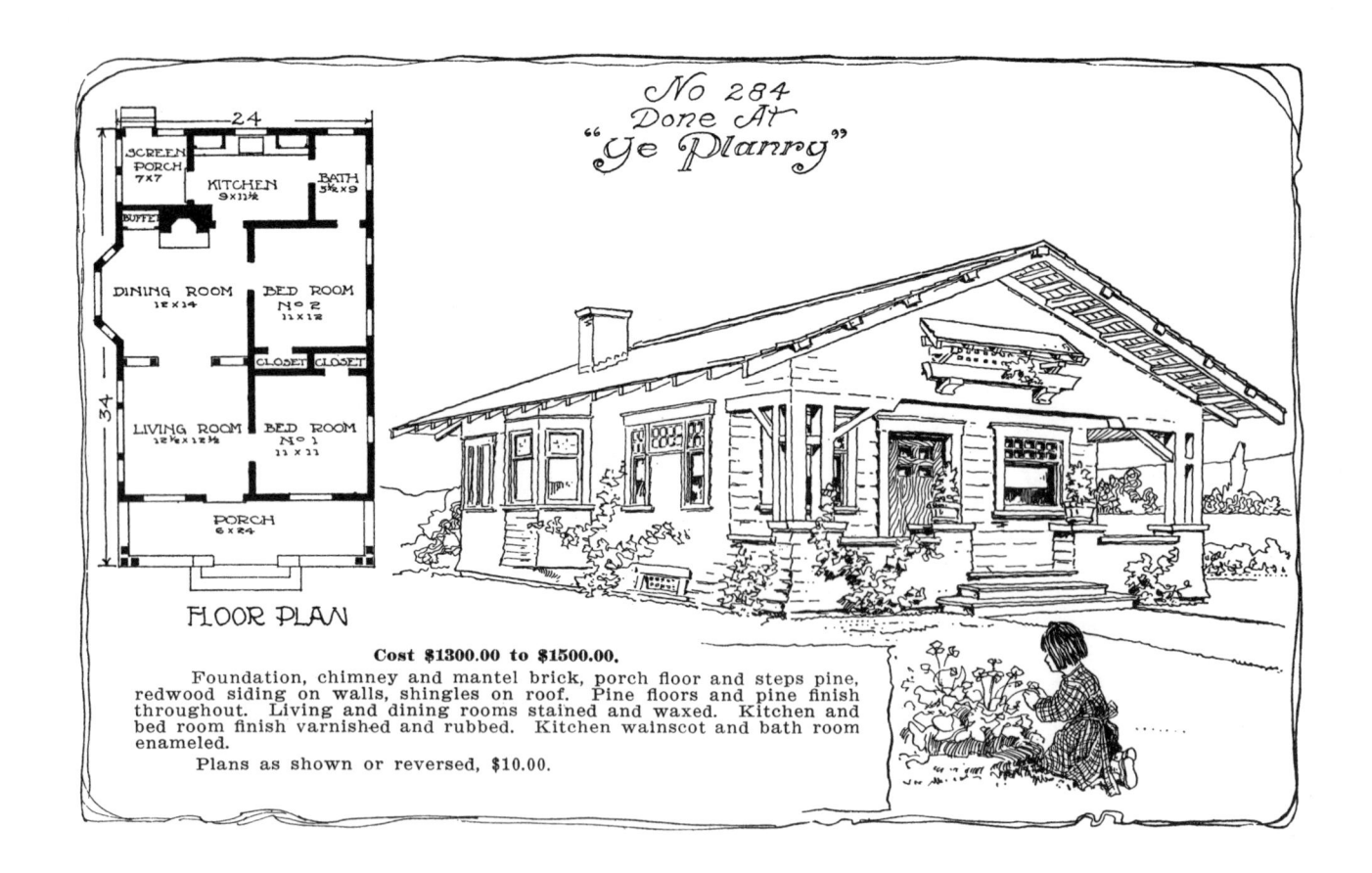

HIPOLITO SELF-REGULATING ROLLER SCREEN AND REVERSIBLE WINDOW

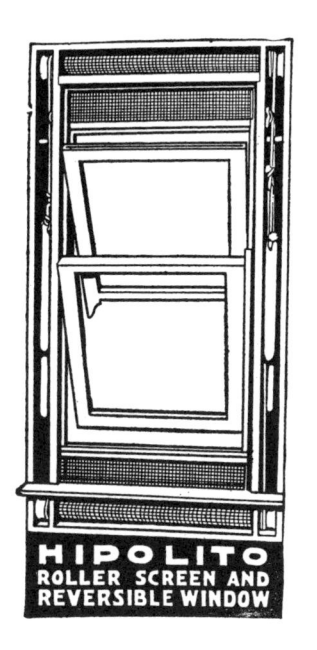

INDISPENSABLE TO EVERY MODERN HOME

Hipolito Self-Regulating Roller Screen and Reversible Window combines all the essential features of the Hipolito Reversible Window and Hipolito Even Tension Screens, with added improvements that make it perfect.

There is a screen for both the upper and the lower sash. When the window is in its ordinary position, the screen is concealed—out of the way. Both windows may then be opened, reversed or placed at any angle. They also slide up and down. Both windows can be cleaned from the inside, thus eliminating all danger and discomfort.

When either window sash is raised or lowered as the case may be, THE SCREEN FOLLOWS IT. Either screen can be operated and used separately.

In rainy or foggy weather, so destructive to screens, the Hipolito Self-Regulating Roller Screen is completely protected from moisture, and will not wear out in years of use.

Hipolito Self-Regulating Roller Screen and Reversible Window costs but very little more. than the ordinary window and screen combined; but it will much more than make up this difference by its superior advantages.

**HAVE YOUR ARCHITECT SPECIFY IT.
SEE THAT YOUR CONTRACTOR USES IT.**

THIS WONDERFUL COMBINATION HAS REVOLUTIONIZED WINDOW AND SCREEN CONSTRUCTION

LET US GIVE YOU A DEMONSTRATION

HIPOLITO SCREEN & SASH CO., 634 MAPLE AVENUE LOS ANGELES, CAL.

No. 383 Done At "Ye Planry"

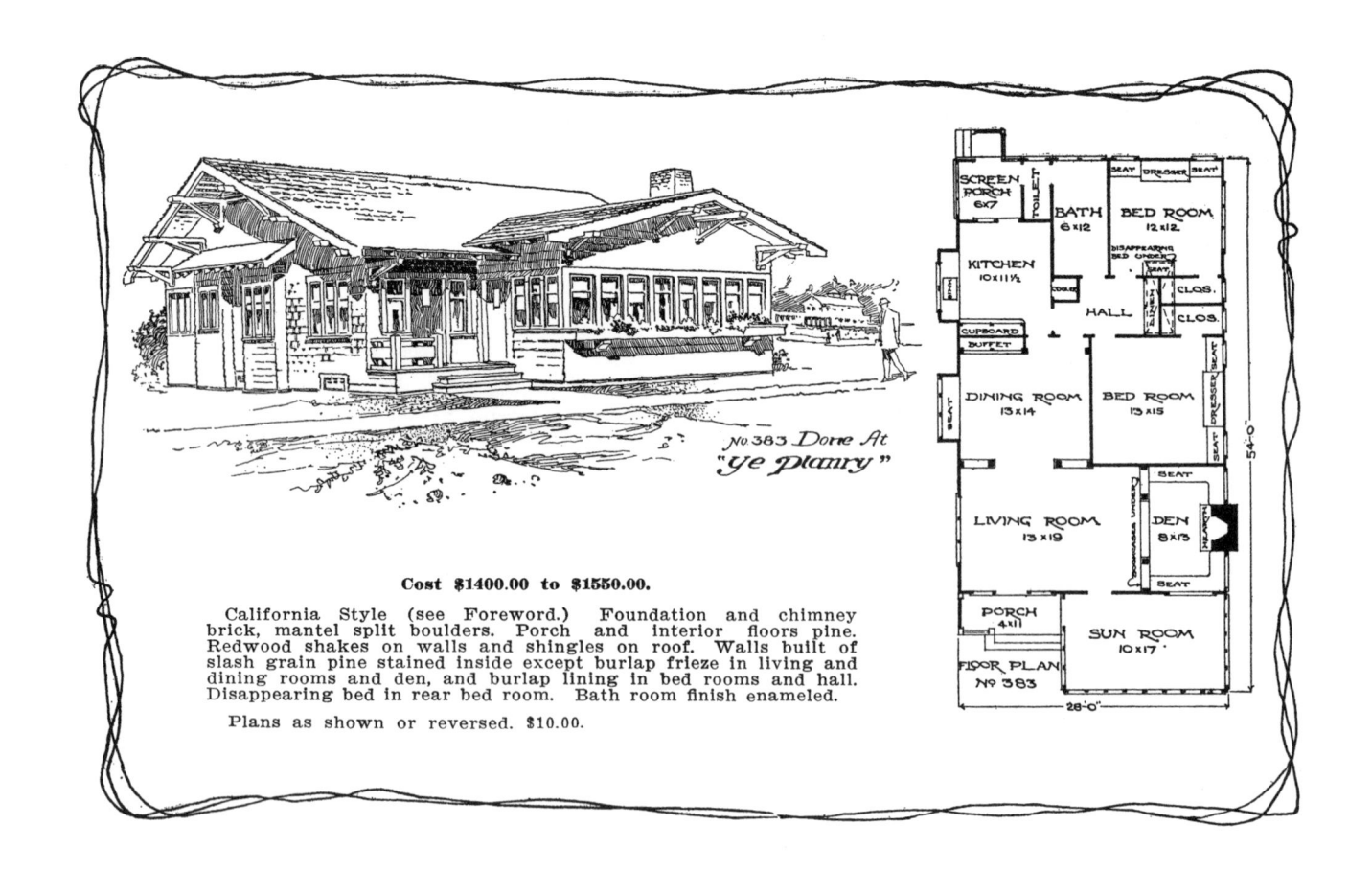

Cost $1400.00 to $1550.00.

California Style (see Foreword.) Foundation and chimney brick, mantel split boulders. Porch and interior floors pine. Redwood shakes on walls and shingles on roof. Walls built of slash grain pine stained inside except burlap frieze in living and dining rooms and den, and burlap lining in bed rooms and hall. Disappearing bed in rear bed room. Bath room finish enameled.

Plans as shown or reversed. $10.00.

E. ARTHUR CLAVELL

Interior Decorating of Residences and Public Buildings

Specialties: — TAPESTRY PAINTING, FIGURAL CEILINGS, VERNIS MARTIN FURNITURE AND PIANO DECORATING, ANTIQUE WALL DECORATING IN BISQUE METALLIC EFFECTS, IN OLD SILVER, BRONZE OR PURE GOLD LEAF. COATS OF ARMS AND HERALDIC EMBLEMS PAINTED TO ORDER. SKETCHES SUBMITTED. ESTIMATES GIVEN

Decorating Carried Out in Either Water or Oil Colors

Tinting and Canvasing   *Special Effects in Wood Finishing*

Phone 21684   Studio : 436 East Twenty-Seventh St.
Los Angeles, California

– SKETCH OF DINING ROOM –

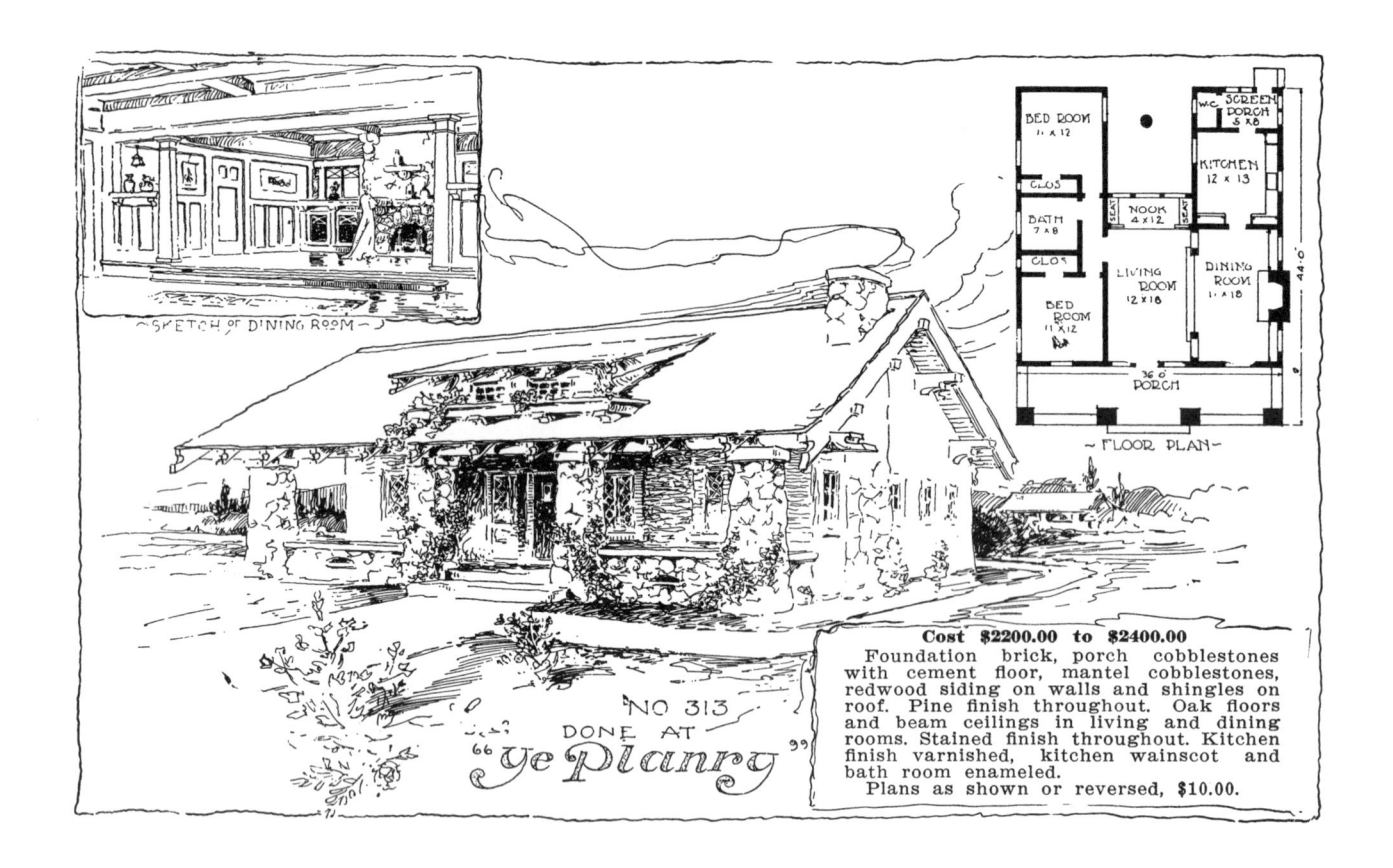

~ FLOOR PLAN ~

NO 313
DONE AT
"Ye Planry"

Cost $2200.00 to $2400.00
Foundation brick, porch cobblestones with cement floor, mantel cobblestones, redwood siding on walls and shingles on roof. Pine finish throughout. Oak floors and beam ceilings in living and dining rooms. Stained finish throughout. Kitchen finish varnished, kitchen wainscot and bath room enameled.
Plans as shown or reversed, $10.00.

Art and Leaded Glass   Mirrors   Electric Fixtures and Wiring

Reproduction of Art Glass Mosaic Panel, Mr. A. Loeb's Residence

ORIGINAL DESIGNS FOR ANY KIND OF WORK

Crescent Art Glass & Mfg. Co.

F 5373, Broadway 2599   818 So. Main Street, Los Angeles, Cal.

No 310. Done At "Ye Planry"

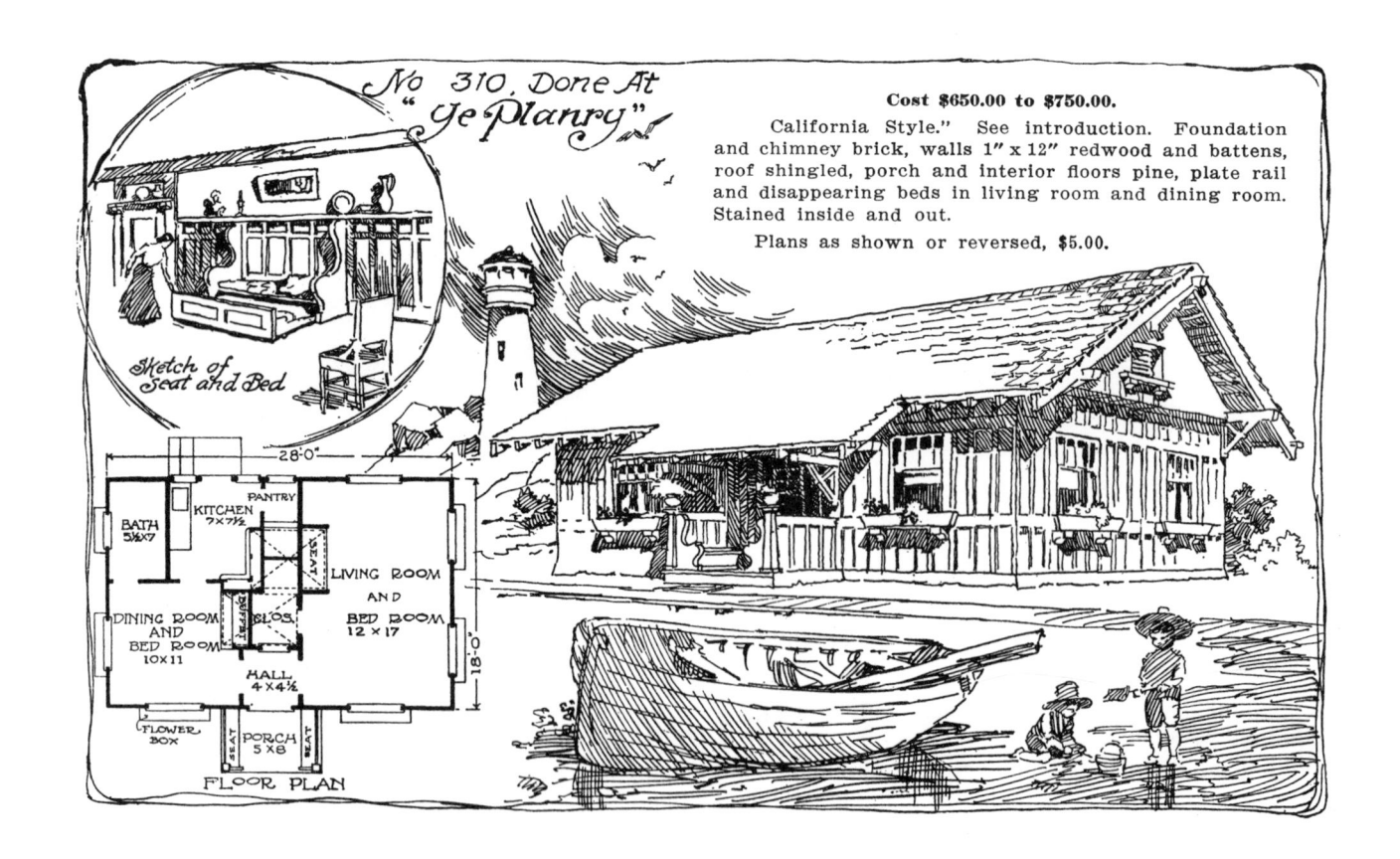

Sketch of Seat and Bed

Cost $650.00 to $750.00.

California Style." See introduction. Foundation and chimney brick, walls 1" x 12" redwood and battens, roof shingled, porch and interior floors pine, plate rail and disappearing beds in living room and dining room. Stained inside and out.

Plans as shown or reversed, $5.00.

FLOOR PLAN

- BATH 5½ x 7
- KITCHEN 7 x 7½
- PANTRY
- DINING ROOM AND BED ROOM 10 x 11
- LIVING ROOM AND BED ROOM 12 x 17
- HALL 4 x 4½
- PORCH 5 x 8
- FLOWER BOX

28'-0"
18'-0"

IMPROVED CLIMAX SOLAR HEATER

Is the safe, standard, satisfactory system of heating water for all purposes in your home at no expense by the sun, winter or summer, day or night.

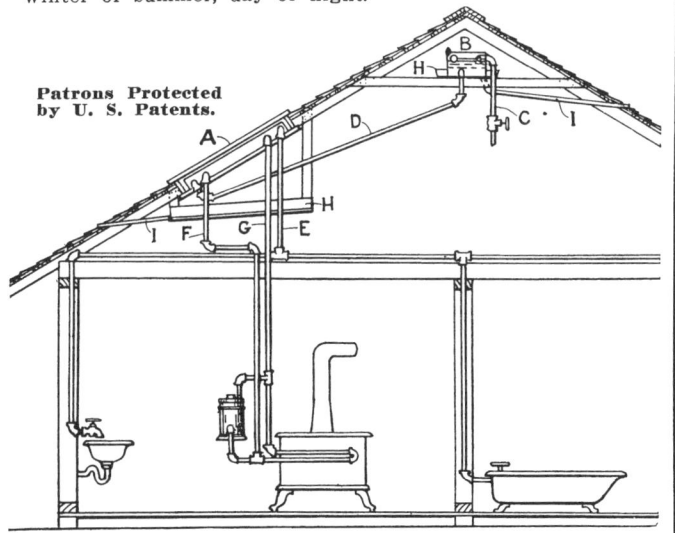

Patrons Protected by U. S. Patents.

The above illustrates the Circulating System whereby the water is heated on a rainy or extremely cloudy day, by the solar heater which is connected to a gas heater and stove. Furnace in basement can also be connected. Solar heater connected in this manner we positively guarantee to give satisfaction. With this system you can ALWAYS have hot water.

Have your architect specify a large size, because we can heat 100 gallons of water as easily as 40 gallons.

SOLAR HEATER CO.
342 New High St.   Los Angeles, Cal.
Main 3932.   Home A 2396.

RILEY-MOORE ENGRAVING CO.

HALF TONE LINE WORK

CUTS FOR PRINTING PURPOSES

PERFECT PLATES PERFECTLY MOUNTED

337 SO. LOS ANGELES ST.
LOS ANGELES, CAL.
MAIN 3021 · HOME A 8637

No 155
Done At
"Ye Planry"

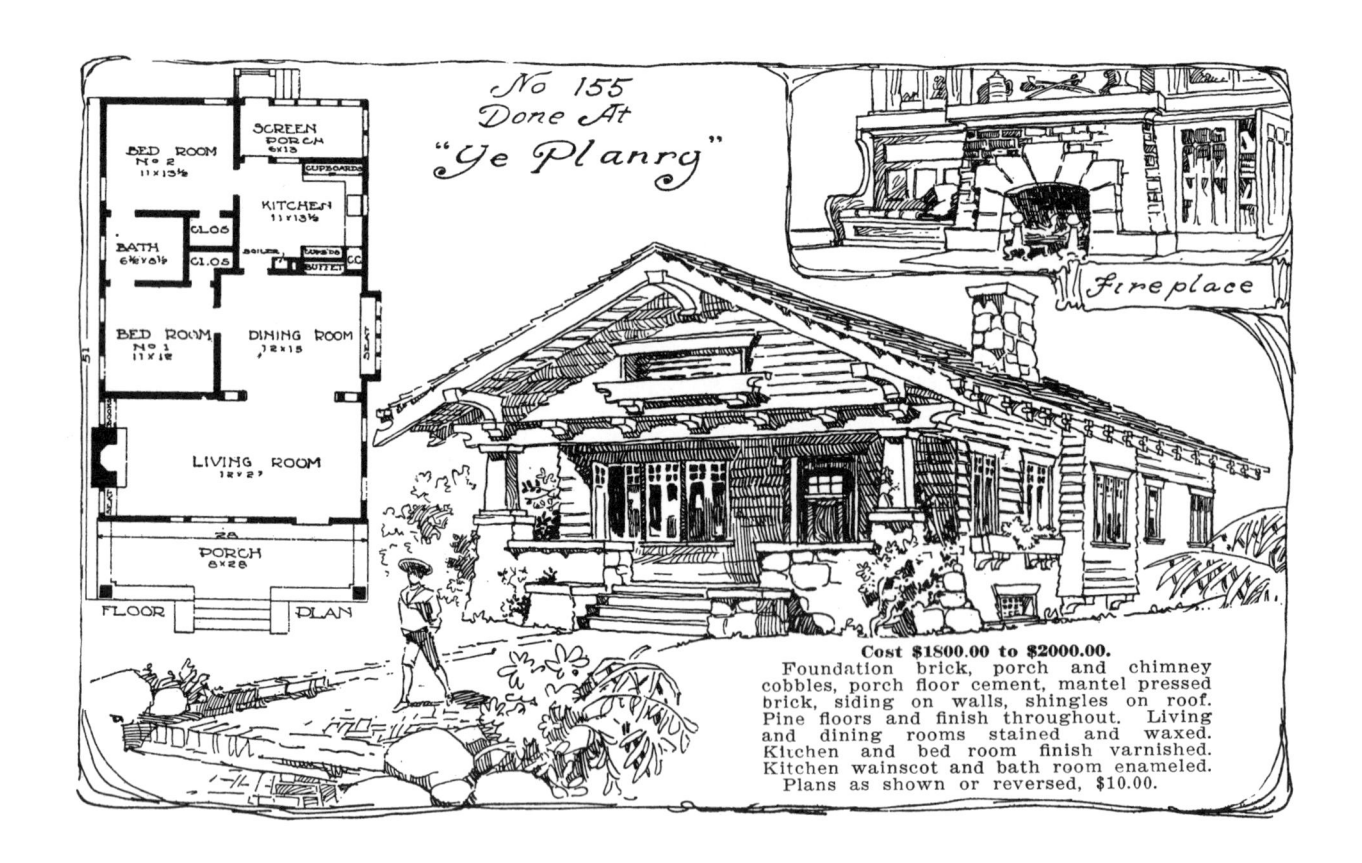

Fireplace

Cost $1800.00 to $2000.00.
Foundation brick, porch and chimney cobbles, porch floor cement, mantel pressed brick, siding on walls, shingles on roof. Pine floors and finish throughout. Living and dining rooms stained and waxed. Kitchen and bed room finish varnished. Kitchen wainscot and bath room enameled.
Plans as shown or reversed, $10.00.

Los Angeles Pressed Brick Company

You are cordially invited to inspect our handsome and comprehensive display at 406-414 Frost Building, 2nd and Broadway, Los Angeles

Hollow Tile—We make a specialty of hollow tile fireproofing known as the ideal type of building material now so popular and extensively used for the modern home.

Ruffled Brick—Reds and blue blacks for facing or veneering, columns, etc. New and artistic.

Pressed Brick and Tile in all shades for attractive mantels.

Roofing Tile—Mission, Spanish, Shingle and Italian equal to the world's best. We are the largest manufacturers of tile roofing west of Ohio.

Paving Brick—For sidewalks, driveways and porches we recommend vitrified brick. Beautiful lasting color, sanitary and durable, economical cost. Price from 12 to 20 Dollars per thousand brick according to size.

No. 217
Done At
"Ye Planry"
212 Mercantile Place, L.A.

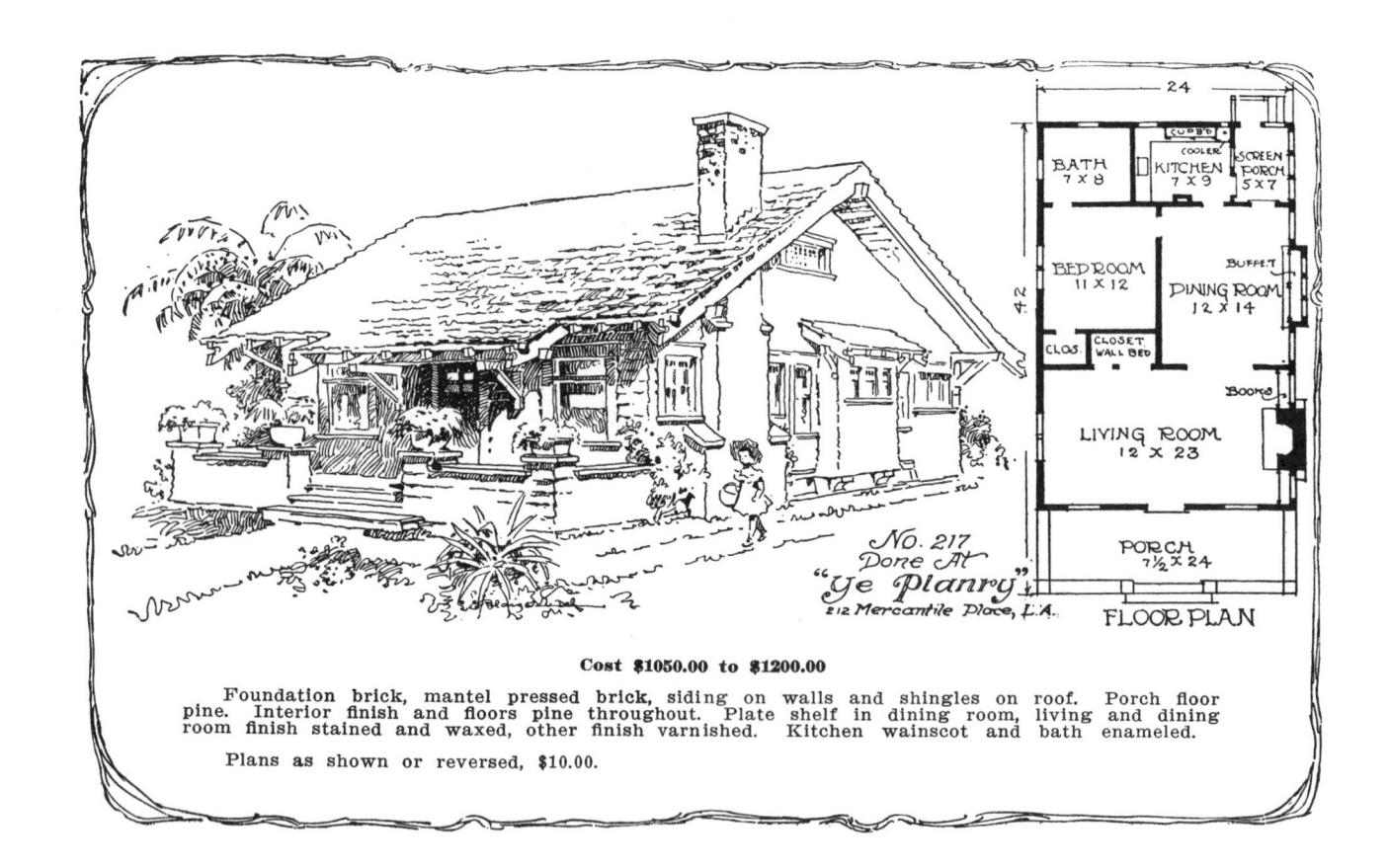

Cost $1050.00 to $1200.00

Foundation brick, mantel pressed brick, siding on walls and shingles on roof. Porch floor pine. Interior finish and floors pine throughout. Plate shelf in dining room, living and dining room finish stained and waxed, other finish varnished. Kitchen wainscot and bath enameled.

Plans as shown or reversed, $10.00.